Justin Batcha

CRCT TEST PREP

7TH GRADE SOCIAL STUDIES

Teaching the Georgia Performance Standards

Louisa Moffitt, Ph.D.
Dr. Emmett Reid Mullins, Jr.

Glen Blankenship, Ph.D., Consultant

Clairmont Press
Atlanta, Georgia

AUTHOR

Louisa Moffitt, Ph.D. is a teacher and department chair of the Social Studies Department at Marist School in Atlanta, Ga. She has taught history and language arts in both public and private schools in Atlanta for over 30 years. Her areas of interest include United States history, Middle Eastern history and politics, and international relations. She has worked on curriculum and test development for the Georgia Department of Education, the College Board, the Educational Testing Service, the Southern Center for International Studies, and the Carter Center of Emory University. She holds undergraduate and specialist degrees from Emory University and two Masters Degrees and a Doctorate in History from Georgia State University. She has been on the National Test Development Committees for AP US History, the SAT II, the PRAXIS Exam, and the NAEP US History exam.

Dr. Emmett Reid Mullins, Jr. is the technology coordinator for a school in Gwinnett County, Georgia. He has over twenty-five years of teaching experience and has done extensive work writing supplemental materials for instruction in social studies and technology integration. He is the author of many learning activities at the **mystatehistory.com** website as well as other resources published by Clairmont Press. Dr. Mullins is a graduate of the University of Georgia.

Consultant	Glen Blankenship, Ph.D
Editors:	Mary Anne Barlow
	Sheila Caudill
	Lynn Thompson
Design:	Cherry Bishop
Production:	New Diameter Creative Services Inc.
Maps:	New Diameter Creative Serivces Inc.

ISBN: 978-1-56733-098-4

Printed in the U.S.A.
Fourth Printing

CONTENTS

TO THE STUDENT

You are beginning the study of several important regions of the world: Africa, Southwest Asia (Middle East), and Southern and Eastern Asia. Each of these regions has an interesting history and geography. You will learn how people have shaped the history of the region. You will learn about how geography and natural resources have affected how people live. You will also learn about the economies of countries in these regions of the world. Learning more about these parts of the world will help you to be a better citizen of your country.

This workbook will guide you and help you focus on the most important parts of what you need to know. You will be given specific information that will be tested on the Georgia CRCT next spring. The CRCT helps you, your teacher, and our state leaders know that you learned the information and skills that will help you become a better citizen of our state.

So get ready to learn about some very interesting parts of our world! You will be given short readings to show you what is important. Then, you will be given some multiple choice questions to answer about the reading to check your learning. Be sure to pay special attention to any questions that you miss. Ask your teacher questions to help you understand why the correct answer was right. This will help you learn the information and be able to use it later.

If you complete this workbook and successfully complete the practice tests, you should be prepared for the CRCT next spring.

Good luck!

INTRODUCTION

All of us want to do well on tests. This book will teach you some techniques to better prepare for tests. After you learn these techniques, you will have the opportunity to practice them as you get ready for the Georgia CRCT.

To become a better test taker, you need to

- Become familiar with the content of the test,
- Become familiar with the format of the test questions,
- Determine if the test is timed, and
- Know if there is a penalty for wrong answers.

CONTENT

Tests are given to find out what you know. To be successful on any test, it is necessary that you know what will be tested. Here are a number of suggestions for preparing for the content of the test.

- Predict what questions will be asked. Look over your notes or assignments or talk with classmates. Think about the information that the teacher emphasized or wrote on the whiteboard or overhead projector. The questions, people, concepts, and so on that are covered in class assignments generally are the things that are tested. Make a list of the important facts and concepts that might be tested.

- Take notes carefully if there is a test review. Note any comments by your teacher such as "This will be on the test," "These are the important people you should know," or "Remember these two points."

- Complete any test review sheet that the teacher might provide. You can use the review sheet as a practice test, or you can make a practice test using the review sheet as a guide.

- Devise methods to study for the test. For example,
  - Make a set of flashcards. Do this by writing a name, date, event, place, vocabulary word, or question on one side of the card. On the other side, write the answer or some information to describe what is listed on the front side of the card.
  - Make an outline of the information. Include major headings, people, events, dates, and so on.
  - Use memory strategies such as mnemonics or graphic organizers (such as concept diagrams, cause and effect charts, Venn diagrams, maps, or timelines) to organize information.
  - Recite the information. Some students are auditory learners and hearing the content helps them to remember.
  - Find a study buddy. Study with a friend or group of friends. Make practice tests for each other or orally ask one another questions.

PACING

It is important to know if a test is timed. Two considerations associated with timed tests are (1) using the allotted time effectively and (2) avoiding text anxiety. There are a number of strategies to help you budget time and, as a result, lessen your anxiety and increase your performance.

One of the biggest problems with timed tests is using the allotted time efficiently. Some students move numerically — from the first question to the last question — on a test. However, the progression of questions often does not move from easy questions at the beginning of the test to more difficult ones at the end. Rather, the degree of difficulty of questions may be random. When you encounter a difficult question, you may spend too much time trying to determine the answer. As a result, the allocated time for the test may elapse before you have completed all the questions.

Through ongoing testing, you can learn to answer the easier questions first. You should skip the harder ones and go back to them at the end of your time. When beginning a test, it is wise to look at the number of items on the test and then figure out how much time you have to answer each one. Following this model ensures that you will answer all the questions you believe you know before time runs out. Try to increase the total number of questions you can complete in a given amount of time.

If the test is not timed, you should work carefully and deliberately. Do not spend an inordinate amount of time on difficult questions, but rather return to those questions later. Do not make random guesses, unless there is no penalty for wrong answers. If there is no penalty, then try to answer all the questions, even if you have not read all of them. When there is a penalty for a wrong answer, answer those questions you know as well as those you can narrow down to two choices. If you have no idea of the answer, do not attempt to answer the question. Later you will learn methods to help you eliminate obviously wrong answers.

Many students have test anxiety, which can increase when the test is timed. The more experience you have with taking tests, the more the anxiety level will decrease. As you feel more comfortable with the content, pacing, and format, you will feel less anxious about the unknown.

COMPLETING ANSWER SHEETS

Many tests require students to bubble in an answer sheet to record their responses. Sometimes, however, students do not clearly understand how to do this simple mechanical process. This lack of understanding can have a bearing on test performance.

Bubbling in an answer sheet requires students to darken a space for their selected response. Many students believe they must fill in the entire space, making it as dark as possible. They spend lots of time, sometimes too much time, darkening in these spaces. In reality, the entire space does not need to be darkened, and it also does not need to be as dark as students sometimes make it.

Ask your teacher for a sample bubble answer sheet and practice filling it in. You may also want to time yourself to see how long it takes to bubble in the answers to a set number of questions. Practice will help you increase the number of bubbles you can darken in a given amount of time.

Another problem with completing answer sheets is that sometimes students skip a question, but they do not skip the corresponding space for its answer. When this happens, the answers to questions are coded incorrectly. Through practice, you can overcome this problem as well. In practice sessions, your teacher may ask you to complete every third or fourth question so you become familiar with skipping answer spaces as well as questions. When you have completed the test, you can go back and check to be sure your answers correctly align with the questions.

You may also want to check the alignment often instead of waiting until you have finished the test. If you only check your answers at the end of the test, you may not have time to make changes, especially if the misalignment began near the beginning.

FORMAT

The test questions on the Georgia CRCT Test are in multiple choice format. Questions that have a multiple choice format are also referred to as selected response questions. These questions, the most common format found on standardized tests, provide a set of choices—one of which is the correct answer. CRCT multiple choice questions contain a phrase or stem followed by 4 choices *(selections)*. Multiple choice formats will ask a student to either answer a question or complete a statement.

When answering multiple choice questions, consider the following suggestions:

- Read the question before looking at the answers.
- If you have an answer, check to see if it is one of the choices. If it is, mark the answer sheet and go on to the next question. If your answer is not one of the choices, discard it and look carefully at the selected responses from which you can choose. Put a mark through choices that are clearly incorrect.

- Identify key words in the stem and selected responses. Check the relationship of the words.
- Locate the verb in the stem. Determine what the verb is asking you to do.
- Note words like *always*, *none*, and *never*. If a choice includes one of these words, it is probably not the correct answer.
- Note words like *often*, *frequently*, and *usually*. If a choice includes one of these words, it is likely to be the correct selection.
- Examine each answer to see how precisely it is written. A precise answer is often the correct one.
- Don't second guess yourself. Generally, your first choice is best.
- Note the use of "All of the above" as a selection. If you know that at least two of the choices are correct, then "All of the above" is probably the correct choice.
- Watch for negative words in the stem. Negative words generally ask you to choose an answer that is not true. When examining a question that contains a negative word, try to find three answers that are correct. This process helps you to narrow down your choices.
- Note similar choices. If two choices are similar, one of them is probably the correct answer. However, if there are two choices that essentially mean the same thing, neither answer is likely to be the correct choice.
- Note selected responses that are complete opposites. Generally, one of the responses is the correct answer.
- Note complex questions. If a question has complex choices, mark each item true or false. This will help you narrow your choices before deciding on the correct answer.

Use the following graphic organizer to analyze a selected response (multiple choice) question. Remember, you should read the sample question and, without looking at the selected responses, answer the question. Check to see if your answer is one of the choices. If it is one of the choices, you would normally mark the answer and move on to the next. For this practice, assume that your answer is not one of the choices. Refer to the list of clues to help you complete the analysis.

Read the stem or question. **Which African country is losing its rainforest most rapidly today?** A. Egypt B. Congo C. Kenya D. Nigeria
Identify key words.
Locate the verb.
Decide what action the verb requires.
Eliminate any choices you know are incorrect.
List the remaining choices.
Make your choice.
Why did you choose that option?

Because multiple choice is the most common test format, especially on standardized tests, it is important to examine a variety of types of questions that test social studies content. Sometimes, before answering questions, you will need to

- Read a long or short passage,
- Use a variety of maps, or
- Interpret data on a graph, table, or chart.

To help you analyze these types of questions, examine the test-taking tips that follow.

Reading a Long Passage

When you are reading a long passage,

- Look at the selected responses (choices) before you read the passage. Knowing what the possible answers are will direct your thinking while you read.
- Read the paragraph and note any key words. Some of the key words might also be found in the selected responses.
- Use the skills you learned for examining multiple choice questions.

Read the following paragraphs and answer the three questions that follow.

The is the largest desert on Earth. It covers over 3.5 million square miles and very few people are able to live there. In the few places where there is water, an (a small place where trees are able to grow and where people can live with grazing animals and a few crops) can be found. Such places are rare in the Sahara Desert. The northern parts of the Sahara Desert are hot and dry, with very little rainfall. Many consider the Sahara one of the most difficult places to live on earth.

Most of the people who live in the Sahara today are . They move from place to place, usually traveling by camel, looking for water or food. Nomadic tribes often trade with each other as they try to fill the needs of their group. These desert nomads were the ones who led the caravan trade across the Sahara in the years before airplanes and desert vehicles were available. Hundreds of years ago, gold and salt came across the Sahara on the backs of camels from central Africa to markets along the Mediterranean coast. Trade goods from the coast then made the return journey. Even today, there are parts of the Sahara that are virtually impossible to get across without a camel. Some of the nomadic tribes who live in the Sahara have been there for centuries. One example is the . Their name means "free men," because their nomadic way of life has not tied them down to one area. Today many of these tribes are finding it difficult to make a living in traditional ways, and many have settled down to live in small villages and towns where they can find steady work.

Despite its harsh environment, the Sahara is home to a number of plants that can tolerate desert conditions. Those areas that do get a little rainfall or that have access to underground water often have grasses and shrubs as well as palm trees, olive trees, and cypress.

_____1. **Which phrase best describes the Sahara region?**
   A. hot, dry desert
   B. rolling grassland
   C. tropical rainforest
   D. scattered grassland and scrub brush

_____2. **What is a nomad?**
   A. plantation owner who lives along the coast
   B. industrial worker who lives in African cities
   C. one who wanders from place to place to find food and water
   D. person who lives and farms in the villages on the edge of the desert

_____3. **What were two of the most important trade goods carried across the Sahara Desert by camel caravan?**
   A. gold and salt
   B. iron and silver
   C. gold and silver
   D. spices and wood

Look at the circle graph below and answer the next two questions.

Religion in South Korea

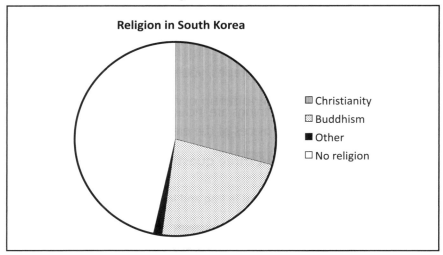

Religion in South Korea

- Christianity
- Buddhism
- Other
- No religion

_____1. **What part of the people in South Korea are Buddhists?**
 A. 1%
 B. 23%
 C. 35%
 D. 47%

_____2. **Which explains information from the graph?**
 A. Most South Koreans do not practice any religion.
 B. Most South Koreans practice some form of religion.
 C. Buddhism has less followers than it once had in South Korea.
 D. Christianity is the second largest religious group in South Korea.

Reading a Chart or Table

A chart or table is a good way to place text into a visual format. Charts are used to categorize data so it is easy to read and understand. Information that would take many pages to put in a text format can be summarized on a chart that may be one page or less.

When you are examining a chart or table, you should

- read the title to determine what the subject is,
- read the column headings and labels,
- draw conclusions from the data, and
- try to identify trends.

Look at the chart below and answer the three questions that follow.

Country	Total Literacy Rate	Literacy of Males	Literacy of Females	GDP – Gross Domestic Product, per capita*
Burkina Faso	21%	21.8%	15%	$1,300
Congo	67%	80.9%	54.1%	$300
Egypt	71.4%	83%	59.45%	$5,500
Ghana	51.9%	66.4%	49.8%	$1,400
Kenya	85.1%	90.6%	79.7%	$1,700
South Africa	86.4%	87%	85%	$9,800
South Sudan	27%	40%	16%	$1,006
Sudan	70%	71%	76%	$2,800
United States (for comparison)	99%	99%	99%	$45,800

*Gross Domestic Product is the value of all goods and services produced within a country in a given year (converted into US dollars for comparison). When divided into a value *per capita* (or per person) it can be used as a measure of the wealth or living conditions in the country. The higher the GDP value, the better the living conditions in the country.

_____1. Which African country has the highest literacy rates?
    A. Ghana
    B. Kenya
    C. Burkina Faso
    D. South Africa

_____2. Which African country has the highest GDP?
    A. Ghana
    B. Kenya
    C. Burkina Faso
    D. South Africa

_____3. Which African country has the lowest literacy rate?
    A. Ghana
    B. Kenya
    C. Burkina Faso
    D. South Africa

Final Thoughts

In addition to all the specific test-taking strategies that you have learned, the following are general suggestions to help you feel confident and ready when the time for the test comes.

The Night Before the Test:

- Review major concepts/objectives.
- Take a break from studying if you get tired.
- Get a good night's sleep.

The Day of the Test:

- Get up early enough to exercise lightly.
- Eat a good, healthy breakfast (avoid sugar and caffeine).
- Wear comfortable clothing to school.
- Arrive at school on time.
- Take any needed materials to the testing site, such as pencils, scrap paper, and a calculator.
- Choose a seat that is free from distractions, for example, in the front of the room or away from the door.
- Take deep breaths if you feel yourself tensing up.
- Listen carefully to any directions. Then, before starting the test, quickly re-read the directions to check for understanding.
- Quickly preview the whole test. Devise a plan to budget your time if the test is timed.
- Be serious. Don't think that any test is unimportant.
- Apply test-taking clues when answering the questions.
- Don't second guess yourself; your first thought is generally best.
- Keep a positive and confident attitude.
- Check your answer sheet periodically to be sure the questions and your answers align properly.
- Reward yourself after the test for a job well done!

AFRICA

GEOGRAPHIC UNDERSTANDINGS

SS7G1 The student will locate selected features of Africa.

a. Locate on a world and regional political-physical map: the Sahara, Sahel, savanna, tropical rainforest, Congo River, Niger River, Nile River, Lake Tanganyika, Lake Victoria, Atlas Mountains, and Kalahari Desert.

Africa is an enormous continent. It has almost every type of climate and geography. The northern coast of Africa runs from the Atlantic Ocean to the Mediterranean Sea. Several hundred miles inland is the **Atlas Mountain Range**, a group of mountains that separate the coastal regions from the great Sahara Desert.

The **Sahara Desert** runs across the entire width of northern Africa. This is the largest desert in the world. It is covered with sand dunes, rolling rocky hills, and wide stretches of gravel that go on for miles and miles. Few people live in the Sahara; however, traders who travel by everything from camel caravan to jeeps and trucks cross its barren miles regularly.

South of the Sahara is a region called the **Sahel**, a dry and semi-arid region that is slowly turning into desert. There is little rain in this region. Generations of people have tried to live there, cutting down trees and allowing animals to overgraze. As the plants have disappeared, the soil has become drier and has begun to blow away.

In the middle of the continent, close to the equator, is the **savanna** region of Africa. It is a vast area of grassland and more tropical habitats. In this part of the continent, one finds many of the animals associated with Africa. The grasslands support lions, elephants, and many other species of animals. Farming is good here when the rains come. However, lack of rainfall can cause difficulties for farmers.

The African **tropical rainforests** are located along the central coast. These are areas with hot and humid climates and dense forests with trees hundreds of feet tall. Many animals and birds live in the African rainforests. The biggest threat to this ecosystem is the rapid population growth in most African nations located in the area. The need for fuel is driving people to cut down the trees faster than they can be replanted.

Africa's other great desert, the **Kalahari Desert**, is located in the southern part of Africa. Like the Sahara in the north, the Kalahari Desert is surrounded by semi-arid areas that are also becoming drier.

Africa also has spectacular rivers. The longest river in the world, the **Nile River**, is found in Africa. The Nile River begins in the central mountains of Africa as the White Nile and the Blue Nile, along with other tributaries. The river flows northward over 4,000 miles until it reaches the Mediterranean Sea at Alexandria, Egypt. The White Nile, the longest tributary of the Nile, begins in Lake Victoria. Lake Victoria is the largest lake in Africa.

The **Congo River** flows through central and west Africa, through the largest rainforest in Africa and second largest rainforest in the world. Only the Amazon rainforest in South America is larger. The Congo River begins in central Africa near Lake Tanganyika and flows almost 3,000 miles before it reaches the Atlantic Ocean. **Lake Tanganyika** is one of the largest freshwater lakes in the world. It is also one of the deepest lakes in the world.

The **Niger River** is the third largest river in Africa, flowing from Guinea over 2,600 miles to the African coast. The mouth of the Niger is a vast delta, sometimes called the "Oil Delta," because of the petroleum industry centered there.

Use the map below to answer the questions 1-7.

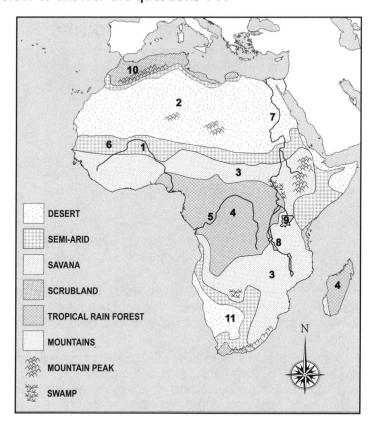

DESERT

SEMI-ARID

SAVANA

SCRUBLAND

TROPICAL RAIN FOREST

MOUNTAINS

MOUNTAIN PEAK

SWAMP

_____ 1. **Which number marks the Nile River?**
   A. 1
   B. 5
   C. 6
   D. 7

_____ 2. **Which number marks the Atlas Mountains?**
   A. 1
   B. 3
   C. 8
   D. 10

_____ 3. **What is marked by the "8"?**
   A. Congo River
   B. Lake Victoria
   C. Kalahari Desert
   D. Lake Tanganyika

_____ 4. **What region is marked by the "3"?**
   A. Sahel
   B. savanna
   C. Sahara Desert
   D. tropical rainforest

_____ 5. **Which number marks tropical rainforest?**
   A. 3
   B. 4
   C. 6
   D. 11

_____ 6. **Which is marked by the "5"?**
   A. Nile River
   B. Niger River
   C. Congo River
   D. Zambezi River

_____ 7. **Which is separated from the coast by the Atlas Mountains?**
   A. the Sahel
   B. the Sahara Desert
   C. the Kalahari Desert
   D. the equatorial rainforest

AFRICA

_____ 8. **Which best describes the Sahara Desert?**
   A. perfectly flat and sandy
   B. the largest desert in the world
   C. impossible for people to go across
   D. located only in the northwest corner of Africa

_____ 9. **Where is the African Sahel located?**
   A. just south of the Sahara
   B. along the Mediterranean coast
   C. along the eastern coast by the Indian Ocean
   D. in the southernmost part of the African continent

_____ 10. **What is causing the Sahel to expand in recent years?**
   A. damming rivers and preventing irrigation
   B. several years of heavy rains and flooding
   C. over-grazing and cutting down trees for fuel
   D. government programs that have moved too many people into the area

_____ 11. **Which describes most of the savanna region?**
   A. desert
   B. grasslands
   C. coastal plains
   D. high mountain ranges

_____ 12. **Where is the largest area of African savanna?**
   A. along the Mediterranean coast
   B. along the edge of the Sahara Desert
   C. in the extreme north of the continent
   D. in the center of the continent along the equator

_____ 13. **Which is the biggest threat to the African rainforests today?**
   A. overpopulation
   B. war and political unrest
   C. extended periods of drought
   D. pollution from nuclear power plants

_____ 14. **Where is the Kalahari Desert located?**
   A. along the equator
   B. in southern Africa
   C. across Egypt
   D. north of the Sahara Desert

_____15. **Which is the longest river in Africa?**
   A. Nile River
   B. Niger River
   C. Congo River
   D. Amazon River

_____16. **Congo River is to Atlantic Ocean as Nile River is to**
   A. Red Sea
   B. Indian Ocean
   C. Atlantic Ocean
   D. Mediterranean Sea

_____17. **Which is the largest lake in Africa?**
   A. Lake Chad
   B. Lake Nasser
   C. Lake Victoria
   D. Lake Tanganyika

_____18. **Which river system flows through the largest rainforest in Africa?**
   A. the Nile River
   B. the White Nile
   C. the Niger River
   D. the Congo River

_____19. **Which is true of both the Niger River and Congo River?**
   A. they begin near the Red Sea
   B. they begin near Lake Tanganyika
   C. they flow into the Atlantic Ocean
   D. they flow into the Mediterranean Sea

_____20. **What is important about the Niger River delta?**
   A. The area is rich in oil deposits.
   B. The delta is poor farming land.
   C. The area frequently dries completely up.
   D. Few people live in the area around the delta.

AFRICA

SS7G1 The student will locate selected features of Africa.

b. Locate on a world and regional political-physical map the countries of Democratic Republic of the Congo (Zaire), Egypt, Kenya, Nigeria, South Africa, Sudan and South Sudan.

The **Democratic Republic of the Congo (Zaire)** is a large country in central Africa with a coastline on the Atlantic Ocean. This country is rich in natural resources and has the added advantage of the Congo River as a route for transportation and commerce. In addition to rainforests, the country is also rich in mineral resources, including copper, cobalt, and diamonds. The Congo has had a troubled history, both with European colonialism and later civil war. The political situation in the Congo remains unstable, which hinders the country's economic development.

Egypt is a large North African country located along the banks of the Red Sea and the Mediterranean coast. The Nile River runs the length of Egypt and empties into the Mediterranean Sea near the Egyptian city of Alexandria. Cairo, Egypt's capital, is a large city located on the Nile River. Most of Egypt is desert, and almost all of the Egyptian people live along the length of the narrow Nile River Valley.

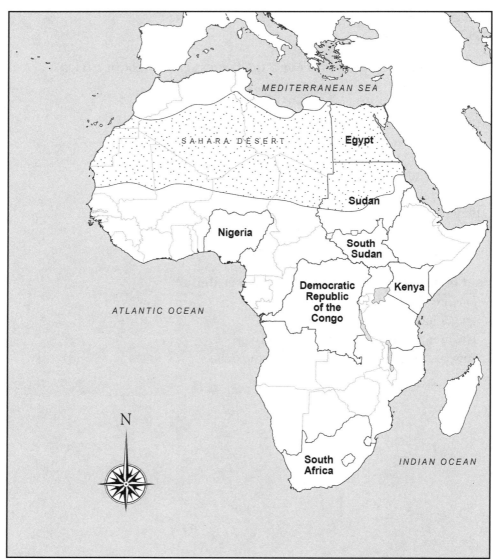

The United Nations, the World Bank, and the United Children's Fund are clean water programs at work in Africa. The African Union had a special meeting on African water issues during the summer of 2008. The problems are large, but African countries are working hard with world organizations to try to find solutions.

_____ 38. **What is one of the major problems facing those who depend on the Nile River for their water?**
A. The Nile River no longer has any fish.
B. The Nile is too shallow to be used for transportation.
C. The river always dries up during the summer months.
D. The water is contaminated with human and industrial waste.

_____ 39. **How did the Aswan High Dam change Egyptian farming?**
A. The Dam washed more silt down the river.
B. The Dam has allowed year-round irrigation.
C. The Dam has increased the annual flooding of the Nile River.
D. The Dam created many jobs in the construction industry.

_____ 40. **What is silt?**
A. a type of chemical fertilizer
B. a chemical used to produce electricity
C. industrial pollution found in the Nile River
D. rich topsoil carried from one location to another by floodwaters

_____ 41. **Continued use of chemical fertilizer causes what to build up in soil?**
A. silt
B. salt
C. animal waste
D. rocks and gravel

_____ 42. **Which part of Africa has access to the Niger River?**
A. Sahel
B. Lake Victoria
C. Sahara Desert
D. Kalahari Desert

_____ 43. **Which BEST describes a major use of the Niger River?**
A. little used because it is too shallow
B. source of much hydroelectric power
C. used for transportation and agriculture
D. used for irrigation projects in the Sahara Desert

_____ 44. **Which BEST describes a major use of the Congo River?**
A. irrigation of farmland
B. supplying water to Egypt
C. water only for rainforest animals
D. transportation of goods and people from the interior of Africa to the Indian Ocean

AFRICA

_____45. **What do some people believe might lead to "water wars" in Africa in the future?**
    A. demands to reroute water to the deserts
    B. competition among countries that share a river system
    C. demands to reroute rivers to supply water to the rainforests
    D. United Nations decrees telling African nations how to share water

_____46. **Why do some governments ignore industrial pollution of major rivers and waterways?**
    A. They want the industries to be profitable.
    B. The people of most countries do not care about pollution.
    C. Industries always have plans in place to clean up polluting wastes.
    D. Most government officials do not recognize pollution as a problem.

SS7G2 The student will discuss environmental issues across the continent of Africa.
b. Explain the relationship between poor soil and deforestation in Sub-Saharan Africa.

The **Sahel** is an area of Africa south of the Sahara Desert. It is an example of how poor farming practices and the destruction of trees and shrubs can lead to an expanding desert. Most historians believe that the Sahel was once rich farmland. Centuries of farming and grazing along with less rainfall have gradually damaged land in the Sahel. Millions of people struggle to farm in its poor soil.

Deforestation is the destruction of trees and other vegetation. This continues to be a problem in the Sahel and elsewhere in Africa. Animals have been allowed to graze too heavily in an area and strip all of the vegetation from the soil. People who need fuel or who hope to be able to clear new farmland cut down the trees that help hold the soil in place. **Droughts**, or periods of little rainfall, have hurt the Sahel, too. The people who live in these areas often face starvation and poverty. Many move into urban areas hoping to find work but most find only more poverty. In recent years, the United Nations and the World Food Bank have come to the aid of those living in parts of the Sahel. They have worked to find solutions to help the people survive and live a better life.

_____47. **What destroyed the grassland and forests that were once found in the Sahel?**
    A. years of heavy flooding
    B. the development of factories
    C. continuous farming and over-grazing
    D. repeated use by nomads and camel caravans

_____48. **Why are droughts a problem for farmers in the Sahel?**
    A. animals move into the desert to find water
    B. the desert stops expanding when there is rain in the Sahel
    C. the soil is of poor quality and dry conditions result in even fewer crops
    D. people do not try to farm in the Sahel any more due to the increased rainfall

SS7G2 The student will discuss environmental issues across the continent of Africa.

c. Explain the impact of desertification on the environment of Africa from the Sahel to the rainforest.

The **Sahel** is one part of Africa that is experiencing severe problems with **desertification**, the process of the desert expanding into areas that had formerly been farmland. As the land is overused, the soil becomes poor and powdery. The winds coming from the **Sahara** gradually blow the dry topsoil away, leaving a barren and rocky land. Periods of drought in recent years have made this situation worse. As the desert expands, people are less able to grow enough food to feed them. People living in areas going through desertification face hunger and hardship. In the Sahel, however, a majority of the desertification is the result of the actions of people rather than climate. Land is being cleared for farming and trees and shrubs are being cut down for firewood. The survival needs of the people living there are clear, but they are destroying major parts of their environment in the process.

Another place on the continent where rapid deforestation is taking place is in Africa's west and central tropical rainforests. Many of the rainforests that once ran from Guinea to Cameroon are already gone. The country in West Africa that is losing rainforests at the fastest rate today is Nigeria. The Food and Agriculture Organization of the United Nations (FAO) estimates that Nigeria has now lost about 55 percent of its original forests to logging, clearing land for farming, and cutting trees to use as fuel.

The same desertification is happening in East Africa as well. In Ethiopia, people who have lived for generations by farming and raising grazing animals like sheep and goats are finding they have less and less land available to them. They have also been hit with long periods of drought or periods of little rain. As cities grow, they expand into areas that were once used for farming. This means those who farm have to reuse the same land. Animals overgrazed their fields and ate more grass than could be grown before the next season. As the soil has worn out, the desert has crept in.

The **Kalahari Desert** is a desert that covers part of the southern tip of Africa. The people around this desert face the same problems as people in the northern part of the continent. Pressure from increasing populations, the need for fuels like firewood and brush, and the constant grazing of animals have worn away the soil and introduced desertification.

The **Nile Delta** shows the differences in the areas of Egypt that are well watered by the Nile River and the point at which the water stops. Some of the western edges of the Nile Delta have begun to show signs of dryness and sandy soil. The Aswan Dam in Upper Egypt and heavy irrigation demands along the river's length limit the amount of water that reaches the Delta every year.

The constant movement of the Sahara Desert can be seen in many of the countries that border that great desert. Some people speak of a "**Green Line**," the place where the cultivated land ends and the desert begins. People work hard to try to replant trees, to build windbreaks to keep out the sand, and to push the desert back whenever they can. In many parts of Africa, this has become a losing battle, as the desert claims more land each year.

_____49. **Which is a result of desertification for the people living in the Sahel region?**
   A. increased tourism
   B. more jobs in manufacturing
   C. increased starvation and poverty
   D. decreased support from the United Nations

_____50. **Which has been a major cause of desertification?**
   A. years of uncontrolled flooding
   B. overuse of the land by the people
   C. heavy seasonal winds coming off the desert
   D. sharp and unexpected changes in the climate

_____51. **Which African country is losing its rainforest most rapidly today?**
   A. Egypt
   B. Congo
   C. Kenya
   D. Nigeria

_____52. **Why is most rainforest area lost today?**
   A. unchecked forest fires
   B. harsh drought and high winds
   C. diseases that attack old growth trees
   D. logging for industry, farming, and fuel

_____53. **In what area are desertification problems the greatest?**
   A. Sahel
   B. Sahara Desert
   C. Kalahari Desert
   D. tropical rainforest

_____54. **What is meant by the "Green Line" when one is talking about desertification?**
   A. the line between the desert and cultivated areas
   B. the line dividing rural and urban neighborhoods
   C. the point in a river at which water pollution begins
   D. a barrier put up around factories to keep people away for their own safety

> **SS7G3 The student will explain the impact of location, climate, and physical characteristics on population distribution in Africa.**
> a. Explain how the characteristics of the Sahara, Sahel, savanna, and tropical rainforest affect where people live, the type of work they do, and transportation.

THE SAHARA

The **Sahara Desert** is the largest desert on Earth. It covers over 3.5 million square miles and very few people are able to live there. In the few places where there is water, an **oasis** (a small place where trees are able to grow and where people can live with grazing animals and a few crops) can be found. Such places are rare in the Sahara Desert. The northern parts of the Sahara Desert are hot and dry, with very little rainfall. Many consider the Sahara one of the most difficult places to live on earth.

Most of the people who live in the Sahara today are **nomads**. They move from place to place, usually traveling by camel, looking for water or food. Nomadic tribes often trade with each other as they try to fill the needs of their group. These desert nomads were the ones who led the caravan trade across the Sahara in the years before airplanes and desert vehicles were available. Hundreds of years ago, gold and salt came across the Sahara on the backs of camels from central Africa to markets along the Mediterranean coast. Trade goods from the coast then made the return journey. Even today, there are parts of the Sahara that are virtually impossible to get across without a camel. Some of the nomadic tribes who live in the Sahara have been there for centuries. One example is the **Tuareg**. Their name means "free men," because their nomadic way of life has not tied them down to one area. Today many of these tribes are finding it difficult to make a living in traditional ways, and many have settled down to live in small villages and towns where they can find steady work.

Despite its harsh environment, the Sahara is home to a number of plants that can tolerate desert conditions. Those areas that do get a little rainfall or that have access to underground water often have grasses and shrubs as well as palm trees, olive trees, and cypress.

_____55. **Which phrase best describes the Sahara region?**
   A. hot, dry desert
   B. rolling grassland
   C. tropical rainforest
   D. scattered grassland and scrub brush

_____56. **What is a nomad?**
   A. plantation owners who live along the coast
   B. industrial workers who live in African cities
   C. one who wanders from place to place to find food and water
   D. those who live and farm in the villages on the edge of the desert

_____57. **What were two of the most important trade goods carried across the Sahara Desert by camel caravan?**
   A. gold and salt
   B. iron and silver
   C. gold and silver
   D. spices and wood

_____58. **What has been the most reliable way to get across the Sahara over the centuries?**
   A. horse
   B. camel
   C. wagon
   D. railroad

_____59. **What is the name for a desert area that gets some rainfall or where there is a spring?**
   A. oasis
   B. Tuarag
   C. nomad
   D. savanna

THE SAHEL

The **Sahel** is the region just south of the Sahara Desert. The Sahel forms a wide band stretching from the Atlantic Ocean to the Red Sea. The word Sahel means "border" or "margin," and this is the region that borders the Sahara. The Sahel covers almost 1.8 million square miles. It is a region between the desert to the north and the grasslands and rainforest to the south. The Sahel is relatively flat with few mountains and hills.

The climate of the Sahel is hot and arid. While there is more rain than in the Sahara desert, rainfall in the Sahel varies from year to year, ranging from 6-20 inches. Even in the years when rainfall is plentiful, farming is difficult. Vegetation is sparse in the Sahel, and grasses and shrubs are unevenly distributed. Some areas have enough grass to support grazing animals. Other areas are dry. Desertification is a problem in the Sahel as the people who live there cut down trees for fuel and shelter.

A majority of the people living in the Sahel follow traditional ways of making a living, herding animals and living semi-nomadic lives. They move when water and grass run out for their animals. Others practice **subsistence farming**, meaning they grow just enough food for their families. Some grow peanuts and millet to sell in the market places, but undependable rain makes farming difficult. Many of countries in the Sahel have rapidly growing populations. This fact is a problem since food and water often are scarce.

_____ 60. **Which phrase best describes the Sahel?**
    A. an area that borders the desert
    B. rolling grasslands and low hills
    C. a desert made up of high sand dunes
    D. cleared land that was once rainforest

_____ 61. **Why is farming so difficult in the African Sahel?**
    A. No rain falls in the Sahel at all.
    B. Thick grass makes farming difficult.
    C. Rainfall can vary widely from year to year.
    D. Farm animals in the Sahel eat up all the crops.

_____ 62. **What is the most common way people make a living the Sahel?**
    A. logging
    B. fishing and shipbuilding
    C. caravan trade in gold and salt
    D. herding and subsistence farming

_____ 63. **Which is a consequence of cutting down trees for fuel in the Sahel?**
    A. civil war
    B. desertification
    C. overpopulation
    D. wealthy loggers

_____ 64. **How large is the region known as the African Sahel?**
    A. The Sahel is found along the Mediterranean coast.
    B. The Sahel makes up the southern half of the country.
    C. The Sahel is found just along the west coast of the continent.
    D. The region extends from the Red Sea to the Atlantic Ocean just south of the Sahara Desert.

THE SAVANNA

The **savanna** is a region where grass is able to grow naturally. Usually there is not enough water to sustain trees and forests. These grasslands are important because they support many animals. Grasses and grains like wheat, oats and sorghum grow in the region, too.

The African savanna is the largest in the world. It covers almost half of Africa. When the summer rains come, the savanna is green and the grass is thick. During the winter dry season, the grass turns brown and grass fires occur. These fires are part of the natural cycle of life in the savanna.

Many animals make their homes in the African savanna. Lions, elephants, buffaloes, giraffes, zebras, leopards, cheetahs, hyenas, and rhinoceros are among the animals found there. Some of these animals, like the giraffes and zebras, feed on the plants and grasses. Others, like the lions and leopards, eat other animals.

The biggest threat to the African savanna is the increasing number of people. The increasing population in Africa has put pressure on people to open more land for farming and ranching. Every year, more savanna grassland is fenced in and plowed for crops. Expanding farmlands mean less land for the animals. Some countries, like Kenya and Tanzania, are working to set aside large areas of the savanna as national parks and game preserves. The savanna regions of Africa have faced pressure from the growth of towns and cities and the need for highways to connect urban areas. As roads are built through isolated savanna wilderness, natural animal habitats disappear.

_____ 65. **Which phrase best describes the savanna?**
A. a semi-arid region just south of the Sahara Desert
B. an area of harsh desert in the north of the continent
C. grasslands making up half of the African continent
D. an area of fertile plain along the Mediterranean coast

_____ 66. **Which is found on the African savanna?**
A. a heavy jungle canopy
B. a wide variety of animals
C. dry areas with just an occasional oasis
D. lots of commercial logging businesses

_____ 67. **Which is the greatest danger for the African savanna today?**
A. seasonal fires
B. logging industries
C. the annual drought
D. activities of people

_____ 68. **What are some African countries trying to do to protect the savanna?**
A. setting land aside as national parks
B. setting up zoos for the animals that are threatened
C. stopping all commercial logging in central Africa
D. refusing to let people move into the savanna area

THE RAINFOREST

Rainforests are found in parts of the world that are warm and humid and usually in an area near the earth's equator. Rich plant life and plentiful water allow thousands of different animals, fish, and insects to live there. Africa has the world's second-largest area of rainforests. The largest of these areas is in the Congo River basin.

There are several levels to life in the rainforest. The floor of a rainforest is home to thousands of varieties of insects, including many types of butterflies. These butterflies play an important role in pollinating the flowers and making it possible for them to reproduce. The rivers and streams in a rainforest support fish, alligators, and crocodiles. Moving higher and up into the trees, one finds the canopy layers of the rainforest, home to birds, frogs, toads, and snakes, as well as monkeys and chimpanzees. Rainforest canopies grow in multiple layers, with taller trees shading those at lower levels and allowing a wide variety of plants and animals to grow.

For most of Africa's history, the rainforests have been home to small groups of people who lived by gathering food from the forest or living on small subsistence farms. They lived simple lives that had little impact on their environment. In the 1800s that changed when European nations discovered the riches in the rainforests. Land was cleared for great plantations, including those that harvested rubber for Europe's industrial revolution. Thousands of the people who had lived in the rainforests were forced to work on these plantations and their traditional ways of life began to disappear.

Today, rainforests continue to be destroyed, but now the cause is commercial logging. This destruction of the rainforest is called **deforestation**. Timber cutting businesses also need roads and heavy equipment to get the trees they cut to cities. These roads destroy more of the natural environment. Deforestation leads to the extinction of species of both plants and animals. **Extinction** means that those species no longer exist anywhere in the world. Destruction of the forests contributes to soil erosion and desertification.

_____69. **Which phrase BEST describes the rainforest?**
A. hot and dry desert
B. semi-arid farmland
C. rolling grassy plains
D. humid and warm with thick vegetation

_____70. **How does the African rainforest rank in the world in terms of size?**
A. the largest in the world
B. the second largest in the world
C. one of the smallest in the world
D. large but not in comparison with most others in the world

_____71. **In what part of Africa is the largest rainforest found?**
A. the Nile River basin
B. the Niger River basin
C. the Congo River basin
D. the Mediterranean coast

_____72. **Beginning in the 1800s, what did European nations do that affected the African rainforest?**
A. cleared large areas of land for great plantations
B. passed laws protecting the rainforests from development
C. moved Europeans who had no homes to land in the rainforests
D. helped African nomads relocate from the desert to farms in the rainforest

_____73. **What is the definition of "deforestation"?**
A. eliminating a species of an animal
B. creating nature preserves to protect forests
C. cutting down and clearing trees from the area
D. forcing people to move from cities into traditional forest villages

_____74. **What does it mean if a plant or animal becomes extinct?**
   A. It begins to smell very bad.
   B. That type of animal can be used for food.
   C. That type of animal becomes too numerous.
   D. There are no more of that type of plant or animal alive in the world.

_____75. **Which is a factor in the destruction of the African rainforest?**
   A. annual grass fires
   B. areas of decreasing desert
   C. rapidly growing population
   D. decreased use of wood as fuel

SS7G4 The student will describe the diverse cultures of the people who live in Africa.
a. Explain the differences between an ethnic group and a religious group.

An **ethnic group** is a group of people who share cultural ideas and beliefs that have been a part of their community for generations. The characteristics they may have in common could include language, religion, a shared history, types of foods, and a set of traditional stories, beliefs, or celebrations.

A **religious group** shares a belief system in a god or gods, with a specific set of rituals and literature. People from different ethnic groups may share the same religion, though they may be from very different cultures.

_____76. **Which would be an example of an ethnic group?**
   A. people who grow similar food
   B. people who share a language or religion
   C. people who share a belief in god or gods
   D. people who like to read the same literature

_____77. **Which would be an example of a religious group?**
   A. people who grow similar food
   B. people who share a language or religion
   C. people who share a belief in god or gods
   D. people who like to read the same literature

AFRICA

ARAB

Arab people began to spread into North Africa in the late 600s AD, when the first Muslim armies arrived in Egypt. From there, Arab armies, traders, and scholars spread across the northern Africa all the way to Morocco. Wherever the Arabs went, they took **Islam** and the Arabic language with them. Arabic was necessary if one was to be able to read the Quran, Islam's holy book. From North Africa, Arab traders began to lead caravans south across the Sahara Desert in the gold and salt trade. This brought Islam and Arab culture to the Sahel region and beyond. Along the east coast of Africa, Arab traders traveled by land and by sea down to present day Kenya, Mozambique, Tanzania, and Zanzibar. They married local women and the process of blending cultures and religions began there as well. The Arabic language, the religion of Islam, and many other aspects of Muslim culture became part of Africa. Today Muslims are found throughout Africa. They make up a majority of the people living along the Mediterranean coast and in some countries along the Indian Ocean in the east.

ASHANTI

The **Ashanti** people are found in the modern country of Ghana. They have been a powerful group in this part of Africa for over three hundred years. Their culture has played a part in the countries around them, including Burkina Faso, Ivory Coast, and Togo. The Ashanti believe that their kingdom was founded in 1701 with the help of a holy man who produced a **Golden Stool** from the heavens and gave it to the first Ashanti king. The Stool came to symbolize Ashanti power and the belief is that the kingdom will last as long as the golden stool remains in the hands of the Ashanti king. The traditional Ashanti religion is centered on a belief in a supreme god, or **Nayme**. His many children, the **Abosom**, represent all the natural powers and forces in the world. The traditional Ashanti believe that all living things have souls. They also believe that witches, demon spirits, and fairies have powers in the lives of men. Ancestors are given great respect, and there are a number of family rituals associated with birth, puberty, marriage, and death.

Other religions are also practiced by many of the Ashanti. **Christianity** has gained many followers in Ghana and along the west coast of Africa. It was introduced by European and American missionaries beginning in the 1800s. There are also a large number of **Muslims**. Like so many other places in Africa, movement of people through the centuries has resulted in a great deal of diversity in nearly all aspects of life among the Ashanti.

BANTU

The **Bantu**-speaking people of Africa migrated in many different waves from the region just south of the Sahara Desert to the central and southern parts of the continent beginning over 2,000 years ago. Today the speakers of the hundreds of Bantu-related languages include many different ethnic groups, though they share a number of cultural characteristics. From their earliest days, the Bantu were known as farmers and animal herders, and they learned iron-making crafts as well. As they spread south and east across the continent, following rivers and streams, they met many new people and learned new skills, even as they shared their own. Bantu-speaking people settled as far south as the southern tip of Africa. They intermarried with the people they met accepting new traditions and blending them with Bantu culture. The Bantu migration was one of the largest movements of people in Africa's history. Today over 60 million people in central and southern Africa speak Bantu-based languages and share some part of Bantu culture.

Many Bantu who settled in areas where there was a strong Arab presence are **Muslim**. Others, living in parts of Africa influenced by missionary efforts are **Christian**. Still others follow traditional **animist religions**. Animists believe that spirits are found in natural objects and surroundings. They may feel a spiritual presence in rocks, trees, a waterfall or particularly beautiful place in the forest.

SWAHILI

The **Swahili** community developed along the coast of East Africa when Arab and Persian traders looking for profitable markets began to settle there and intermarry with the local Bantu-speaking population. The resulting Swahili culture is a mix of people who can claim ancestors in Africa, in Arabia, and even across the Indian Ocean. Many people in the countries of Kenya, Tanzania, and Mozambique share the Swahili culture, language, history and traditions. While the Swahili language is considered a Bantu language, there are many Arabic words and phrases included as well. The word Swahili comes from the Arabic word "Swahili," which means "one who lives on the coast." Most Swahili today are city dwellers rather than traditional farmers and herdsmen. Many are engaged in fishing and trade, as their ancestors were.

Because contact with Arab traders was such a big part of their history, most of the Swahili today are Muslims. Islam has been one of the factors that helped create a common identity for such a diverse group of people. It is not unusual for Swahili men to wear charms around their necks containing verses of the Quran to protect them from harm. The Quran is the holy book of the Muslims. Many among the Swahili also follow local beliefs that have been part of the culture of eastern Africa since before Muslim traders arrived over a thousand years ago. These local beliefs are known as **mila**. One belief that is part of mila is that there are spirits that can possess a person. Many Swahili also see a close link between their religious beliefs and the practice of medicine and healing. Herbal medicines are often given along with prescribed prayers and rituals that are all thought to be part of the cure.

_____ 78. **What religion did the Arabs bring with them to Africa?**
   A. Islam
   B. Judaism
   C. Animism
   D. Christianity

_____ 79. **Why was learning Arabic important for those who became Muslims?**
   A. The Quran is written in Arabic.
   B. Arabic is an easy language to learn.
   C. Arabic was the only written language.
   D. Muslims are required to speak only Arabic.

_____ 80. **Which were goods Arab traders carried across the Sahara by caravan?**
   A. salt and gold
   B. silk and wool
   C. grains and olives
   D. books and writing utensils

_____ 81. **Where do most Muslims live in Africa?**
   A. only in the Sahel
   B. near the southern tip of Africa
   C. in Northern and Eastern Africa
   D. few Muslims live in Africa today

_____82. **In which country do most Ashanti live?**
   A. Egypt
   B. Kenya
   C. Ghana
   D. Morocco

_____83. **What is the significance of the Golden Stool for the Ashanti people?**
   A. It symbolizes the power of the Ashanti people.
   B. The stool was meant to encourage equal rights for all.
   C. The Ashanti would become rich making furniture and household goods.
   D. The Ashanti people could only worship if they were sitting on the Golden Stool.

_____84. **Those who practice the traditional Ashanti religion**
   A. use the Quran as their holy book.
   B. believe there is one supreme god.
   C. believe that Jesus is the son of God.
   D. must pray facing Mecca five times a day.

_____85. **What are the main religions found among the Ashanti people today?**
   A. a traditional religion and Hinduism
   B. a belief in Judaism and Christianity
   C. a traditional Shanti religion, Christianity, and Islam
   D. There is little formal practice of religion among the Ashanti today.

_____86. **Which BEST describes the Bantu people?**
   A. The Bantu are nomadic people in the Sahara Desert.
   B. The Bantu are a separate race in the northern part of the African continent.
   C. The Bantu live only in cities and towns; none of them farm or herd animals anymore.
   D. They are many different people who share a related language and some cultural characteristics.

_____87. **Why is the Bantu migration so important in the study of Africa?**
   A. The Bantu migration led to the first settlements in the Sahara.
   B. The migration was forced by the African governments in the north.
   C. The Bantu migration brought language and iron tools across Africa.
   D. During the Bantu migration, the people refused to intermarry with Arabs or Muslims.

_____88. **How many people in Africa today are part of the Bantu culture?**
   A. only a very few
   B. over 60 million
   C. several hundred thousand
   D. those living in the southern part of the continent

_____89. **Which best describes the religion of the Bantu people?**
    A. most are Muslims
    B. most Bantu practice Animism
    C. nearly all Bantu are Christians
    D. the Bantu practice a wide variety of religions

_____90. **Where are the majority of the Swahili people found?**
    A. the Sahel
    B. East Africa
    C. North Africa
    D. South Africa

_____91. **The Swahili language is a mixture of Bantu and**
    A. Arabic
    B. Muslim
    C. Ashanti
    D. English

_____92. **What does the word "Swahili" mean in Arabic?**
    A. forest dweller
    B. nomad wanderer
    C. one who herds animals
    D. one who lives on the coast

_____93. **What religion is most common among the Swahili today?**
    A. Islam
    B. Hinduism
    C. Buddhism
    D. Christianity

_____94. **What are the "mila" that are part of Swahili belief?**
    A. spirits that can possess a person
    B. rituals of the pilgrimage to Mecca
    C. special foods eaten on the holidays
    D. prayers that must be said five times a day

AFRICA

SS7G4 The student will describe the diverse cultures of the people who live in Africa.

c. Evaluate how the literacy rate affects the standard of living.

Literacy, or the ability to read and write, has a big effect on the standard of living of a country. Those who cannot read or write have a very difficult time finding decent jobs. Lack of education also prevents many young people from becoming the engineers, doctors, scientists, or business managers that countries need in order to improve. Many parts of Africa have lower literacy rates than one finds in Europe or the United States. Often schooling is only available to those who can afford to pay to attend. Many countries in this region are working hard to raise literacy rates among young people. Girls tend to have less opportunity to go to school than boys in many areas of Africa. The United Nations and the World Bank are currently working with many African countries to try to bring educational opportunities to their people.

Use this chart to answer questions 95 - 99.

Country	Total Literacy Rate	Literacy of Males	Literacy of Females	GDP – Gross Domestic Product, per capita*
Burkina Faso	21%	21.8%	15%	$1,300
Congo	67%	80.9%	54.1%	$300
Egypt	71.4%	83%	59.45%	$5,500
Ghana	51.9%	66.4%	49.8%	$1,400
Kenya	85.1%	90.6%	79.7%	$1,700
South Africa	86.4%	87%	85%	$9,800
South Sudan	27%	40%	16%	$1,006
Sudan	70%	71%	76%	$2,800
United States (for comparison)	99%	99%	99%	$45,800

Gross Domestic Product is the value of all final goods and services produced within a country in a given year (converted into US dollars for comparison). When divided into a value *per capita* (or per person) it can be used as a measure of the wealth or living conditions in the country. The higher the GDP value, the better the living conditions in the country.

____95. **Which African country has the highest literacy rates?**
   A. Ghana
   B. Kenya
   C. Burkina Faso
   D. South Africa

____96. **Which African country has the highest GDP?**
   A. Ghana
   B. Kenya
   C. Burkina Faso
   D. South Africa

____97. **Which African country has the lowest literacy rate?**
   A. Ghana
   B. Kenya
   C. Burkina Faso
   D. South Africa

____98. **Which country demonstrates GDP will not always be high just because the literacy rate is high?**
   A. Egypt
   B. Congo
   C. Burkina Faso
   D. South Africa

____99. **How do the literacy rates for men and women compare in most of the countries represented on this chart?**
   A. It costs more for a country to educate women.
   B. The chart proves that most women do not want to go to school.
   C. There is very little difference in the literacy rates for men and women.
   D. In nearly all the countries women have a lower literacy rate than men.

GOVERNMENT/CIVICS UNDERSTANDINGS

SS7CG1 The student will compare and contrast various forms of government.
a. Describe the ways government systems distribute power: unitary, confederation, federal.

A **unitary government system** is one in which the central government holds nearly all of the power. In a unitary system, local governments such as state or county systems may have some power at certain times, but they are under the control of the central government. The central government has the power to change the way state or county governments operate or remove them altogether. Some unitary governments have elected officials who, once elected, may make and enforce laws without taking the opinions of those at lower levels of government into consideration. A **monarchy**, where a king and his advisors make most of the decisions, would be a good example of a unitary government. Some of the countries in Africa have unitary forms of government. Other African countries have kings, but most of them are kings of particular tribes or ethnic groups and do not play a major role in the day-to-day government of the countries.

A **confederation government system** is one in which the local governments hold all of the power and the central government depends on the local governments for its existence. The central government has only as much power as the local governments are willing to give it. The United Nations is a good example of a confederation. The UN can only offer advice and assistance when the member nations agree to cooperate.

A **federal government system** is a political system in which power is shared among different levels of government. It is a government made up of an executive branch, a legislative branch, and a judicial branch. Power is shared between the national government and the local governments.

_____ 100. In a unitary government system who holds most of the power?
   A. the individual voters
   B. the local governments
   C. the central government
   D. both the central and local governments

_____ 101. In a confederation government system who holds most of the power?
   A. individual voters
   B. local governments
   C. central government
   D. central and local governments

_____ 102. In a federal system of government, who holds most of the power?
   A. the president
   B. the local governments
   C. the central government
   D. power is shared among different levels of government

Copyright © Clairmont Press, Inc. DO NOT DUPLICATE. 1-800-874-8638

SS7CG1 The student will compare and contrast various forms of government.
b. Explain how governments determine citizen participation: autocratic, oligarchic, and democratic.

People who live under different kinds of governments often find there are great differences in the rights given to individual citizens.

An **autocratic government** is one in which the ruler has absolute power to do whatever he wishes and make and enforce whatever laws he chooses. Individuals who live under autocratic governments do not have any rights to choose leaders or vote on which laws are made and put into practice. Some autocratic governments may allow the people rights in certain areas like managing local affairs, but the central government keeps control of all the most important aspects of the country's life. In an autocratic system, people usually have little or no power to use against the government if they disagree with decisions that government or ruler has made.

An **oligarchy** means "government by the few." In this form of government, a political party or other small group makes all of the major decisions. The people of the country have little choice but to go along with the decisions they make. This sort of government can be very similar to an autocratic government.

In a **democratic** government system, the people play a greater role in deciding who the rulers are and what decisions are made. "**Democracy**" comes from the Greek word "demos" which means "people." In this form of government, a great deal of power is left in the hands of the people. Decisions are often made by majority votes, but there are also laws in place to protect individual rights. If a person living in a democracy feels his rights have been violated, he has the power to ask the government for help in correcting the situation.

_____ 103. **In an autocracy, who makes most of the important governmental decisions?**
A. the courts
B. the people
C. an individual ruler
D. an elected legislature

_____ 104. **Which describes the decision-makers in an oligarchy?**
A. voting citizens
B. judges and lawyers
C. a king and his family
D. a group of powerful leaders

_____ 105. **Why do the individual voters have more power in a democracy than they do in an autocracy or an oligarchy?**
A. Kings are always cruel rulers.
B. The people play a role in deciding who rules.
C. All of the power stays in the hands of the local governments.
D. Voters in democratic countries always choose qualified leaders.

SS7CG1 The student will compare and contrast various forms of government.

c. Describe the two predominant forms of democratic governments: parliamentary and presidential.

In a **parliamentary** form of democratic government, the people vote for those who represent the political party they feel best represents their views. The legislature they elect, the **Parliament**, makes and carries out the laws for the country. The leader of a parliamentary form of government is usually chosen by the party that wins the most seats in the legislature. This leader is often called a Prime Minister or Premier and is recognized as the head of the government. The Prime Minister leads the executive branch of the government and must answer directly to the legislature for the actions and policies recommended. In many parliamentary governments, a "Head of State" is more of a ceremonial leader.

In a **presidential** form of government, a **president**, or chief executive, is chosen separately from the legislature. The legislature passes the laws, and it is the duty of the president to see that the laws are enforced. The president holds power separately from the legislature, but he does not have the power to dismiss the legislature or force them to make particular laws. The president is the official head of the government. The legislature does not have the power to dismiss the president, except in extreme cases. The president is both the Head of State and the head of the government.

_____ 106. **Which branch of government is responsible for making and carrying out the laws in a parliamentary system of government?**
  A. courts
  B. monarch
  C. president
  D. legislature

_____ 107. **What is the leader of a parliamentary system often called?**
  A. king
  B. president
  C. governor
  D. prime minister

_____ 108. **Which BEST describes the two predominant forms of a democratic government?**
  A. dictatorship and republican
  B. presidential and dictatorship
  C. presidential and confederate
  D. parliamentary and presidential

_____ 109. **The leader of a parliamentary type of government is called the**
  A. dictator.
  B. president.
  C. prime minister.
  D. prime negotiator.

_____ **110. Who chooses the country's leader in a parliamentary form of government?**
   A. the monarch
   B. popular vote of the people
   C. decision by the national courts
   D. the party with the most representatives in the legislature

_____ **111. Which BEST describes a head of state in a parliamentary government system?**
   A. person who has no role in government
   B. ceremonial figure without much actual power
   C. the most powerful person in the national government
   D. one who can veto or cancel laws passed by the legislature

_____ **112. Which branch of government passes laws in a presidential system of government?**
   A. judicial
   B. executive
   C. legislative
   D. bureaucracy

_____ **113. In a presidential system of government how is a president chosen?**
   A. separately from the legislature
   B. by a decision of the national courts
   C. by a majority vote of the legislature
   D. by the political party with the most representatives in the legislature

_____ **114. What is the role of the president regarding the laws passed by the legislature?**
   A. The president is supposed to enforce those laws.
   B. The president can change the laws he does not like.
   C. The president sends the laws to the states for approval.
   D. Laws passed by the legislature do not have to go to the president for approval.

_____ **115. What is one main difference between a president and a prime minister?**
   A. A prime minister has more power than a president.
   B. A president has to be elected while a prime minister does not.
   C. A prime minister does not belong to a particular political party, while a president always does.
   D. A president is separate from the legislature, while a prime minister answers directly to the legislature.

AFRICA

SS7CG2 The student will explain the structures of the modern governments of Africa.

a. Compare the republican systems of government in the Republic of Kenya and the Republic of South Africa, distinguishing the form of leadership and the role of the citizen in terms of voting and personal freedoms.

The countries of Kenya and South Africa have very different governmental systems today. Though both are described as "republics," the reality is very different in each country.

Use this chart to answer questions 116 - 121.

Country	Type of Government	Head of State	Who Can Vote	Degree of Personal Freedom for Citizens	Year of Independence from Colonial Rule
Republic of Kenya	Republic, with one-house legislature called the National Assembly	President leads the Kenyan African National Union (KANU) political party	All citizens 18 years of age or older can vote.	Freedoms are written into the constitution but government is dominated by the president. There have been improvements in citizens' rights in recent years though.	Kenya became independent from Great Britain in 1963.
Republic of South Africa	Republic, with a two-house National Assembly	President elected by the National Assembly	All citizens 18 years of age or older can vote.	Personal freedoms are numerous. Apartheid (legal separation of the races) has ended. Literacy rates are high.	South Africa became independent from Great Britain in 1910. The racially segregated government was ended in 1994, when majority rule was established.

(Source: CIA World Factbook)

116. **What is confusing about the fact that both of these countries are called "republics"?**
   A. Both countries are ruled by kings.
   B. These countries do not allow women to vote.
   C. The governments of both work in different ways.
   D. Only one of the countries has a legislature or representative assembly.

117. **Which country has been independent of colonial control for the longest time?**
   A. Kenya
   B. Sudan
   C. South Africa
   D. still under colonial control

118. **Which term correctly defines "apartheid"?**
   A ruled by a king
   B. a two-house legislature
   C. legal separation of races
   D. ruled by European colonial country

119. **How is the president of South Africa chosen?**
   A. He is appointed by the king.
   B. He is elected by the National Assembly.
   C. He is chosen by the country's religious leader.
   D. He is identified by the people in a national election.

120. **Which European country once controlled these countries as a colonial power?**
   A. Egypt
   B. France
   C. Germany
   D. Great Britain

121. **Where are individual rights applied and protected?**
   A. African National Union
   B. National Assembly
   C. Kenya
   D. South Africa

AFRICA

Copyright © Clairmont Press, Inc. DO NOT DUPLICATE. 1-800-874-8638

SS7CG3 The student will analyze how politics in Africa impacts the standard of living.

a. Compare how various factors, including gender, affect access to education in Kenya and Sudan.

The Republics of Kenya, Sudan, and South Sudan present very different pictures when looking at how these countries provide education for their children. Factors like money, political stability, and even traditions play a part in shaping the educational systems of the three countries.

KENYA

The country of Kenya currently has a national literacy rate of about 87 percent. The Kenyan government has made improving education a priority. They have started a number of government programs for building schools and eliminating fees for children who want to go to school. About 85% of Kenya's school-age children attend elementary school. That number drops to 24% for high school, and only 2% for college. Kenya has a Ministry of Education whose motto is "Quality Education for Development." Literacy and school attendance are much higher for both boys and girls in cities. Teachers still have to work to get many rural families to see the importance of education for girls. The traditional view is that girls only need to prepare for marriage. Early marriages are very common in rural parts of Kenya and a marriage brings a dowry to the bride's family. A dowry is money or gifts the groom and his family give to the bride and her parents as a wedding gift.

SUDAN

The Republic of Sudan has not made quite the progress in education that one sees in Kenya. The Republic of Sudan has been involved in a civil war for five decades, resulting in the creation of South Sudan in July, 2011. Sudan has a national literacy rate of about 61 percent, and a wide gap in the literacy of boys and girls. Sudan's boys have a literacy rate of about 72 percent, while girls have only 50 percent. Children living in cities have the best chance to get an education. Sudanese girls face many of the same problems as girls throughout Africa who live in rural or traditional communities. Many parents are concerned that allowing girls to go to public schools will result in their learning bad behavior. Daughters are often seen as needing only to prepare for marriage. A married daughter means wealth for both families, dowry money for the bride's family and a new household worker for the family of the groom.

SOUTH SUDAN

The civil war in Sudan created much chaos and more than two million lost lives in the southern and western parts of the country resulting in the creation of South Sudan on July 9, 2011 as the world's 196th independent country. The military conflict in the countryside has left many schools in South Sudan in ruins. South Sudan models its educational programs after Sudan. The national literacy rate is 27%. South Sudanese boys have a literacy rate of 40% and the girls' literacy rate is 16%. Only one schoolchild in four is a girl and female illiteracy is the highest in the world. These children have not had educational opportunities due to the civil war with Sudan, but education is a priority for the Southern Sudanese and they are working to improve their education system.

_____ **122. What is the literacy rate in Kenya?**

     A. 25 percent

     B. 85 percent

     C. 75 percent

     D. 50 percent

_____ **123. What is the literacy rate in the Republic of Sudan?**

     A. 50 percent

     B. 61 percent

     C. 70 percent

     D. 85 percent

_____ **124. How do the literacy rates for boys and girls compare in these three countries?**

     A. Literacy rates for girls are higher.

     B. Literacy rates for boys are higher.

     C. There is no difference in literacy rates.

     D. Literacy rates are not reported by gender.

_____ **125. What percentage of Kenyan children attends elementary school?**

     A. 55 percent

     B. 65 percent

     C. 75 percent

     D. 85 percent

_____ **126. What organization is primarily responsible for improvements in Kenya's educational system?**

     A. Kenyan parents

     B. Teachers' Union

     C. Students' Initiative

     D. Kenyan Ministry of Education

_____ **127. Why are literacy rates for girls lower than those for boys in Kenya, Sudan and South Sudan?**

     A. Very few schools have been opened for girls in either country.

     B. Girls have shown they cannot do schoolwork as easily as boys.

     C. Most girls in these countries have no interest in going to school.

     D. Traditional views say that girls should be married rather than educated.

_____ **128. What would be the correct definition of a "dowry"?**

     A. the gifts wedding guests give to the bride and groom

     B. money paid to the government to get a marriage license

     C. the household goods a bride must give the groom's family

     D. money or gifts given by the groom to the bride's family at marriage

AFRICA

_____ 129. **What is one factor that has caused the Republics of Sudan and South Sudan to pay less attention to education?**
   A. civil war
   B. lack of interest
   C. education system needs improvement
   D. no education beyond elementary school

_____ 130. **What is the literacy rate in the Republic of South Sudan?**
   A. 10%
   B. 27%
   C. 54%
   D. 70%

> **SS7CG3 The student will analyze how politics in Africa impacts the standard of living.**
> b. Describe the impact of government stability on the distribution of resources to combat AIDS and famine across Africa.

Sub-Saharan Africa has one of the highest HIV-AIDS infections in the world. Estimates are that there are about 23 million people living in Africa with AIDS and another 1.5 million have died from the disease. Because so many of the victims are young and middle aged adults, their deaths have left Africa with over eleven million orphans. Some of these children are able to move in with relatives. Many thousands of others have no one to take care of them and they must try to survive on their own. The extent of the disease in Africa is just being understood. Most health officials expect the numbers of those infected and of those who die will increase in the next ten years. Poor health care systems, poverty, and lack of government organization, as well as ignorance about the disease and its prevention all contribute to the rapidly expanding number of cases. The **antiretroviral drugs (AVTs)** that are able to slow down the progress of the disease are expensive and beyond the budgets of many who are infected.

South Africa is a different story. Health officials at the United Nations have estimated that one in five South Africans may be infected with HIV/AIDS, yet few people can get the drugs they need to slow the disease. AIDS took hold in South Africa first in the 1990s when the country was trying to end the old apartheid system of racial segregation. The early days of the HIV epidemic were overshadowed by the nation's other problems. Some see HIV/AIDS as a disease only of the poor. Some men blame it on the women. Ignorance has a real impact on how rapidly this disease spreads.

Zimbabwe has one of the highest rates of HIV/AIDS infection in the world. Government corruption, civil unrest, and suspicion of offers of help from other countries have made Zimbabwe's problems even greater. Zimbabwe's poor economy has made expensive antiretroviral drugs impossible for most people to afford. Political turmoil and a harsh government have created many refugees in Zimbabwe, making the health crisis even worse.

Nigeria has a 3.1 percent HIV/AIDS infection rate, relatively low in comparison to some other African countries. However, Nigeria has a very large population, so that 3.1 percent translates into almost 3,000,000 people who are currently infected. Though Nigeria has oil, most Nigerians are relatively poor, and the Nigerian government did not make HIV/AIDS a priority until the late 1990s. Since then, Nigeria has made HIV/AIDS prevention, treatment, and care a main concern. While Nigeria still has to struggle with the HIV/AIDS problem, the government is working hard to educate the people and make treatment available.

SS7E1 The student will analyze different economic systems.

b. Explain how most countries have a mixed economy located on a continuum between pure market and pure command.

A MIXED ECONOMY

In reality, nearly all modern economies in the world today have characteristics of all three types of economic systems, and the countries of Africa are no exception. That is why they are called mixed economies.

A **mixed economy** is located on a continuum between a pure market and a pure command economy.

_____ 147. **Why are most modern economies referred to as mixed economies?**

A. Poverty is always highest in countries with market economies.

B. Government planners do not know how to handle economic problems.

C. Products made by traditional economies have no markets in the modern world.

D. Most countries have aspects of all three economic types at work in their economies.

Today no countries in the world have economic systems that are all traditional, all command, or all market systems. Nearly all countries of Africa today would best be described as mixed economies, as they have the characteristics of free market and free enterprise as well as some government planning and control. As African nations join the world economic market, they are finding that there is a place in the economic world for many different approaches to what they produce, how to do it, and for whom.

_____ 148. **Why do most economies in the world today operate somewhere in between a market economy and a command economy?**

A. Government control always makes a market economy profitable.

B. Most consumers prefer government control to a free market system.

C. Government control of some aspects of the economy has never been successful in the modern world.

D. Most economies have found they need a mix of free market and some government control to be successful and protect consumers.

AFRICA

Copyright © Clairmont Press, Inc. DO NOT DUPLICATE. 1-800-874-8638

SS7E1 The student will analyze different economic systems.
c. Compare and contrast the economic systems in South Africa and Nigeria.

Use this chart to answer questions 149 - 153.

Area of Comparison	South Africa	Nigeria
Type of economy	A technologically advanced market economy with some government control; one of the strongest economies in the region	Poorly organized economy after a long period of military dictatorship and corruption; now trying to reorganize with more private enterprise allowed; want to be able to take advantage of strong world oil market
Goods produced	Mining (platinum, diamonds, and gold), automobile assembly, machinery, textiles, iron and steel chemicals, fertilizer	Oil and petrochemicals are the primary market goods; Nigeria once exported food and other agricultural products but now must import them.
Leading Exports	Gold, diamonds, platinum, other minerals, machinery and equipment	Oil and petrochemical products
GDP per capita	$10,700	$2,500
GDP Composition by Sector	Agriculture – 2.5% Industry – 30.5% Services – 67%	Agriculture – 30% Industry – 32% Services – 38%
Unemployment Rate	25%	4.9%

_____ 149. **The economies of the two countries on the chart could best be described as**
A. mixed.
B. market.
C. command.
D. traditional.

_____ 150. **What is South Africa's main export?**
A. oil
B. textiles
C. gold and diamonds
D. agricultural products

_____ 151. **Which country has the largest per capita GDP?**
A. Nigeria
B. South Africa
C. GDP information is not available.
D. The GDPs are almost all the same.

_____ 152. **Why was Nigeria formerly under a command economic system?**
A. The country was under military rule.
B. Most people did not know how to produce anything on their own.
C. The government wanted to control the gold and diamond exports.
D. They were forced by the United Nations to use a command system.

_____ 153. **What does the chart indicate that might be a concern about the economy of South Africa?**
A. The GDP is lower than that of Nigeria.
B. The country has a high unemployment rate.
C. There is not much of a world market for gold and diamonds.
D. Few of their people are able to work in the services sector of the economy.

AFRICA

A **tariff** is a tax placed on goods when they are **imported** (brought into one country from another country). The purpose of a tariff is to make the imported item more expensive than a similar item made locally. This sort of a tariff is called a "**protective tariff**" because it protects local manufacturers from competition coming from cheaper goods made in other countries. If a country in Africa wanted to be sure only locally grown grain was purchased, the government might place a tariff (a tax) on any grain imported from other countries. That tariff makes the imported goods more expensive than the locally produced goods. Therefore, sales of imported grain would go down, and sales of locally grown grain would go up.

A **quota** is a different way of limiting the amount of foreign goods that can come into a country. A quota sets a specific amount or number of a particular product that can be imported or acquired in a given period. By limiting imports, more people will buy products made locally. A quota can also be a limit placed on how much of a particular product can be produced. Nigeria is a major producer of oil. Nigeria is also a member of the **Organization of Petroleum Exporting Countries (OPEC)**. OPEC places quotas on how much oil each member nation can produce for the world market in order to keep prices at levels they want. This quota is designed to regulate the supply and the price of oil. The goal is for OPEC to make as much profit as possible.

A third type of trade barrier is called an **embargo**. An embargo is when one country announces that it will no longer trade with another country. The goal is to isolate the country and cause problems with that country's economy. Embargoes usually come about when two countries are having political problems. One example of an embargo involves South Africa. This country once practiced an official policy of **apartheid** (the legal separation of the races). Many countries in the United Nations thought this was wrong. They decided to stop selling weapons to South Africa. The embargo lasted for many years. More products and money were kept from South Africa. In the 1990s, South Africa officially dropped its apartheid system and the nations of the world began trading with South Africa again.

_____ 161. **What is a tariff?**
  A. a tax paid by the purchaser when goods are sold
  B. a tax placed on goods coming into one country from another
  C. a tax placed on goods made by local craftsmen or manufacturers
  D. a fee paid when goods are shipped from one state to another in the United States

_____ 162. **What is a quota?**
  A. a tax placed on imported goods when they enter the country
  B. a limit on the amount of foreign goods allowed into a country
  C. a decision to prevent certain goods from being imported at all
  D. a tax placed on goods when they are purchased in the market place

_____ 163. **What is an embargo?**
  A. a tax placed on goods coming into the country from overseas
  B. a limit on the amount of certain goods allowed into the country
  C. a tax paid by the producer before he can sell his goods in another country
  D. a halt to trade with a particular country for economic or political reasons

_____ 164. **How could a high tariff on imported grain help the people in the country charging the tariff?**
  A. The grain process would be lower if tariffs were in place.
  B. Local grain would always be of a higher quality than grain from other countries.
  C. Local grain would be more plentiful because it was grown closer to the markets.
  D. Local farmers would be able to sell their grain since it would be cheaper than imported grain.

_____ 165. **Why did a number of the countries of the United Nations have an embargo on South Africa?**
    A. South Africa refused to take part in international trade.
    B. They wanted South Africa to end its system of apartheid.
    C. Some were hoping for better oil deals from the South African government.
    D. They wanted South Africa to lower the world price of gold and diamonds.

> **SS7E2 The student will explain how voluntary trade benefits buyers and sellers in Africa.**
> b. Explain why international trade requires a system for exchanging currencies between nations.

EXCHANGING CURRENCIES IN INTERNATIONAL TRADE

In order for countries to trade with each other, a system of exchanging currencies is necessary. Most countries have their own individual types of money. Currency from countries with stronger economies is usually easier to exchange because it has a more dependable value. Many of the currencies of African nations are harder to exchange because there has been so much political unrest and economic problems.

Parts of Africa have already begun to use a currency that can be exchanged between nations. This currency is called the **CFA franc**. This currency was created after World War II when economies around the world were unstable. The value of the currency was tied to the French franc, because France has been in power in parts of Africa.

Today there are two versions of the **CFA franc**. One is called the **West African CFA franc** and the other is the **Central African CFA franc**. They now have their value linked to the Euro, which is used in the European Union.

_____ 166. **Why is a system of currency exchange necessary for international trade?**
    A. Nearly all world currencies are worthless on the world market.
    B. Those buying goods on the world market want to be paid in gold and silver.
    C. Most goods bought on the international market must be paid for in US dollars.
    D. There must be a way to pay for goods purchased from countries with different types of currencies.

_____ 167. **The CFA Franc is used in what part of Africa?**
    A. along the Atlantic coast
    B. in West and Central Africa
    C. along the Indian Ocean coast
    D. in the southern part of the continent

Human capital means the knowledge and skills that make it possible for workers to earn a living producing goods or services. The more skills and education workers have, the better they are able to work without mistakes and to learn new jobs as technology changes. Companies that invest in better training and education for their workers generally earn more profits. Good companies also try to make sure working conditions are safe and efficient, so their workers can do their jobs with less risk.

Gross domestic product, or **GDP**, is the total value of all the final goods and services produced within a country in a single year. Wealthy countries have a much higher **per capita GDP** (amount of goods and services produced divided by the total population) than do developing or underdeveloped countries.

Companies that have invested in human capital through training and education are more likely to have profitable businesses and more satisfied workers than companies that do not make these investments. Countries where training and education are more easily available often have higher production levels of goods and services. The countries in Africa have widely different GDP levels. Those countries that make it possible for workers to receive training and education tend to be wealthier than those that do not.

South Africa has invested heavily in human capital. They have a diversified economy and one of the highest Gross Domestic Products on the continent. The electronics industry in South Africa requires workers with skills and training, and the mining industry relies on workers who can deal with technology that is more sophisticated. In spite of these positive factors, South Africa still has one of the highest unemployment rates in Africa. Over 25 percent of the country's workers are unemployed. Most of them are black people who are still suffering the effects of the apartheid system that was in place in South Africa for many years.

Nigeria is an example of a country that should have a strong economy because they have rich deposits of oil and an educated population. However, years of government corruption, civil war, and military rule have left Nigeria poor. Nearly 70 percent of the people in Nigeria have to live on less than one dollar a day. Even though it has good farmland, it must import food to keep its people from starving.

_____ **168. Which is a part of a country's human capital?**
   A. skills and knowledge workers have
   B. taxes collected from a country's workers
   C. money paid to workers for producing goods
   D. the amount of goods sold in foreign trade in a year

_____ **169. Why has the country of South Africa made a big investment in human capital?**
   A. South Africa has no natural resources to develop.
   B. They were forced to provide training and education by the United Nations.
   C. Some of that country's most important industries need educated, skilled workers.
   D. Most schools and universities are free because of foreign investment in the country.

SS7E4 The student will explain personal money management choices in terms of income, spending, credit, saving, and investing.

When people go to work, they earn an income. An **income** is the total of a person's earnings that they can then decide how to use. Broadly speaking, an individual has only two choices about what to do with income: spending money now on goods and services or saving for the future.

Savings are after tax income minus consumption spending, that is, the money that you have not spent after buying things you want. To help people make decisions about using their limited income, a budget can be developed. A **budget** is a spending-and-savings plan, based on estimated income and expenses for an individual or an organization, covering a specific time. From an individual point of view, savings typically becomes a form of **investing**, because the savings is put into a bank account, stock, bond or mutual fund that pays a rate of return (interest). Investing refers to postponing current consumption or rewards to pursue an activity with expectations of greater benefits in the future. **Financial investment** refers to the decisions by individuals (and firms) to invest money in financial assets such as bank accounts, certificates of deposit, stocks, bonds and mutual funds.

Real investment or **physical capital investment** refers to the decisions by businesses to purchase equipment and physical plants and new homes by consumers. The amount of real investment is critical to economic growth. Financial investment and real investment are connected, but they are not the same.

Credit refers to the ability to borrow money. Some forms of credit commonly used by consumers are car loans, home mortgage loans and credit cards. Firms also use credit regularly, either by borrowing from a bank or issuing corporate bonds. Government also uses credit when it needs to borrow money to finance a budget deficit (e.g., savings bonds, treasury notes). Those who can borrow moderate or large sums of money at a reasonable rate of interest are sometimes said to have good credit, while those who cannot borrow such amounts are said to have bad credit.

Credit is extremely useful to the economy. Most people would have great difficulty in buying a house if they couldn't borrow the money. Many people also use credit to further their education. Many firms would be unable to build new factories if they had to save all the money first. In addition, short-term credit is often used by people (through credit cards) as a simple and convenient method of paying for purchases.

However, excessive borrowing can be a problem for households, firms and government. Making interest payments because you borrowed money for the house that you live in, a car that you drive or a factory that produces goods can make good economic sense. However, credit should not be used to pay for goods or consumption in the present that were completely consumed in the past.

_____ **184. Which BEST describes income?**
   A. money borrowed from a credit union
   B. credit offered on the basis of a person's salary
   C. money you earn working or get from investing
   D. taxes paid to the government based on annual salary

_____ **185. What is the definition of savings?**
   A. money sent to the government as taxes
   B. money used to pay off loan obligations
   C. money left over after buying what is needed and wanted
   D. money used to buy things one needs like food and shelter

_____ **186. Which is a plan for saving and spending?**

    A. a will

    B. a budget

    C. a savings account

    D. a checking account

_____ **187. When an individual invests money in bank accounts, certificates of deposit or mutual funds, it is called**

    A. real investment.

    B. a checking account.

    C. risking one's savings.

    D. a financial investment.

_____ **188. When firms invest money in equipment, factories, or real estate, that is called**

    A. real investment.

    B. a checking account.

    C. a financial investment.

    D. risking one's savings.

_____ **189. The ability to borrow money is called**

    A. credit.

    B. savings.

    C. investment.

    D. mutual funds.

_____ **190. Credit becomes a problem when**

    A. banks begin to issue their own credit cards.

    B. credit is used to pay for things like college tuition.

    C. credit card companies offer people additional credit cards.

    D. a person cannot find the money to pay their monthly bills.

_____ **201. Which European country first colonized South Africa?**
A. France
B. Germany
C. Great Britain
D. The Netherlands

_____ **202. When Great Britain took over South Africa and the Dutch settlers moved farther North, which African group fought that expansion?**
A. Zulus
B. Berbers
C. Ashanti
D. Mau Mau

_____ **203. What valuable natural resources were discovered in South Africa after the British took control of that country?**
A. coal and iron
B. salt and silver
C. oil and natural gas
D. gold and diamonds

_____ **204. Which organization was formed to work for equality in the country of South Africa?**
A. African Union
B. Pan African Congress
C. African National Congress
D. Organization of Petroleum Exporting Countries

_____ **205. What is the apartheid system?**
A. equality for all
B. segregation of races
C. constitutional monarchy
D. western-style democracy

_____ **206. What was significant about Nelson Mandela's election to political office in South Africa in 1994?**
A. He was the first black president of South Africa.
B. He was elected as a representative of the Zulu nation.
C. He united the Zulu and Ashanti people in order to win the election.
D. He was the overwhelming choice of British citizens living in South Africa.

_____ **207. Why was the government of Kenya criticized after independence, even though it was led by Africans?**
A. They voted to bring the old king back to power.
B. The government was controlled by only one party.
C. They put an apartheid system of government in place.
D. The new government refused to trade with western countries.

AFRICA

_____ **208. What conflict broke out in Nigeria after independence was declared?**

      A. religious conflict between Muslims and Christians

      B. a government decision that handed rule over to a dictator

      C. protests by women in Nigeria who demanded equal rights

      D. arguments over writing a constitution that called for apartheid

_____ **209. How could the political situation in Nigeria today be described?**

      A. The government is still unstable.

      B. Ghana took over Nigeria in a regional war several years ago.

      C. The United Nations has taken over the government of Nigeria.

      D. Nigeria currently has a government that is able to deal effectively with all its problems.

Apartheid means the legal separation of the races. Apartheid was the law of the Union of South Africa from the earliest creation of the state in 1948. The country had a complicated system of racial identification, classifying citizens as either black, colored, Asian, or white. Blacks were allowed to own only a very little land, even though they made up over 70 percent of the population. All sorts of public facilities were segregated, including schools, libraries, movie theaters, restaurants, and even beaches. People were not allowed to marry anyone who was of a different race. The apartheid system lasted until well into the 1980s, with the white minority population making all of the laws for the nonwhite majority.

Throughout these years, two groups were working to end this South African regime, the African National Congress led by **Nelson Mandela**, and the Pan African Congress. Many countries around the world were critical of South Africa for its discriminatory government. Some refused to do business with South Africa. Riots and fighting took place constantly, and Nelson Mandela was sentenced to life in prison for his work against the regime. The repressive measures did not slow down the protests however. Eventually the South African government had to admit that their policy of apartheid had no place in the modern world. In 1990, South African **President F. W. de Klerk** agreed to allow the African National Congress to operate as a legal party and he released Nelson Mandela from prison after he had served 27 years in prison. De Klerk also began to repeal the apartheid laws. In 1994, South Africa had its first elections that were open to all races. The African National Congress won the most delegates to the new government and Nelson Mandela was chosen South Africa's first black president. Rather than be bitter about being jailed, Mandela announced that one of his goals was to get the races in South Africa to work together and try to overcome the hatred that had grown during the apartheid years.

_____ 210. **What percent of the population of South Africa was black when that country achieved independence?**

A. 20 percent

B. 40 percent

C. 50 percent

D. 70 percent

_____ 211. **What was the name of Nelson Mandela's political party?**

A. Zulu Nation

B. African Union

C. African National Congress

D. Kenyan National Unity Party

_____ 212. **What decision did South African President F.W. de Klerk eventually make about the country's apartheid laws?**

A. He added many new and even harsher laws.

B. He began to recommend that the laws be repealed.

C. He lifted segregation restrictions on those living in South African cities.

D. He worked to spread apartheid laws to nations neighboring South Africa.

_____ 213. **What was Nelson Mandela's attitude toward the people who had been responsible for the old government of South Africa?**
  A. Many of the old leaders were sent to jail on his orders.
  B. He turned the leaders over to the United Nations for punishment.
  C. He tried to have all the old government officials exiled to other countries.
  D. He felt the different races needed to try to work together in the new government.

SS7H1 The student will analyze continuity and change in Africa leading to the 21st century
d. Explain the impact of the Pan-African movement.

The **Pan-African movement** began as a reaction to the terrible experiences of colonial rule and the desire for people of African descent, no matter where they lived in the world, to think of Africa as a homeland. The first people to support the idea of Pan-Africans were Africans who were living in other parts of the world. They felt all Africans, no matter where they lived, shared a bond with each other. They also called for Africans all over the continent to think of themselves as one people and to work for the betterment of all. They wanted to end European control of the continent and to make Africa a homeland for all people of African descent. Those in the movement also hoped that African countries could work together to improve each country's economy.

While the peaceful unification of Africa has never taken place, the Pan-African movement can take a lot of credit for sparking independence movements that left nearly all African nations free of colonial rule by the 1980s.

_____ 214. **The main goal of the Pan-Africa movement was to**
  A. end any support for the African National Congress.
  B. immediately overthrow all of the ruling governments in Africa.
  C. get all African nations to become members of the United Nations.
  D. get Africans to think of themselves as one people and to work together.

Use the graph to answer questions 215-217.

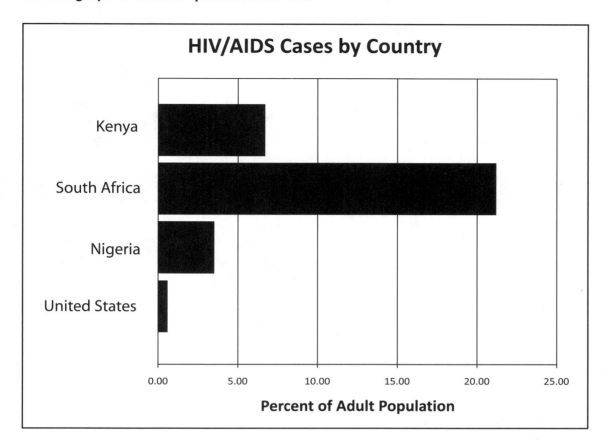

HIV/AIDS Cases by Country

Kenya

South Africa

Nigeria

United States

0.00   5.00   10.00   15.00   20.00   25.00

Percent of Adult Population

_____ **215. What part of the adult population of Kenya has HIV/AIDS?**
A. about 7%
B. over 10%
C. nearly 22%
D. less than 5%

_____ **216. Which question can be answered using the graph?**
A. How many people in Africa have HIV/AIDS?
B. What part of the population of Nigeria has HIV/AIDS?
C. Which of the countries listed have the most adults with HIV/AIDS?
D. Which African country has the highest percentage of adults with HIV/AIDS?

_____ **217. What is the BEST reason for including data from the United States on the graph?**
A. only three African countries have adults with HIV/AIDS
B. many people in the U.S. have ancestors that came from Africa
C. to compare data from African countries with data from our own
D. the U.S. has assisted people from many countries in fighting HIV/AIDS

AFRICA

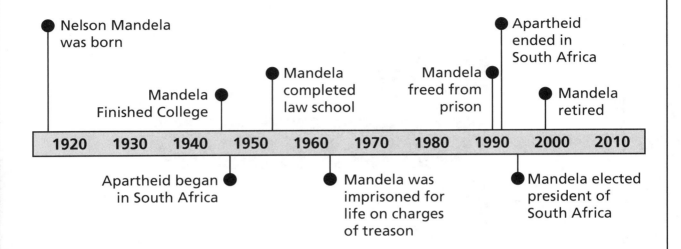

Events in the Life of Nelson Mandela

Nelson Mandela was born

Mandela Finished College

Mandela completed law school

Mandela freed from prison

Apartheid ended in South Africa

Mandela retired

1920　1930　1940　1950　1960　1970　1980　1990　2000　2010

Apartheid began in South Africa

Mandela was imprisoned for life on charges of treason

Mandela elected president of South Africa

_____ **218. In what year was Nelson Mandela born?**
    A. 1918
    B. 1945
    C. 1962
    D. 1999

_____ **219. About how long after Mandela was imprisoned did he become president of South Africa?**
    A. about 30 years
    B. nearly 20 years
    C. less than 10 years
    D. more than 40 years

_____ **220. Which event in Mandela's life happened before the official beginning of apartheid?**
    A. Mandela completed college.
    B. Mandela finished law school.
    C. Mandela was convicted of treason.
    D. Mandela retired as president of South Africa.

AFRICA

SOUTHWEST ASIA (MIDDLE EAST)

GEOGRAPHIC UNDERSTANDINGS

SS7G5 The student will locate selected features in Southwestern Asia (Middle East).
a. Locate on a world and regional political-physical map: Euphrates River, Jordan River, Tigris River, Suez Canal, Persian Gulf, Strait of Hormuz, Arabian Sea, Red Sea, and Gaza Strip.

The **rivers of Southwest Asia** (the Middle East) are important because much of this region of the world is dry and desert or semi-desert. One of the longest rivers in the region is the **Euphrates River**, which begins in Turkey, and flows through Syria and Iraq. In southern Iraq, the Euphrates River joins with the Tigris River to form one waterway called the **Shaat al-Arab**, which then flows along the border between Kuwait and Iran before emptying into the Persian Gulf.

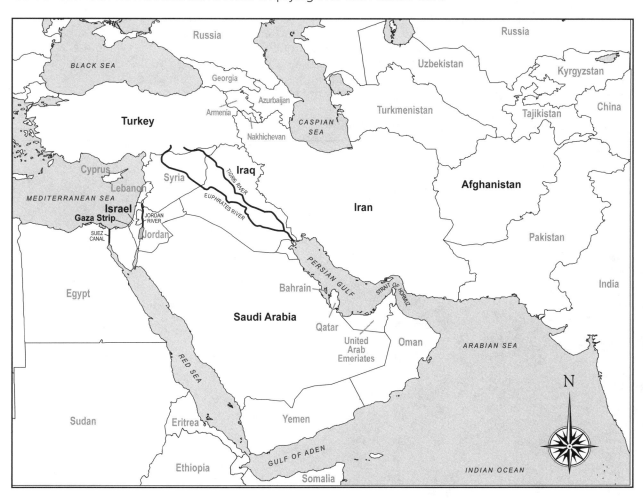

The **Tigris River** begins in the mountains of Turkey and flows south through Iraq. It joins the Euphrates in southern Iraq. These two rivers provide water for both drinking and farming. The countries that share these rivers have had problems over how the water will be shared among them. The **Shatt al-Arab**, the waterway formed when the Euphrates River and Tigris River come together, is also important because it is the boundary between Kuwait and Iran.

The **Persian Gulf** is one of the main ways oil is shipped from the rich fields of Kuwait, Saudi Arabia, Iran, and the other countries that line its shores. All of the countries that produce oil in that region depend on the Persian Gulf as a shipping route. Any ships coming out of or into the Persian Gulf must navigate through the very narrow **Strait of Hormuz**, located at one end of the Persian Gulf. This waterway connects the Persian Gulf to the **Arabian Sea**.

Once in the Arabian Sea, ships can sail west into the **Red Sea**, which is bordered by Saudi Arabia to the east and Egypt to the west. At the northern end of the Red Sea, ships can enter the man-made **Suez Canal**, which will allow them to get to the Mediterranean Sea without having to sail all around the continent of Africa.

The **Jordan River** is a much smaller river than either the Tigris or the Euphrates, but it is still very important. The waters that form the Jordan River begin in the mountains of Lebanon and Syria and flow down into the Hula Valley in northern Israel before reaching the Sea of Galilee. The Jordan River begins at the southern end of the Sea of Galilee and flows south until it reaches the Dead Sea. This river is one of the main sources of water for Israel, Jordan, parts of Syria, and many of those living in the West Bank and the Gaza Strip. Because so much water is taken out of the Jordan River by the different groups that depend on it, less and less water reaches the **Dead Sea**. The Dead Sea has no outlets. Water that flows in stays there and because so much evaporates in the desert air, the water remaining is high in salts and other chemicals. There are no fish living in the Dead Sea, and that is the reason for its name. The Jordan River is also important because it is the political boundary between Israel and the West Bank, a small part of Syria, and the country of Jordan.

Use the map to answer questions 221-224.

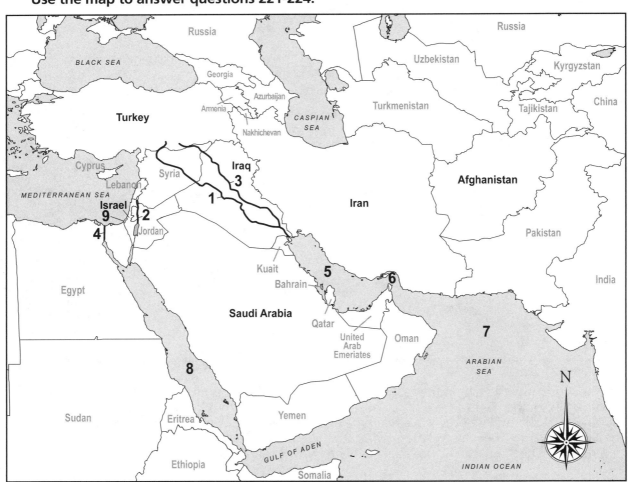

_____ **221. Which marks the Suez Canal?**
   A. 1
   B. 2
   C. 3
   D. 4

_____ **222. Which marks the Red Sea?**
   A. 5
   B. 6
   C. 7
   D. 8

_____ **223. Which is marked with a "9"?**
   A. Dead Sea
   B. Gaza Strip
   C. Tigris River
   D. Euphrates River

_____ **224. Which is marked with a "1"?**
   A. Dead Sea
   B. Gaza Strip
   C. Tigris River
   D. Euphrates River

_____ **225. Which bodies of water are connected by the Strait of Hormuz?**
   A. the Red Sea and the Arabian Sea
   B. the Persian Gulf and the Arabian Sea
   C. the Mediterranean Sea and the Red Sea
   D. the Mediterranean Sea and the Persian Gulf

_____ **226. Which bodies of water are connected by the Suez Canal?**
   A. the Red Sea and the Arabian Sea
   B. the Persian Gulf and the Arabian Sea
   C. the Mediterranean Sea and the Red Sea
   D. the Mediterranean Sea and the Persian Gulf

_____ **227. The Tigris and Euphrates rivers come together to form the border between which countries?**
   A. Turkey and Iraq
   B. Kuwait and Iran
   C. Saudi Arabia and Israel
   D. Iraq and Saudi Arabia

_____ **228.** **Why is the Suez Canal so important to international shipping?**
  A. The Suez Canal is Iraq's only waterway leading into the Persian Gulf.
  B. The Suez Canal is the only way for ships to get out of the Persian Gulf.
  C. The Suez Canal makes it possible to get to the Mediterranean Sea from the Arabian Sea without having to sail around the continent of Africa.
  D. The Suez Canal connects the Jordan River to the Persian Gulf, making it less expensive to ship products to other parts of Southwest Asia.

SS7G5 The student will locate selected features in Southwestern Asia (Middle East).
  b. Locate on a world and regional political-physical map the nations of Afghanistan, Iran, Iraq, Israel, Saudi Arabia, and Turkey.

The country of **Afghanistan** is located at the far eastern edge of the region of Southwest Asia. This country is **landlocked**, which means it has no seacoast. Afghanistan is very mountainous, and the people who live there are divided into a number of different ethnic groups or tribes.

Iran, to the west of Afghanistan, is one of the largest countries in Southwest Asia. Iran is mountainous as well, but this country also has long seacoasts and is able to use both the Persian Gulf and the Arabian Sea. Iran uses the Persian Gulf and the Strait of Hormuz to transport its exports to the Arabian Sea and then on to many different world markets.

Just to the west of Iran is the country of **Iraq**. Iraq has the added advantage of having two of the largest rivers in the region, the Tigris and the Euphrates rivers, flowing through its territory. In southern Iraq, these two rivers join and form a waterway called the Shatt al -Arab, a river that runs for about 125 miles before it empties into the Persian Gulf. This river forms part of the international boundary between Iraq and Iran, and a number of disputes have occurred there over access to the waterway.

The Kingdom of **Saudi Arabia** is the largest country of the Arabian Peninsula. The Persian Gulf lies to the northwest of the country and the Red Sea is to its west.

Turkey is located to the north and west of Iraq. Turkey shares a border with Iraq, Syria, and Iran. Turkey is also the country in which the Euphrates and the Tigris rivers begin. Turkey has built a number of dams in recent years to try saving water from these two rivers for use by Turkish farms, villages, and towns.

South of Turkey is the country of Lebanon, and south of Lebanon is Israel. **Israel** was created by the United Nations in 1948 as a homeland for the Jewish people of the world. The country of Israel is bound by the **Gaza Strip** along the southern coast and the **West Bank** to the east. The Jordan River forms the boundary between the West Bank and the country of Jordan.

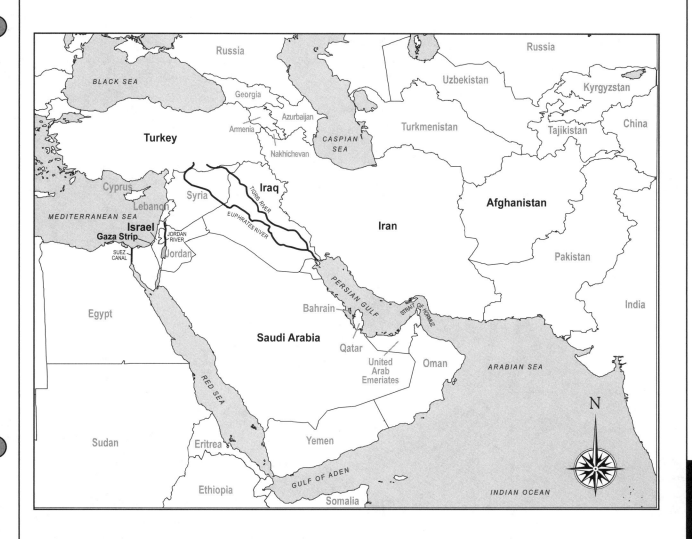

Use this map to answer questions 229-232.

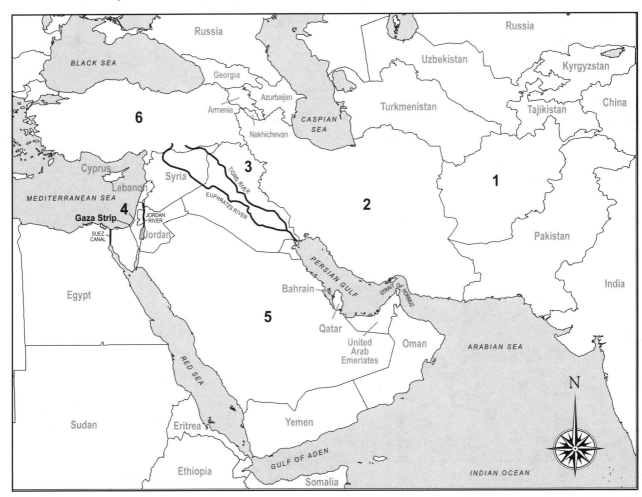

_____ **229. Which number marks Israel?**

     A. 1

     B. 2

     C. 3

     D. 4

_____ **230. Which number marks Iraq?**

     A. 2

     B. 3

     C. 4

     D. 6

_____ **231. Which number marks Saudi Arabia?**

     A. 1

     B. 4

     C. 5

     D. 6

_____ **232. Which country is marked by a "6"?**

     A. Iran

     B. Jordan

     C. Turkey

     D. Afghanistan

SOUTHWEST ASIA (MIDDLE EAST)

Water is a natural resource that is distributed unevenly in Southwest Asia. Some countries, like Turkey and Iraq, have major rivers that provide enough water for farming communities. These two countries share the **Tigris and Euphrates river systems**. Israel, Syria, and Jordan share the **Jordan River**. Others, like Saudi Arabia, have almost no water. They are mostly made up of desert. Others, like Iran, have areas with access to rivers and areas that are made up of deserts. Because water is in short supply in so many parts of Southwest Asia, irrigation has been necessary for those who want to farm and raise animals for market.

Many types of **irrigation** can be found in Southwest Asia as farmers struggle to bring water to their fields from local rivers and from **underground aquifers** (layers of underground rock where water runoff from rains and streams is trapped). Some farmers use water from wells that tap into **fossil water** (water that has been underground for centuries). Rains and streams do not replace this water, and once it is used, is gone forever. Farmers in very rural areas still use methods used by their ancestors to irrigate their fields, including water wheels, irrigation ditches and canals, and animal power to lift water from underground wells. Farmers in countries with more technology use modern irrigation techniques. Israel and Saudi Arabia have developed systems of **drip irrigation** using computers that measure out how much water each plant receives. There has also been a lot of work done to learn how to take water from the ocean and desalinate it to use for drinking and irrigation. **Desalination** (the process of removing salt and other chemicals from seawater) is very expensive and requires complex technology.

As countries in Southwest Asia have worked to modernize their systems of agriculture, **water pollution** has been a growing problem. Increased demand for irrigation to expand farming has led to overuse of rivers and streams. Many farmers have begun to use chemical fertilizers, which have contaminated water supplies through runoff into these same rivers and streams. Constant planting and fertilizer use have led to the build-up of salt levels in soils, eventually making it impossible to farm in those areas. In the rush to develop industry, many cities and towns have grown rapidly, but the people living there have been slow to create effective ways to manage garbage and treat sewage. Access to water is also a source of conflict, especially among countries that share a river system. Dams built along a river to create lakes for irrigation and the production of **hydroelectric power** (electricity produced from the energy of running water) in one country reduce the amount of water available to other countries located further downstream.

_____ 233. **Which river do Syria, Israel, and Jordan share?**
A. Nile
B. Tigris
C. Jordan
D. Euphrates

_____ 234. **How has the building of dams created problems for countries sharing rivers in Southwest Asia?**
A. Dams are too expensive to build to be practical.
B. Dams limit the water available to countries further downstream.
C. Few countries have the technology needed to be able to build dams.
D. Countries in Southwest Asia are not allowed to build dams along shared rivers.

_____ **235. What is one problem chemical fertilizers cause for farmers?**

    A. Chemical fertilizers make farm animals sick.

    B. Chemicals have led to the build-up of salt levels in the soil.

    C. Fertilizers are too expensive for anyone in Southwest Asia to use.

    D. Few countries in Southwest Asia have factories to make fertilizers.

_____ **236. How has the use of chemical fertilizers affected water supplies in many countries in Southwest Asia?**

    A. Use of chemical fertilizers means crops must be watered constantly.

    B. Enormous amounts of water must be used to produce chemical fertilizers.

    C. Chemical fertilizers have had very little effect on local water supplies in Southwest Asia.

    D. Water supplies have been contaminated by the chemicals through runoff from the fields.

_____ **237. Why aren't desalinization and drip irrigation used more in Southwest Asia?**

    A. Most countries do not know about these technologies.

    B. Drip irrigation is not very effective in a hot, dry climate.

    C. Few countries in Southwest Asia have access to seawater.

    D. These technologies are very expensive for the countries to use.

SS7G7 The student will explain the impact of location, climate, physical characteristics, distribution of natural resources, and population distribution in Southwest Asia (Middle East).

a. Explain how the distribution of oil has affected the development of Southwest Asia (Middle East).

Two of the most important **natural resources** found in Southwest Asia are **natural gas** and **oil**. These two resources bring wealth into the region because they are needed for much of the world's economy. Deposits of underground oil and natural gas were discovered in Southwest Asia at the beginning of the 1900s. At first, companies from the United States and Europe controlled the drilling and refining of most of this oil, but now most of the oil operations are controlled by the countries themselves. Over half of the world's known oil reserves are found in this part of the world This has made some of these countries extremely rich and has led them to have a lot of control over the global economy.

In the 1960s, several of these Southwest Asian countries joined with other oil-rich countries around the world to create the **Organization of Petroleum Exporting Countries (OPEC)** in order to have more control over the price of oil on the world market. OPEC has called for an embargo, or a slow-down or temporary halt, to oil supplies at different times in the past to get political and economic agreements from the other countries in the world. While some countries in Southwest Asia have grown very rich due to their oil production, others have struggled to help their populations make a decent living.

The Southwestern Asian countries with the greatest reserves of natural gas and oil are Saudi Arabia, Iraq, Iran, and Kuwait. Some other countries have smaller reserves, especially those found around the Arabian Gulf. These countries have enjoyed tremendous growth in national wealth and an improved standard of living in the past fifty years. Those countries without oil reserves have had a much harder time improving living conditions for their populations. This difference in wealth in some of the Southwest Asian countries has led to conflicts among the nations.

_____ 238. **What are the two most valuable natural resources in Southwest Asia?**
   A. water and cotton
   B. phosphates and oil
   C. oil and natural gas
   D. sulfur and natural gas

_____ 239. **How much of the world's oil supply is found in Southwest Asia?**
   A. 25 percent
   B. 40 percent
   C. 50 percent
   D. 75 percent

_____ 240. **How has the discovery of oil in some Southwest Asian countries affected the economic development of this area?**
   A. Those with oil need less water than the other countries around them.
   B. Having oil has made very little difference in the economy in this region.
   C. The discovery of oil has meant that no other industries have developed in the region.
   D. Those countries with oil reserves are much richer than those countries that have not found oil in their territory.

_____ **241. Which countries are the most oil-rich in the Southwestern Asian region?**

    A. Iran, Iraq, Jordan, Israel

    B. Iraq, Kuwait, Israel, Lebanon

    C. Jordan, Israel, Syria, Lebanon

    D. Iran, Iraq, Kuwait, Saudi Arabia

_____ **242. Why does the organization of OPEC play a powerful role in the world economy today?**

    A. OPEC is a part of the United Nations.

    B. OPEC controls the oil in the world market.

    C. OPEC builds dams along rivers shared by several countries.

    D. OPEC membership includes many oil companies owned by firms in the United States.

SS7G7 The student will explain the impact of location, climate, physical characteristics, distribution of natural resources and population distribution on Southwest Asia (Middle East).

b. Describe how the deserts and rivers of Southwest Asia (Middle East) have affected the population in terms of where people live, the type of work they do, and how they travel.

Three major river systems are located in Southwest Asia: the **Euphrates River** that runs through Turkey, Syria, Iraq, and Kuwait; the **Tigris River**, which runs through Turkey, Iraq, and Kuwait; and the **Jordan River**, which forms part of the border for Syria, Jordan, the West Bank and Israel. In addition to being important sources of water, these rivers also provide boundaries between nations. These three rivers are important because they furnish water for drinking and irrigation, as well as routes for transportation and trade for those who live along their routes. Many of the major cities in Southwest Asia are located on or near these rivers. These cities and towns are also centers of industry, as that is where workers can most easily be found.

Southwest Asia has a number of very large desert areas: the great **Syrian Desert** shared between Syria and Iraq, and the **Rub al-Khali**, or "**empty Quarter**," in southern Saudi Arabia. These deserts have historically provided Southwest Asia with natural barriers against invasion. They have also led to a way of life that developed around the need to survive in such harsh surroundings. Some people have always managed to live in and around the desert, living in tent camps and surviving as sheep and camel herders and making a living by trading animals and handmade goods with those who lived in the towns on the desert's edge. These people are known as "**Bedouins**," or desert nomads, and their way of life is gradually disappearing.

The countries of Southwest Asia generally have a very hot and dry climate. The climate is the type of weather a region has over a very long period. Four large oceans or bodies of water, the Mediterranean Sea, the Red Sea, the Arabian Gulf, and the Indian Ocean border Southwest Asia. Even so, mountain ranges close to many of the coastal areas block rains coming from these bodies of water and the result is that much of the interior of Southwest Asia is desert. Because there are coastal areas as well as a number of large rivers, other parts of this region have enough water to support agriculture and towns and cities of significant size.

Southwest Asia is located between three major continents: Europe, Africa, and Asia. For this reason, the region has played a major role in trade among these continents through the centuries. Ships loaded with trade goods from Asia would travel to the coast of Southwest Asia. These goods would then be loaded unto caravans that traveled across the desert to the coast on the other side of Southwest Asia. Today the **Suez Canal** in Egypt links the Mediterranean Sea with the Red Sea and Indian Ocean, making it possible to continue the trade among continents without having to use overland caravans.

Many people in Southwest Asia practice **subsistence agriculture**, growing small amounts of crops, to take care of their local needs. Because the climate is so dry, agriculture nearly always depends on irrigation, directing water from small rivers and streams to the farmers' fields. There is some commercial agriculture (growing crops for industrial markets), but even that is limited by lack of water.

Water is a critical resource in Southwest Asia, both as a source of life and as a route for trade. Because the Tigris and Euphrates rivers run through more than one country, access to the water has led to many political conflicts in recent years. Several countries have built dams along their portion of these rivers, to create lakes for irrigation and to generate **hydroelectric power** (electricity created using the energy of running water). Each dam cuts down on the water available to the countries further downstream.

No agriculture or animal herding can take place without access to adequate sources of water. People in this region have used many creative ways to bring water to the fields where it is needed, using water wheels and pumps powered by animals or electricity, digging wells and **qanats** (underground tunnels that bring water from the hills to dry plains), and building canals. An additional problem comes with irrigation. Irrigated land usually needs chemical fertilizers. Repeated use of fertilizer eventually causes salts to build up in the soil, making it hard to grow anything. Many places in Southwest Asia that have been irrigated for many years no longer produce crops as well as they once did.

_____ 243. **Many of the largest cities in Southwest Asia are located on or near**
  A. deserts.
  B. major rivers.
  C. large grasslands.
  D. mountain ranges.

_____ 244. **The "Bedouins" are Southwest Asians who have traditionally lived in and around**
  A. oil fields.
  B. urban areas.
  C. major deserts.
  D. large river systems.

_____ 245. **People living in the deserts in Southwest Asia have usually made their living by**
  A. farming.
  B. mining and hired labor.
  C. working in the oil industry.
  D. trading animals and handmade goods.

_____ 246. **How have the major rivers of Southwest Asia become a part of political conflict?**
  A. Many rivers dry up during the hot summers.
  B. The rivers have nothing to do with the area's political conflict.
  C. Most countries do not allow water to be taken out of rivers for irrigation.
  D. Several countries have built dams along their portion of the river, cutting off water to those living downstream.

_____ **247. Which describes the climate of much of Southwest Asia?**
   A. hot and dry
   B. windy and cold
   C. tropical and rainy
   D. moderate and cool

_____ **248. Because mountains block winds coming from the oceans, much of the interior of Southwest Asia is**
   A. desert.
   B. grasslands.
   C. inland lakes.
   D. rich farming areas.

_____ **249. The major rivers in Southwest Asia have become political issues because**
   A. deserts prevent the rivers from being large enough to be useful.
   B. they can be used only for trade and travel but not for drinking water.
   C. farmers have not been able to find ways to use the water for irrigation.
   D. everyone needs to be able to use the water and there is only a limited amount.

_____ **250. People living along the rivers of Southwest Asia have built canals, qanats, and water wheels to use the water for**
   A. shipping.
   B. irrigation.
   C. swimming.
   D. flood control.

_____ **251. Dams built along the rivers have caused problems for people living further downstream because**
   A. dams are expensive to build.
   B. a river can only be dammed in one place along its path.
   C. no fish can live in the rivers after they have been dammed.
   D. less water comes down the river to those people once the dam is built.

_____ **252. Which do Turkey, Syria, Iraq, and Kuwait share?**
   A. Tigris River
   B. Jordan River
   C. Euphrates River
   D. Afghanistan River

SOUTHWEST ASIA (MIDDLE EAST)

SS7G8 The student will describe the diverse cultures of the people who live in Southwest Asia (Middle East).

a. Explain the differences between an ethnic group and a religious group.

An **ethnic group** is a group of people who share cultural ideas and beliefs that have been a part of their community for generations. The characteristics they may have in common could include a language, a religion, a shared history, types of foods, and a set of traditional stories, beliefs, or celebrations. These things make up a common culture shared by those in a particular ethnic group.

An example of an ethnic group from Southwest Asia is the Kurds. This group lives in a mountain region that spans Iran, Iraq, Syria, and Turkey. Kurds speak Kurdish, and most are Muslim. Kurds do not have their own homeland or government. They are a minority group ruled by the country where they live.

A **religious group** shares a belief system in a god or gods, with a specific set of rituals and literature. People from different ethnic groups may share the same religion, though they may be from very different cultures. Religion has been important to the history of Southwest Asia. Christianity, Islam, Judaism were started in this region. People who follow Judaism are called Jews. Followers of Christianity are called Christians. Followers of Islam are called Muslims.

_____ 253. **Which do Kurds share as part of their ethnic group?**
   A. the Kurdish language
   B. they live in the same country
   C. self-rule in the land of Kurdistan
   D. the ability to move freely to other countries

_____ 254. **Which are the three main religious groups of Southwest Asia?**
   A. Hinduism, Islam, Judaism
   B. Christianity, Islam, Judaism
   C. Buddhism, Hinduism, Islam
   D. Christianity, Islam, Shamanism

SS7G8 The student will describe the diverse cultures of the people who live in Southwest Asia (Middle East).

b. Explain the diversity of religions within the Arabs, Persians, and Kurds.

Southwest Asia is home to many different ethnic groups who share similar religions. The **Arabs** of Southwest Asia believe themselves to be descendants of Abraham in the Bible, through his son Ishmael. They make up the majority of those who live throughout the region known as Southwest Asia, though there are many differences among them. Most Arabs practice the religion of **Islam** and call themselves **Muslims**.

Those who call themselves Muslims are further divided, as some call themselves **Sunni Muslims**, while others are **Shia Muslims**. Many Arabs are **Christians**. Most Arabs, whether they are Muslim or Christian, speak the Arabic language.

Persians are those who live in the modern country of **Iran**. The Persian people are descended from a different group than those who are Arabs and Jews. Their ancestors were Indo-Europeans, from Central Europe and Southern Russia.

The country of Persia became known as **Iran** after World War I. Persians, or Iranians, speak **Farsi**, a language that uses the Arabic alphabet but is actually a different language. They practice **Islam**, but most belong to the **Shia group of Muslims**. About 15 percent of the Muslims in the world are Shia. The other 85 percent are Sunni Muslims.

The **Kurds** are an ethnic group that lives in several different countries in Southwest Asia. Most Kurds are found in the mountainous areas where Syria, Turkey, Iran, and Iraq come together. The Kurds see themselves as a distinct ethnic group from others in the area. They speak their own language, known as **Kurdish**, and have a separate history, literature, music, and set of traditions. Many Kurds hope to have a nation of their own some day, a hope that has caused conflict with the countries in which Kurdish people live. Most Kurds are Sunni Muslim, though there is a small minority who are Shia Muslims.

_____ **255. Which ethnic group is most numerous in Southwest Asia?**
   A. Jews
   B. Kurds
   C. Arabs
   D. Persians

_____ **256. What modern country is the home to those who call themselves Persians?**
   A. Iran
   B. Iraq
   C. Israel
   D. Syria

_____ **257. What is the religion of most Persians?**
   A. Judaism
   B. Christianity
   C. Shia Muslim
   D. Sunni Muslim

_____ **258. What is the religion of most of the Arabs in Southwest Asia?**
   A. Judaism
   B. Christianity
   C. Shia Muslim
   D. Sunni Muslim

_____ **259. What is the religion of most of the Kurds?**
   A. Catholicism
   B. Christianity
   C. Shia Muslim
   D. Sunni Muslim

Judaism, **Christianity**, and **Islam** have their origins in the lands that make up the countries of Southwest Asia. Though these three religions have much in common, historically there has been a great deal of religious conflict in this part of the world. Today, Israel is the only country in the area that is mostly Jewish. All of the other countries in the region are mostly Muslim, although most also have a Christian minority. There are further divisions within all three religions. Muslims are divided into a number of sects, or groups. The most important are the Sunni Muslims and the Shia Muslims. Christians have many different denominations, which include Protestants, Catholics and various Orthodox sects. Different groups are found among Jews as well, including those who are Orthodox and those who are Reform. Religion has played a big role in the history and politics of Southwest Asia.

JUDAISM

Judaism is a monotheistic religion, meaning its followers believe in only one God. Judaism traces its origins back to Abraham, a man born in Mesopotamia in approximately 2000 BC. He was one of the first people to profess the belief in a single God, even though the society in which he lived worshipped many different gods. The Torah, the first five books in the Hebrew Scriptures, says that God made a covenant (agreement) with Abraham, promising to set him as the head of a new nation if he would dedicate himself and the Hebrew people to the worship of one God. Abraham left Mesopotamia and eventually came to the land of Canaan (part of the present day state of Israel) on the Mediterranean coast, which he believed God had promised to him and his descendants. Here the Hebrews lived, worshipping Yahweh, the God they believed would protect them for their faithfulness. At a very old age, he and his wife Sarah had a son, Isaac. Abraham, his son Isaac, and his grandson Jacob, are seen as the patriarchs, or founders, of the Hebrew nation. Jacob's twelve sons, in turn, are viewed as the ancestors of the Twelve Tribes of Israel.

The Hebrew people lived in an area surrounded by more powerful kingdoms, and the Bible says that around 1300-1200 BC the Hebrews were forced into slavery in Egypt. After years of suffering Moses, who took them into the Sinai desert to escape capture, led them out of slavery. This escape is known as the "Exodus" and is remembered each year by the celebration of Passover in the Jewish religious calendar. While wandering in the Sinai desert, the Jewish faith teaches that God renewed his covenant with the Hebrew people, revealing to them the Ten Commandments. After many years, they were able to return to Canaan where they lived in twelve generally self-governing tribes. They gradually extended their territory to the south along the Jordan River. The largest of these tribes was that of Judah, from which the names Judaism and Jews developed.

Around 1000 BC, the Hebrew people united under a series of kings, Saul, David, and Solomon, in the kingdom of Israel. David established his capital in the city of Jerusalem, and Saul later built a great temple there and dedicated it to the one true God of the Jewish people. Struggles with more powerful neighbors continued however, and eventually the kingdom was divided with Judah in the south and Israel in the north. A period of Babylonian rule followed, ended by a revolt of the Maccabeus in 167 BC, which restored Hebrew control of the area. Independent rule in the area was ended finally by a Roman takeover, and the Temple in Jerusalem was destroyed in 70 AD. Only a portion of the Western Wall of the Temple was left standing. The Jewish people were forced out of the lands around Jerusalem and for many generations lived in what was called "The Diaspora," or the scattering of the Jews to other parts of the world. The importance of Jerusalem and of the remaining western wall of the Temple continued to be central to Jews during the long centuries of the Diaspora. They believed that the lands of ancient Israel and Judea remained part of the covenant they had made with God.

_____ 260. **What is the main belief that distinguished the Jewish faith from the others in the ancient world?**

   A. the belief in life after death

   B. the organization of believers into a separate state

   C. the worship of a single god rather than many gods

   D. the offering of sacrifices during religious ceremonies

_____ 261. **Which is the holy writing of Judaism?**

   A. Torah

   B. Quran

   C. Constitution

   D. New Testament

_____ 262. **The "Exodus" in the history of the Jewish people was the time when**

   A. Jews were in captivity in Babylon.

   B. the Romans forced the Jews out of Jerusalem.

   C. Abraham left Mesopotamia and moved to Canaan.

   D. Jews were freed from slavery in Egypt and returned to the land of Canaan.

CHRISTIANITY

Christianity is a religious movement that grew out of Judaism during the time of Roman rule in Palestine. The founding figure in Christianity is Jesus, a man who was born in Bethlehem in Judea to a Jewish family in about 4 BC. Tradition holds that he lived a modest life in Nazareth as a carpenter until he began to attract attention as a teacher and preacher when he reached the age of about thirty years of age. While he followed Jewish law and belief, he spoke of a more personal relationship with God, focusing on both the love of God and the generous treatment of neighbors and acquaintances. He had a number of followers who became known as his disciples, and their writings provide much of what is known about the life and teachings of Jesus. The first four books of the New Testament are made of these writings. They are known as the Gospels.

Many among both the Romans and the Jewish leaders worried about the attention Jesus attracted among the common people. Some of his followers went so far as to claim that he was the long awaited Messiah, or "savior of man." Jewish leaders claimed Jesus encouraged such beliefs and was therefore guilty of crimes against Jewish teachings. The Roman ruler, Pontius Pilate, saw him as a threat to his authority and that of the Roman Empire. As a result, Jesus was sentenced to death by crucifixion, a form of execution in those days in which a person either was tied or nailed to a cross and suspended there until dead.

After his death, his followers believed that he was able to rise from the dead and walk among them again before going to heaven. They continued to call him the Messiah or the Greek "Christos," which was shortened to "Christ." They called him the "Son of God." Word of Jesus' rising from the dead began to spread quickly, and along with his teachings became the basis for a new religion called **Christianity**. His followers emphasized this new religion's willingness to take in all who wished to believe. They angered the Romans, as they refused to worship Roman gods and goddesses. Many of the early Christians were put to death by Roman authorities in the years following the time of Jesus, but the religion continued to have growing appeal among many who did not like Roman rule and who wanted a religion that emphasized both Old Testament teachings and the loving and forgiving God described by Jesus. By the year 300 AD, Christianity had spread to most parts of the Roman world. In 313 AD, the Roman Emperor Constantine officially ended the harsh treatment of Christians and made Christianity a religion approved by the empire.

_____ 263. **Why did Jesus have trouble with both the Jewish leaders and the Roman authorities?**
   A. Jesus urged people to tear down the Temple in Jerusalem.
   B. The new religion of Christianity was opened only to a very few people.
   C. He encouraged the people to form an army and revolt against the government.
   D. Jews accused him of crimes against their teachings; Romans saw him as a threat to the Roman Empire.

_____ 264. **What basic belief made Christianity different from Judaism?**
   A. Christians believed Jesus was the Messiah, or savior of man.
   B. Only Judaism accepted and believed in the Ten Commandments.
   C. Jews never had problems with Roman authorities, while the Christians did.
   D. Christians allowed the worship of many of the Roman gods, while Judaism did not.

_____ 265. **Why was Christianity finally accepted by the Roman Emperor as a legal religion?**
   A. Christian armies defeated the Roman Emperor in battle.
   B. There were few other religions left in the Roman Empire by 313 AD.
   C. Emperor Constantine recognized that many Romans had become Christians.
   D. Christians made the worship of Roman gods and goddesses part of their religion as well.

ISLAM

Islam is a religion that began in the city of Mecca in the Arabian Peninsula in the 600s AD. Mecca was a trading center located along a main route on the Red Sea coast connecting the Byzantine Empire with the shipping and trading centers coming from the Indian Ocean and the Far East. As a stop on the trade route, many different people visited the city of Mecca. In the center of the town stood a rectangular building, the Ka'aba, which held several hundred different idols inside. Meccans believed the building had originally been built by Abraham and his son, Ishmael, to honor God for saving them from dying in the desert. Over the centuries, however, statues of many other idols and gods were placed in the building.

Muhammad was born in Mecca in 570 AD. Orphaned at an early age, he was taken in by his uncle and trained to become a merchant. He married an older woman and took over her caravan business, becoming a respected member of the Mecca community.

At the age of forty, while spending an evening in one of the cool caves in the hills around Mecca, Muhammad began to hear the voice of the angel Gabriel, calling on him to tell the word of God to the people. After much worry and after talking with his wife, Muhammad decided the voice was real, and he began to tell others in Mecca about what he had heard. He told people they needed to rededicate themselves to the worship of one God, whom he called Allah. Those who were willing to agree to this belief became known as "Muslims," or "ones who submit" to the will of God. Many in Mecca worried that his teachings would hurt their trade by angering those who worshipped other gods, and some of his followers began to face threats and violence.

To escape these threats, in 622 AD, Muhammad and his followers moved about 200 miles north to Yathrib, a city Muhammad renamed Medina, which means "the city of the prophet." This move came to be known among Muslims as the "Hijrah," and the date serves as the first year of the Islamic calendar. The people of Medina accepted Muhammad as both a political and a religious leader, and many joined the new religion of Islam.

Muhammad returned to Mecca as the head of an army in 630 AD, and the city surrendered rather than face a war. One of his first acts on entering Mecca was to go to the Ka'aba and remove all the idols. He then dedicated the building to Allah, the one God. Mecca and the Ka'aba remained central to Muslim worship.

After Muhammad's death, his followers collected the teachings from the angel Gabriel into the Quran (the holy book of Islam). Muslims believe there is only one God, and they view Muhammad as his final prophet. Much of the Old Testament and the New Testament are also included in the Quran, so Muslims see the Quran and Islam as the final and complete word of God. All Muslims believe they must meet five basic obligations, known as the Five Pillars. The first is called Shahada, the belief that "There is no God but Allah and Muhammad is his prophet." The second is Salat, or praying five times a day facing the direction of Mecca. Zakat, or charity to the poor is the third, followed by Sawm, or eating or drinking nothing during the daylight hours of the month of Ramadan, the tenth month in the Muslim calendar. The final Pillar is to make the Hajj, or pilgrimage to Mecca, sometime during one's lifetime.

For Muslims, the Quran offers a handbook for leading a respectable life. Some Muslim countries base their legal code on the law of Quran, a system known as shariah law. Because so much of both the Old and New Testaments are a part of the Quran, Muslims view Jews and Christians as "People of the Book," who should be accorded special respect though they were expected to pay a tax as they were not required to give Zakat to the poor.

After Muhammad's death, the religion of Islam spread rapidly throughout the Arabian Peninsula and parts of the Persian and Byzantine Empires. Led by four men who had been friends of Muhammad, the "Rightly Guided Caliphs," Muslim armies were able to easily conquer areas where these older empires had weakened over the years. The word "Caliph" means leader or ruler. Many people welcomed the Muslims and converted to Islam, finding it a simple and direct religion.

_____ **266. What is the relationship between Judaism, Christianity, and Islam?**
    A. The three religions all believe in different gods.
    B. All three religions accept Jesus as the "Son of God."
    C. Unlike Judaism and Christianity, Islam won new converts only by war and force.
    D. Islam includes much of the Old and New Testaments in its holy book, the Quran.

_____ **267. What did Muhammad believe the angel Gabriel was asking him to do?**
    A. tell the word of God to the people
    B. bring an end to all religions other than Islam
    C. develop Mecca into a more powerful trading center
    D. tear down the Ka'aba because idols had been stored there

_____ **268. What is the importance of the Ka'aba to Muslims?**
    A. The Ka'aba was the original home of Muhammad.
    B. They believe it was originally built by the prophet Abraham.
    C. This building is where most important business deals were made in Mecca.
    D. They believe it is the place where Gabriel gave Muhammad the word of God.

_____ **269. Why did Islam spread so quickly after the death of Muhammad?**
    A. Muslim armies conquered empires that had weakened over the years.
    B. Muslims refused to trade with anyone who would not convert to Islam.
    C. There were no religions in that part of the world to compete with Islam.
    D. Jews and Christians were forced to convert to Islam or face prison or death.

270. What are the Five Pillars?

A. the first five books of the Quran

B. the five columns that support the roof of the Ka'aba

C. five beliefs shared by Judaism, Christianity, and Islam

D. five basic obligations that Muslims are supposed to meet in their lives

271. Why do Muslims call Jews and Christians "People of the Book"?

A. People belonging to these religions could read.

B. Followers of all three religions were taken in census records.

C. Much of the Old and New Testament is included in the Quran.

D. Jews and Christians were the first groups in Southwest Asia who had a written language.

SS7G8 The student will describe the diverse cultures of the people who live in Southwest Asia (Middle East).

d. Explain the origin of the division between Sunni and Shia Muslims.

After Muhammad died, there was disagreement about who should lead the **Muslim** community, or the ummah. This question was settled for a time by agreeing to place power in the hands of men who had been friends of Muhammad's in his lifetime. They ruled one after the other, and they were known as the "Four Rightly Guided Caliphs." When the last of these men died, a new argument arose over who should lead the Muslim community. One group thought leadership should go to whoever was most able to keep the community together. These people came to be known as the **Sunni** Muslims, those who saw themselves closely following Muhammad's example. The second group felt leadership should go to a direct descendant of Muhammad. They wanted to choose one of Muhammad's grandsons, the children of his son-in-law Ali, for leadership. They became known as the Shia-Ali, or "supporters of Ali." This name has been shortened to **Shia**. A battle for control soon followed, resulting in the death of one of Muhammad's grandsons and the transfer of power to the Umayyad family and the Sunni supporters. These divisions in the Muslim community remain even today, though there is little difference in their basic religious beliefs. The Sunni Muslims have always been in the majority, making up about 85 percent of those who call themselves Muslims today. The Shia Muslims have always been a minority, but they are a major portion of the populations of a number of countries today including Iran, Iraq, and Lebanon. Iran is over 90 percent Shia.

272. What issue led to the split between the Sunni and Shia in Islam?

A. The Shia believed only Arabs could be Muslims.

B. Arguments began over what should be included in the Five Pillars.

C. The Shia wanted to change the direction of prayer to Jerusalem rather than Mecca.

D. They disagreed over who should lead the Muslim community after the death of Muhammad.

273. Why were the first four leaders of the Muslims after Muhammad's death called the "Four Rightly Guided Caliphs"?

A. They had been friends of Muhammad.

B. They had studied leadership for many years and were well prepared to rule.

C. They arranged for a split in the community between Sunni and Shia Muslims.

D. These men all ruled together so there could be no question about their decisions.

_____ **286. Which Southwest Asian country is an example of a federal system of government?**

A. Iran

B. Israel

C. Kuwait

D. Saudi Arabia

SS7CG4 The student will compare and contrast various forms of government.

b. Explain how governments determine citizen participation: autocratic, oligarchic, and democratic.

People who live under different kinds of governments often find there are great differences in the rights given to individual citizens.

An **autocratic government** is one in which the ruler has absolute power to do whatever he wishes and makes and enforces whatever laws he chooses. Individuals who live under autocratic governments do not have any rights to choose leaders or vote on which laws are made and put into practice. Some autocratic governments may allow the people rights in certain areas like managing local affairs, but the central government keeps control of all the most important aspects of the country's life. In an autocratic system, people usually have little or no power to use against the government if they disagree with decisions that government or ruler has made. There are many different kinds of autocratic governments. A monarchy such as Saudi Arabia, where the king has ultimate power, is one example.

An **oligarchy** means "government by the few." In this form of government, a political party or other small group takes over a government and makes all of the major decisions. The people of the country have little choice but to go along with the decisions they make. This sort of government can be very similar to an autocratic government. There are several countries in Southwest Asia that might be described as oligarchies. In Syria, the ruling political party, the Ba'ath Party, controls much of the government. Syria has a nationally elected assembly, but most of the major decisions are made by the delegates of the Ba'ath Party and then handed down to the people. Iran could also be described as an oligarchy, because a small group of religious and political leaders makes many of the important decisions.

In a **democratic government system**, the people play a much greater role in deciding who the rulers are and what decisions are made. "Democracy" comes from the Greek word "demos," which means "people." In this form of government, a great deal of power is left in the hands of the people. People who live in a democracy generally recognize that there must be some rules to organize society, but the goal is to leave as much individual freedom as possible. Decisions are often made by majority votes, but there are also laws in place to protect individual rights. If a person living in a democracy feels his rights have been violated, he has the power to ask the government for help in correcting the situation. Among the countries of Southwest Asia, Israel is a good example of a democracy. Those organizing the new government of Iraq are hoping to establish a democratic system in that country as well.

_____ **287. Who makes most of the important governmental decisions in an autocracy?**

A. the ruler

B. the people

C. the court system

D. the elected legislature

_____ 288. **Which Southwest Asian country is an autocracy?**
   A. Iraq
   B. Israel
   C. Turkey
   D. Saudi Arabia

_____ 289. **Who makes most of the important governmental decisions in an oligarchy?**
   A. the king
   B. the people
   C. the legislature
   D. a small group of powerful leaders

_____ 290. **Why do the individual voters have more power in a democracy than they do in an autocracy or an oligarchy?**
   A. Kings are always cruel rulers.
   B. The voters get to choose the people who make the laws.
   C. All of the power stays in the hands of the local governments.
   D. Voters in democratic countries always choose qualified leaders.

_____ 291. **Which Southwest Asian country has a democratic system of government?**
   A. Iran
   B. Israel
   C. Kuwait
   D. Saudi Arabia

Use information in the passage to answer the next two questions.

> *The Saudi royal family controls the national government of Saudi Arabia. The king is the son of the previous king, and his son will rule after him. All government leaders serve by appointment from the king. The king appoints the governors of the provinces, as well. The king has the ability to remove any government official from a village, town, or province. The governments of the provinces and towns have no rights or authority.*

_____ 292. **Which type of government is described in the passage?**
   A. unitary
   B. federation
   C. confederation
   D. parliamentary

_____ 293. **Which BEST describes the government of Saudi Arabia?**
   A. oligarchy
   B. monarchy
   C. democracy
   D. dictatorship

_____ **307. What is Shariah law?**
   A. laws made by the king alone
   B. laws based on parliamentary democracy
   C. laws based on the teachings of the Quran
   D. laws calling for a separation of church and state

_____ **308. What is the definition of a "theocracy"?**
   A. a government that sees God as the supreme ruler
   B. a government that allows the people to choose the leaders
   C. a system in which religious law and civil law are separate
   D. a system in which only religious leaders are allowed to vote

_____ **309. Why is Iran sometimes called a theocratic republic?**
   A. Iran's religious leaders make all the laws for the country.
   B. Religious leaders decide which Iranian citizens can vote.
   C. The people of Iran have no say in choosing their government leaders.
   D. Iran's government is led by both an elected parliament and powerful religious leaders.

_____ **310. What is an Ayatollah?**
   A. a Christian priest
   B. a Shia religious leader
   C. the title of a local governor
   D. a leader of a Jewish congregation

Use the diagram to answer questions 311-312.

Government of Iran

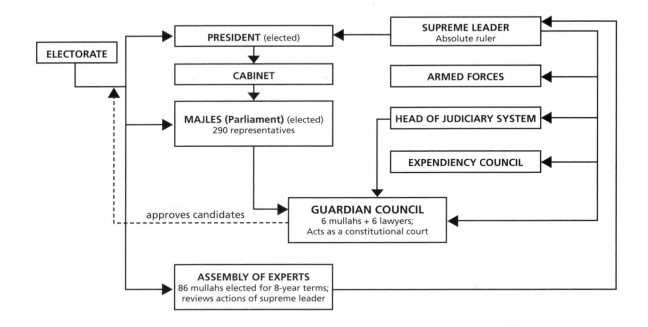

_____ **311. Who is the most powerful elected official in Iran?**
A. president
B. electorate
C. Supreme Leader
D. head of the judiciary

_____ **312. How does the Guardian Council affect elections?**
A. the mullahs tell people who to vote for
B. the mullahs and lawyers must agree on the Supreme Leader
C. they approve candidates that will be placed on the ballots in elections
D. they cannot affect elections since they are appointed by the Majles and Supreme Leader

_____ 319. **Why do most economies in the world today operate somewhere in between a market economy and a command economy?**

A. Most consumers want government control of the economy.

B. Government control makes a market economy more profitable.

C. Government control of some aspects of the economy has never been successful in the modern world.

D. Most economies have found they need a mix of free market and some government control to be successful and protect consumers.

SS7E5 The student will analyze different economic systems.
c. Compare and contrast the economic systems in Israel, Saudi Arabia, Turkey and Iran.

Israel, Saudi Arabia, and Iran are very different countries in terms of location, residents, and economic systems.

Israel is located along the Mediterranean coast and has a relatively small geographic area and almost no natural resources. Israel was founded in 1948 as a homeland for the world's Jews, and most of the citizens are Jewish. Though they have many problems with their Arab neighbors, Israel has good relations with much of Western Europe and with the United States. The Israelis have built an economy based on advanced technology that has allowed them to make up for much of what they lack in farmland and natural resources.

Saudi Arabia is one of the largest countries in Southwest Asia, and it is located to the south of Israel on the Arabian Peninsula. Most Saudis are Sunni Muslims, and Saudi Arabia is the location of Mecca, the holiest city for Muslims. Though much of Saudi Arabia is desert, the country has rich oil reserves that allow the Saudis to buy most of the goods they cannot produce themselves. The king of Saudi Arabia and his advisors make most of the decisions about how and where to use oil profits, but they have invested a lot of the nation's wealth in technologies that allow them to produce goods they would not be able to do otherwise in a desert climate.

Iran is located across the Persian Gulf from Saudi Arabia. Iran has great oil wealth, like Saudi Arabia, though there is also a more mixed economy that has grown in spite of government attempts to keep tighter control. Iran's command economy has not been very efficient in recent years. Even though there is oil wealth, many Iranians do not share in the money.

Turkey is located in the northwestern part of the Middle East. The city of Istanbul in Turkey is seen as the gateway to Asia from Europe, and for thousands of years, traders have crossed Turkey traveling from Europe to Asia. Turkey has the least economic freedom of the three countries. Industries such as airlines and railroads have been controlled by the government. The government has controlled the telephone and television industries, as well. However, in recent times, the government has been loosening its hold on these key businesses. More private ownership has been allowed. More laws have been passed to protect business owners.

_____ 320. **The economies of Israel, Saudi Arabia, Turkey and Iran could best be described as**

A. mixed.

B. market.

C. command.

D. traditional.

SOUTHWEST ASIA (MIDDLE EAST)

_____ **321. How have the Israelis made up for their lack of natural resources?**

   A They have put everyone to work and have no unemployment.

   B. They have relied primarily on farming to keep their economy going.

   C. They have developed strong technology companies in their economy.

   D. Israelis have refused to import oil, saving huge amounts of money each year.

_____ **322. Which industry does the government of Saudi Arabia heavily control?**

   A. oil

   B. technology

   C. agricultural

   D. textile manufacturing

_____ **323. How has the Saudi king used the profits from oil to help other areas of his kingdom?**

   A. Money is distributed directly to all Saudi citizens.

   B. The King has ended unemployment in Saudi Arabia.

   C. Oil profits have paid for modern technology and services.

   D. The King has let the Saudi people decide how to invest oil profits.

Not every country can produce all of the goods and services it needs. Because of this, countries specialize in producing those goods and services that they can provide most efficiently. They then look for others who may need those goods and services so they can sell their products to those who need them. The money earned by such sales then allows the purchase of goods and services the first country is unable to produce.

In international trade, no country can be completely self-sufficient (produce all the goods and services it needs). **Specialization** (products a country makes best and that are in demand on the world market) is a way to build a profitable economy and to earn money to buy items that cannot be made locally.

Some countries in Southwest Asia are very rich in oil and natural gas, but they lack farmland and the ability to produce enough food. Saudi Arabia is able to specialize in the production of oil and gas and sell these products at great profit on the world market. The money earned in this trade can then be used to purchase food and the technology needed to make their agriculture system more efficient.

Israel has little in the way of oil wealth, but they have become leaders in agricultural technology even though they have a limited supply of land suitable for farming. They can sell this technology to earn the money to supplement their limited production of food.

_____ 324. **What is "economic specialization"?**
   A. directly swapping goods from one country to another without having to use money
   B. trying to avoid investing in industry and technology because of the expense involved
   C. producing all goods and services needed for a country's growth, so that trade with other countries is not needed
   D. producing those goods a country can make most efficiently so they can trade them for goods made by others that cannot be produced locally

_____ 325. **Saudi Arabia specializes in the production of**
   A. oil and gas.
   B. oil and sugar.
   C. olive and orange.
   D. beef and chicken.

_____ 326. **Israel specializes in**
   A. medical technologies.
   B. industrial technologies.
   C. scientific technologies.
   D. agricultural technologies.

SS7E6 The student will explain how voluntary trade benefits buyers and sellers in Southwest Asia (Middle East).

b. Compare and contrast different types of trade barriers such as tariffs, quotas, and embargos.

Trade barriers are anything that slows down or prevents one country from exchanging goods with another. Some trade barriers are put in place to protect local industries from lower priced goods made in other countries. Other times trade barriers are created due to political problems between countries. Trade is stopped until the political issues are settled. The countries in Southwest Asia, as in most parts of the world, have experienced trade barriers at one time or another.

A **tariff** is a tax placed on goods when they are brought (imported) into one country from another country. The purpose of a tariff is usually to make the imported item more expensive than a similar item made locally. This sort of tariff is called a "protective tariff" because it protects local manufacturers from competition coming from cheaper goods made in other countries. Most countries have tariffs on goods imported from other countries. Other countries also place tariffs on goods coming to their markets from other parts of the world.

A **quota** is a different way of limiting the amount of foreign goods that can come into a country. A quota sets a specific amount or number of a particular product that can be imported or acquired in a given period. Israel could decide, for example, that only 1500 cars could be brought into the country from Japan in a given year. That would make it more likely that people buying cars would have to buy Israeli-made cars if Japanese cars were not available.

A third type of trade barrier is called an **embargo**. An embargo is when one country announces that it will no longer trade with another country in order to isolate the country and cause problems with that country's economy. Embargos usually come about when two countries are having political disputes. Embargos often cause problems for all countries involved. A good example of an embargo is the decision by the OPEC countries to stop all sales of oil and gas to the countries supporting Israel in the 1973 Arab-Israeli war.

_____ **327. What is a tariff?**
   A. a tax paid by the purchaser when goods are sold
   B. a tax placed on goods coming into one country from another
   C. a tax placed on goods made by local craftsmen or manufacturers
   D. a tax paid when goods are shipped from one state to another in the United States

_____ **328. What is a quota?**
   A. a decision to prevent certain goods from being imported
   B. a tax placed on imported goods when they enter the country
   C. a tax placed on goods when they are purchased in the market place
   D. a limit to the number or amount of a foreign-produced good that is allowed into the country

_____ **329. What is an embargo?**
   A. a tax placed on goods coming into the country from overseas
   B. a limit to the amount of a certain good allowed into the country
   C. a tax paid by the producer before he can sell his goods in another country
   D. a formal halt to trade with a particular country for economic or political reasons

SS7E6 The student will explain how voluntary trade benefits buyers and sellers in Southwest Asia (Middle East).

c. Explain the primary function of the Organization of Petroleum Exporting Countries (OPEC).

The **Organization of Petroleum Exporting Countries (OPEC)** was created in 1960 by some of the countries with large oil supplies who wanted to work together to try to regulate the supply and price of the oil they exported to other countries. The first five countries to belong to OPEC were Kuwait, Iraq, Saudi Arabia, Iran, and Venezuela. All of these countries, with the exception of Venezuela, are located in Southwest Asia. These countries, along with others who have joined since 1960, continue to decide how much oil they will produce and that determines the price on the world market. When they produce less, the price on the world market goes up. When they increase production, the price on the world market goes down.

_____ 330. **Why was OPEC created?**

        A. to regulate the supply and price of oil

        B. to help the Palestinians in their problems with Israel

        C. to design new machinery to get oil out of the ground

        D. to keep countries that are not members from producing any oil

_____ 331. **What happens to the price of oil when OPEC countries decide to limit production?**

        A. prices rise

        B. prices drop

        C. prices stay the same

        D. oil stops being sold

_____ 332. **Where are most of the OPEC countries located?**

        A. Africa

        B. South America

        C. North America

        D. Southwest Asia

Most of the countries in Southwest Asia have their own type of **currency**. In order for them to pay for goods as they trade with each other, they had to establish a system of changing from one type of currency to another. This system is known as an **exchange rate**. They also have to be able to exchange their currencies with those used by other countries around the world. The currency of the United States is based on the dollar. In most of Western Europe, currency is called the Euro. In Southwest Asia, there are many different types of currency. In order for them to trade with each other, they have to be able to figure out what goods cost in each currency.

_____ 333. **Why is it important for nations to have a system to convert from one currency to another?**

A. Converting to different currencies makes goods cost less.

B. Banks are not able to handle different kinds of currencies.

C. The dollar is the most valuable currency in the world today.

D. This makes it possible to buy and sell goods between nations with different types of money.

Human capital means the knowledge and skills that make it possible for workers to earn a living producing goods or services. The more skills and education workers have, the better they are able to work without mistakes and to learn new jobs as technology changes. Companies that invest in better training and education for their workers generally earn more profits. Good companies also try to make sure working conditions are safe and efficient, so their workers can do their jobs without risk.

Gross domestic product, or **GDP**, is the total value of all final goods and services produced within a country in a single year. Wealthy countries have a much higher **per capita GDP** (amount of goods and services produced divided by the total population) than do developing or underdeveloped countries.

Companies that have invested in their human capital through training and education are more likely to have profitable businesses and more satisfied workers than companies that do not make these investments. Countries where training and education are more easily available often have higher production levels of goods and services, therefore higher gross domestic product, than countries that do not offer these opportunities. The countries in Southwest Asia have widely different gross domestic product levels. Those countries that make it possible for workers to receive training and education tend to be wealthier than those that do not.

Israel has wide access to education and an economy that depends on technology industries to make up for the country's lack of natural resources. Many Israelis work in industries related to medical technology, agricultural technology, mining, and electronics. They also have highly developed service industries (businesses that supply the needs of the rest of the working population). The Israeli GDP is very high because they have invested heavily in their human capital.

Saudi Arabia's main industry is as an exporter of oil (petroleum) and petroleum products. The technology involved in the oil industry is complicated and requires a well-trained and educated labor force. Saudi Arabia also has modern communications and transportation systems, as well as enormous building projects, all of which require investments in human capital. By contrast, some Saudi citizens still practice traditional economic activities such as farming and herding animals. Because oil is such an important part of the world's economy, however, the Saudi GDP is high.

Iran is the world's fifth largest producer of oil. As in Saudi Arabia, oil wealth in Iran has led to the use of advanced technology that has required highly trained workers. Iran has always had highly regarded schools and universities that have meant educated workers were available for industry. Even so, in recent years the Iranian government has not always done a good job of regulating the parts of the economy that are under government control.

_____ 334. **What is human capital?**

      A. skills and education workers have

      B. taxes collected from a country's workers

      C. money paid to workers for producing goods

      D. the amount of goods sold in foreign trade in a year

_____ **335. Why have the Israelis made a big investment in human capital?**
   A. Their main industry is the oil industry.
   B. Investing in human capital takes very little money.
   C. They have to bring in workers from other countries.
   D. They need well-trained workers because their economy depends on advanced technology.

_____ **336. Why would the Saudi oil industry need a large investment in human capital?**
   A. The technology in the oil industry is very complicated.
   B. The Saudis have found it hard to make a profit in the oil industry.
   C. Most people working in the Saudi oil industry have little or no real training.
   D. They hope to have machines take over most of the jobs now done by workers.

_____ **337. One of Iran's biggest problems with their state-run oil industry is**
   A. few remaining large oil deposits.
   B. lack of a market for their product.
   C. inefficiency and poor organization.
   D. a labor force that does not want to work.

_____ **338. If a country does not invest in its human capital, how can it affect the country's gross domestic product (GDP)?**
   A. Investment in human capital has little effect on a country's GDP.
   B. Most workers want to keep their jobs and do not care about GDP.
   C. GDP is only affected if workers pay for the investment out of their own pockets.
   D. GDP may go down because poorly trained workers will not be able to do their jobs as well.

> **SS7E7 The student will describe factors that influence economic growth and examine their presence or absence in Israel, Saudi Arabia, and Iran.**
> b. Explain the relationship between investment in capital (factories, machinery, and technology) and gross domestic product (GDP).

Capital goods (the factories, machines, and technology that people use to make other goods) are important to economic growth. Advanced technology and the organization of this technology into factories, where many workers can work together, increases production and makes that production more efficient. Producing more goods for sale in a quicker and more efficient way leads to economic growth and greater profit. This greater profit leads to a higher gross domestic product (GDP).

Israel has invested heavily in capital goods, as so much of their economy depends on technology and industrial production, as well as advanced communications systems. Israel has also invested heavily in the technology involved in the defense industry.

Saudi Arabia has invested heavily in capital goods, especially the technology related to oil production, transportation, and communication.

Iran has made great investments in capital goods related to oil production, technology, and communication. Iran also spends a great deal on technology for its defense industry.

_____ **339. What are capital goods?**

    A. the workers who make the goods and services

    B. the factories and machines used to make goods

    C. the money spent to train workers to use new technology

    D. the goods and services that are produced for a country's economy

_____ **340. Israel has invested heavily in capital goods in all of the following areas EXCEPT**

    A. oil.

    B. defense.

    C. communication.

    D. farming and agriculture.

SS7E7 The student will describe factors that influence economic growth and examine their presence or absence in Israel, Saudi Arabia, and Iran.
c. Explain the role of oil in these countries' economies.

Natural resources are the raw materials a country has that make life and production of goods possible. Land, water, forests, rich soil, and minerals are all types of natural resources. In Southwest Asia, one of the most important natural resources for some countries is oil. Some natural resources can be replaced once they are used, like the trees cut for lumber or fuel. Others, like oil or coal, cannot be replaced once they are used.

Oil is one of the most important and valuable natural resources in Southwest Asia. Oil and natural gas are called fossil fuels, which mean they were created when plants and animals that lived centuries ago decayed underground. Oil and natural gas are also considered non-renewable natural resources, meaning they cannot be replaced once they are taken out of the ground. Most of the world's industrial nations depend on a steady supply of oil and natural gas. The United States has to import nearly half of all the oil it uses, almost 18 million barrels every day. Many other industrial countries have to do the same, even though they also use other sources of energy such as coal, wind power, and nuclear power. For this reason, countries in Southwest Asia with large reserves of these products have steady markets for all the oil and gas they can produce. Many of these countries have become very rich in the last fifty years, as the world demand for oil and gas has increased. Saudi Arabia and Iran are two of the world's largest producers of oil. Over half of the world's known supplies of oil are found in countries in Southwest Asia.

Israel has very few natural resources and practically no oil at all. Israel does have a highly developed industrial economy, so the world price of oil has a huge impact on the Israeli economy. Because they have no oil of their own and an industrial economy that requires purchases of oil and natural gas to operate, this country has had to find other natural resources to develop in order to help their economy grow. Minerals are mined commercially in Israel including phosphates. Salts are also taken from the Dead Sea. Israel's economy depends more on technology than on the development of natural resources, but this also means Israel must always purchase oil to keep industries going.

Saudi Arabia has very few natural resources, but the one they do have plenty of is oil. Oil production and the production of natural gas (petrochemicals) make up the majority of Saudi Arabia's economic wealth. Because Saudi Arabia has such large oil deposits, this country has become very influential in the world economy and in the Organization of Petroleum Exporting Countries (OPEC). The great wealth oil production has brought to Saudi Arabia has enabled the country to modernize agriculture, spending billions of dollars on irrigation and desalinization technology. Many modern Saudi cities have been built in areas that were once remote desert areas. They have modernized roads, schools, airports, and communications systems. Even though the oil wealth of the country technically belongs to the royal family, the al-Saudis, enormous sums of money have been spent to improve the lives of ordinary citizens. Saudi Arabia has gone from being a "desert kingdom" to a modern nation in less than 100 years.

Iran's most valuable natural resource is oil, although Iran also has rich farmland and access to water for irrigation and farming. Iran has a varied economy, with oil and petroleum products production being the largest contributor to the country's national wealth. Eighty-five percent of the government's money comes from the sale of oil and petrochemicals on the world market. Even so, much of Iran's population works in other industries as well, with almost a third engaged in agriculture. Iran has had political problems in recent decades that have led to economic difficulties in spite of their large supply of oil. Iran is a member of the Organization of Petroleum Exporting Countries (OPEC) and benefits from that organization's decisions to keep the price of oil on the world market at high levels.

_____ 341. **Why are oil and gas such valuable natural resources?**
   A. Large deposits of oil and gas are found in most countries.
   B. It is easy to replace oil and gas supplies after they are used.
   C. Industrial countries depend on oil and gas as their energy supply.
   D. Oil and gas are the only sources of energy used around the world.

_____ 342. **How much of the oil used by the United States has to be imported every day?**
   A. 33 percent
   B. 50 percent
   C. 75 percent
   D. nearly 100 percent

_____ 343. **How has the Saudi government used its national wealth to change the country?**
   A. All Saudi citizens are given an equal share of the national wealth.
   B. The Saudi government has spent very little to improve the lives of ordinary citizens.
   C. A majority of the national wealth has been given to religious organizations in the country.
   D. The government has paid for improvements in transportation, education, health care, and agriculture.

_____ 344. **How do Iran and Saudi Arabia benefit from belonging to the Organization of Petroleum Exporting Countries (OPEC)?**
   A. OPEC keeps the price of oil high on the world market.
   B. Countries in OPEC are able to share water resources with each other.
   C. The organization sets up tariffs to protect Southwest Asian manufacturing.
   D. OPEC makes it possible for Southwest Asian countries to buy oil at low prices.

_____ 345. **How has Israel's lack of oil affected that country's economy?**

    A. Israeli businesses use little oil to operate.

    B. Israel has little industry dues to their lack of oil.

    C. The Israeli economy is built around large-scale farming.

    D. The Israeli economy depends on technology rather than natural resources, such as oil.

> **SS7E7 The student will describe factors that influence economic growth and examine their presence or absence in Israel, Saudi Arabia, and Iran.**
> d. Describe the role of entrepreneurship.

Entrepreneurs are creative, original thinkers who are willing to take risks to create new businesses and products. Entrepreneurs think of new ways to combine productive resources (natural, human, and capital) to produce goods and services that they expect to sell for a price high enough to cover production costs. These business people are willing to risk their own money to produce these new goods and services in the hope that they will earn a profit. Because no one can tell how popular their new products and services will be, not all entrepreneurs can count on making a profit. Many businesses are not successful. Only about 50% percent of all new businesses are still operating three years after they begin.

_____ 346. **What is an entrepreneur?**

    A. people who enjoy saving all their money

    B business people who try not to take risks with their money

    C. someone who is always successful in whatever he attempts

    D. someone who is willing to take a risk to begin a new business

SOUTHWEST ASIA (MIDDLE EAST)

HISTORICAL UNDERSTANDINGS

SS7H2 The student will analyze continuity and change in Southwest Asia (Middle East) leading to the 21st century.

a. Explain how European partitioning in the Middle East after the breakup of the Ottoman Empire led to regional conflict.

THE OTTOMAN EMPIRE IN 1914

The **Ottoman Empire** controlled much of the area known as the Middle East, or Southwest Asia, from the 1300s until the end of World War I. At its most powerful in the 1500s, the Ottoman Empire's capital was the city of Istanbul. By the beginning of World War I in 1914, the Ottoman Empire had shrunk in size but still included much of what is known today as Southwest Asia. The Ottoman Empire had weakened because it tried to rule such a huge empire with leaders who could not manage to hold on to the territory. European countries had also become more powerful. When World War I began, the Ottoman Empire decided to join forces with Germany, Austria-Hungary, and Bulgaria to form the Central Powers. They fought against the Allies, Russia (dropped out in 1917), France, United Kingdom, Italy (joined in 1915), and the United States (joined in 1917). Their side lost the war, and as a result, the Ottoman Empire was overthrown, and Ottoman territory was broken up into a number of smaller countries. The treaty that was announced in 1920, that defined the new boundaries was called the San Remo Agreement. These countries are part of what is known today as the modern Middle East, or Southwest Asia.

The European politicians who decided where the boundaries of these new countries would be often paid little attention to the ethnic and religious groups who were already living in these areas. The new boundaries that were drawn did not take into consideration the concept of nationalism (the idea that countries are most successful if the people who live there share some common cultural, historic, or religious beliefs). As a result, there has been a lot of conflict. Many different groups tried to live together in countries that were created by those who did not realize the problems some of these new boundaries would cause.

_____ 347. **What led to the end of the Ottoman Empire at the close of World War I?**
   A. The Ottomans were on the losing side of the war, along with Germany and Italy.
   B. The Empire spent too much money on buildings and new roads and went bankrupt.
   C. The people in the Empire were starving because a long drought had ruined agriculture.
   D. The Ottoman government was overthrown by a revolt of factory workers who were unemployed when the war ended.

_____ 348. **Who drew up the boundaries of the new countries created from the Ottoman Empire at the end of World War I?**
   A. United States
   B. Ottoman rulers
   C. European politicians
   D. Middle Eastern governments

SOUTHWEST ASIA (MIDDLE EAST)

SS7H2 The student will analyze continuity and change in Southwest Asia (Middle East) leading to the 21st century.

b. Explain the historical reasons for the establishment of the modern State of Israel in 1948; include the Jewish religious connections to the land, the Holocaust, anti-Semitism, and Zionism in Europe.

One of the areas created from the old Ottoman Empire at the end of World War I was Palestine. This area was important to Jews, Christians, and Muslims because this is where much of what is written in the Old Testament, the New Testament, and the Quran took place. There are many religious sites in Palestine sacred to all three religions. The most important of these is Jerusalem.

In the years before World War II, Palestine was divided again into Transjordan, on the eastern side of the Jordan River, and an area still known as Palestine on the western side of the river. The British were given the responsibility for ruling in Palestine until a decision could be made about how to establish a permanent government there. Most of the people living in Palestine before World War II were Palestinian Arabs. However, since the late 1800's large numbers of Jewish settlers had been immigrating to the area from both Western and Eastern Europe. Some of these Jewish settlers wanted to create a homeland for the world's Jews in Palestine, because they believed land in this area had been promised to them by God many thousands of years ago, as told in the stories of the Old Testament. These groups were known as **Zionists** (those who felt the world's Jews deserved to return to a homeland in Zion, or those parts of Palestine where the Jewish people had lived in Biblical times). Conflicts began to break out between the settlers and the Palestinian Arabs, as each group tried to hold onto the land.

During World War II, the Jewish people in Europe suffered terribly at the hands of the Nazi government of Germany. There was widespread **anti-Semitism** (hatred of the Jews simply because they practiced the Jewish faith) in Europe. Over six million European Jews were killed in concentration camps set up by Germany and many thousands of others had to leave Europe to avoid death. This terrible time came to be known as the **Holocaust**.

At the end of the war, the Jewish people of the world wanted to take steps to be sure nothing like this could ever happen again. Many countries in the world felt tremendous guilt over the Holocaust as they began to learn the details of what had gone on in the German-run concentration camps. A number of Jewish groups living in Europe and the United States, even before the Holocaust, had talked of trying to set up a homeland for the Jewish people in the region of the Middle East or Southwest Asia known as Palestine. At the end of the war, the newly created United Nations also believed something should be done for the Jewish people because of their suffering.

In 1948, the United Nations voted to create a homeland for the Jews in part of Palestine. The Jews who were living there accepted the offer and declared the creation of the State of **Israel**. However, not everyone was happy with this new state. There were Palestinian Arabs living in the area who felt the United Nations had unfairly given their land away, and they along with many other Arab countries refused to accept the new state. War broke out in May 1948 between the new state of Israel and the Palestinians. Other Arab countries in Southwest Asia agreed with the Palestinians and helped them during this war. The Israelis were able to win this war and the new state of Israel survived, taking over even more land than had originally been planned.

_____ **349. Which describes the Holocaust?**

        A. the murder of millions of European Jews during World War II

        B. the destruction of all European governments during World War II

        C. the bombing of towns and villages in England and Germany during World War II

        D. the Russian policy of burning ground behind them as they retreated to stop the German invasion

SOUTHWEST ASIA (MIDDLE EAST)

_____ 350. **Why did so many countries in the United Nations feel it was right to create Israel in 1948?**
   A. There was no one else living on the land at that time.
   B. Many felt the Jews deserved help due to their suffering in the Holocaust.
   C. Arab countries in the area supported the creation of a homeland for the Jews in Palestine.
   D. All national groups in the former Ottoman Empire were being given homelands at the same time.

_____ 351. **What is Zionism?**
   A. the idea that all religious groups should have their own states
   B. the plan to let Arabs and Jews share the land in Palestine equally
   C. the hope that all governments will be based on religious principles
   D. the belief that Jews deserved to return to a homeland in Zion where they had lived in Biblical times

_____ 352. **What world organization created the new state of Israel in 1948 as a homeland for the Jews?**
   A. the United Nations
   B. the European Union
   C. the League of Nations
   D. the Organization of Petroleum Exporting Countries

_____ 353. **How did Arabs living in Palestine in 1948 feel about the creation of the new state of Israel?**
   A. They supported it fully.
   B. They rejected it as unfair to them.
   C. The Arab population in Palestine was largely unaffected by the new state.
   D. They agreed to try to work it out although they were unhappy about the decision.

_____ 354. **When war broke out in Palestine, what countries joined with the Palestinian Arabs to try to stop the creation of the new state of Israel?**
   A. the United States
   B. neighboring Arab countries
   C. the major nations of Europe
   D. the countries belonging to the United Nations

Use the map below to answer questions 355-357.

Israel

_____ **355. Which countries border the Gaza Strip?**

    A. Iraq and Jordan

    B. Israel and Egypt

    C. Lebanon and Syria

    D. Israel and the West Bank

_____ **356. What is the approximate location of the Dead Sea from Jerusalem?**

    A. nearly 25 miles east

    B. nearly 25 miles west

    C. about 15 miles southeast

    D. about 15 miles southwest

_____ **357. What country is found at 31° N, 34° E?**

    A. Egypt

    B. Israel

    C. Jordan

    D. Saudi Arabia

SS7H2 The student will analyze continuity and change in Southwest Asia (Middle East) leading to the 21st century.

c. Describe how land and religion are reasons for continuing conflicts in the Middle East.

In May 1948, war broke out in Palestine between the Jews who supported the creation of the new state of Israel and the Palestinian Arabs who also lived there. The neighboring Arab countries supported Palestinian claims to land now in the new state of Israel. The Israelis were able to win this war and the new state of Israel survived, taking over even more land than had originally been planned. Many Palestinians became refugees (people who had to leave their homes as the result of the war). In the last 50 years, there have been additional wars between the Israelis and the Palestinians. Israel has continued to exist, and many of the Palestinians and their descendants still live in refugee camps or in parts of Israel that they feel should be a Palestinian state. The problems between these two people still exist, even though people on both sides of the conflict continue to look for ways to find a peaceful solution to their disagreements. Arab countries in the area are strong supporters of the Palestinians, while the United States is a powerful supporter of the Israelis. The Arab-Israeli conflict plays a major role in the difficulties that the United States and the rest of the world face when trying to find peaceful settlements to Southwest Asian, or Middle Eastern, conflicts.

_____ 358. **What was the outcome of the 1948 War between the new state of Israel and the Arabs living in and around Palestine?**

A. The conflict ended and all Palestinian Arabs became citizens in the new State of Israel.

B. Israel won the war and the new State of Israel was even larger than originally planned.

C. Almost no Jewish people were willing to go to Israel because of the country's angry Arab neighbors.

D. The United Nations decided to withdraw the proposal to create a State of Israel because of all the problems it caused in the area.

_____ 359. **What is a "refugee"?**

A. a person who had to leave their home as a result of war

B. a person who opens his home to those who need a safe place to stay

C. a person who refuses to take in someone who is without a safe place to stay

D. a person who refuses to leave his home even though it is dangerous to stay there

_____ 360. **What has become of many of the Palestinians who became refugees in 1948?**

A. Many still live in refugee camps.

B. Most have become Israeli citizens.

C. They have been given a state of their own in which to live.

D. They have given up any claim to return to the land they lost in 1948.

The United States has had significant political and economic interests in Southwest Asia, or the Middle East, since the 1800s, when merchants, missionaries, and tourists began to visit the region. In addition, vast supplies of oil are found in this area, oil that is critical to United States' energy supplies. Since the end of World War I, the United States has played an important role in the diplomacy following the break-up of the Ottoman Empire. The United States support for the creation of the state of Israel in 1948 also focused attention on this part of the world.

In August 1990, the country of Iraq invaded Kuwait in an effort to control Kuwait's large supplies of oil. The leader of Iraq, Saddam Hussein, claimed that Kuwait was taking more oil than they were allowed to from shared oil fields. He also claimed that when the Ottoman Empire was broken up at the end of World War I, the area that became the country of Kuwait should have been a part of Iraq. The creation of the country of Kuwait in 1920 meant that Iraq no longer had any coastline on the Persian Gulf. The United States was concerned about the invasion because the United States gets a large portion of its imported oil from Kuwait and Saudi Arabia, another country in the area. Kuwait belonged to the United Nations, a world organization which will come to the aid of a member nation that is attacked without cause by another country. The United Nations voted to raise a military force to liberate Kuwait from the Iraqi invasion. Because of the threat to the oil supply, the United States sent troops to be a part of this United Nations military force to drive Iraq out of Kuwaiti territory. This effort was known as the **Persian Gulf War**, or **Operation Desert Storm**. Thirty-nine countries joined in and within three months, by February 1991, the Iraqi government accepted a truce and agreed to withdraw from Kuwait.

In 2001, after the destruction of the World Trade Center in New York City, the United States began a military operation in **Afghanistan** aimed at capturing the people responsible for the attack. Intelligence sources identified an organization known as Al-Qaeda, or the Force, as the group of terrorists that planned and carried out the attack. Its leader was a man who was born in Saudi Arabia named Osama bin-Laden. His family was very wealthy and he had used his money to finance this organization. One of the aims of Al-Qaeda is to bring about an end to western influence in the Middle East, or Southwest Asia. Sources in the United States government believed that the radical Muslim government of Afghanistan, the Taliban, allowed Al-Qaeda to hide in the mountains of their country. The United States launched a series of attacks on these mountain hideouts in October 2001 in an attempt to capture bin-Laden and destroy al-Qaeda. United States troops were also sent in and the government of the Taliban collapsed. Since 2001, United States troops have continued fighting in Afghanistan in an attempt to find bin-Laden and destroy his organization. The United States is still working to help the people of Afghanistan reorganize their government.

In 2003, the United States launched an **invasion of Iraq**, after claiming that the Iraqi government, led by Saddam Hussein, was developing nuclear weapons and offering aid to groups like al-Qaeda, who were a threat to United States interests in the region. The United States called this military action **Operation Iraqi Freedom**. The government of Saddam Hussein collapsed quickly because many of the Iraqis also felt he was a cruel leader. However, problems followed as the United States did not have a plan ready to help reorganize the country once the old government was gone. American forces have remained in Iraq ever since, trying to stop the fighting between the different religious and ethnic groups who are competing with each other for power as they try to organize a new government.

SOUTHWEST ASIA (MIDDLE EAST)

_____ **361. What is the United States' main economic interest in Southwest Asia?**

    A. oil

    B. tourism

    C. trade routes

    D. selling American-made products

_____ **362. Why did the United Nations try to stop Iraq from taking over Kuwait in 1990?**

    A. The United Nations wanted to destroy the country of Iraq.

    B. The only job of the United Nations is military action around the world.

    C. The economies of many countries depend on oil and Iraq's actions threatened that supply.

    D. The United Nations has to intervene whenever any member nation has a conflict with another country.

_____ **363. Who are the "Taliban"?**

    A. the government of Iraq

    B. the government of Kuwait

    C. a group of radical Muslims

    D. a part of the United Nations

_____ **364. Why did the United States bomb and invade Afghanistan in 2001?**

    A. Afghanistan invaded the country of Kuwait and threatened the United States supply of oil.

    B. The United Nations asked the United States to overthrow the Taliban government of Afghanistan.

    C. The United States was afraid that Afghanistan was working to develop nuclear weapons and they wanted to put a stop to the program.

    D. They believed the government was offering safety to al-Qaeda, the organization that attacked the United States on September 11, 2001.

_____ **365. Why did the United States go to war against Iraq in 2003?**

    A. Iraq was threatening Afghanistan with nuclear weapons.

    B. The United Nations believed Iraq was about to invade Kuwait a second time.

    C. Iraqi troops launched an attack on Saudi Arabia, a close ally of the United States.

    D. The United States government saw the Iraqi leader, Saddam Hussein, as a threat to peace and United States interests in the region.

SOUTHERN AND EASTERN ASIA
GEOGRAPHIC UNDERSTANDINGS

SS7G9 The student will locate selected features in Southern and Eastern Asia.

a. Locate on a world and regional political-physical map: Ganges River, Huang He (Yellow River), Indus River, Mekong River, Yangtze (Chang Jiang) River, Bay of Bengal, Indian Ocean, Sea of Japan, South China Sea, Yellow Sea, Gobi Desert, Taklimakan Desert, Himalayan Mountains, and Korean Peninsula.

The southern and eastern parts of Asia are home to almost half of the world's population. The geography of this large area is varied, containing some of the world's longest rivers, highest mountain ranges, and most extensive deserts.

The **Indus River** begins in the mountains of Tibet and flows almost 2000 miles through the country of Pakistan before emptying into the Arabian Sea. The Indus River valley is one of the richest farming areas in this region. Many different civilizations have lived along this river throughout the centuries.

The **Ganges River** is India's most important river. It begins in the Himalayan Mountains and flows southeast through India and Bangladesh before emptying into the **Bay of Bengal**. The water of the Ganges carries tons of rich **sediment** (topsoil, silt and minerals from the mountains) that is gradually spread along its path enriching the farmland and creating a large, fertile delta at the mouth of the river. Because so many people live and work along the Ganges, the water in the river is heavily polluted.

The country of Bangladesh is located almost completely in the Ganges River delta. Heavy flooding in this part of the world during the **monsoon season** (a seasonal prevailing wind, lasting several months, bringing heavy rains) often causes great hardships for those living in this country. Further out to sea is the **Indian Ocean**, which is the third largest ocean in the world.

The **Himalayan Mountains** form the southern border of China. This high ground spreads to the north to form the Tibetan Plateau. The area is sometimes called "the roof of the world" because of its high altitudes. This wide area of mountains and high plateau blocks any moisture coming from the rivers and seas to the south. The Himalayan Mountains form India's eastern border with China and Nepal. These high mountains form a barrier between India and countries to her north and east. The Himalayan Mountains stretch for almost 200 miles. The highest mountain in the world, Mount Everest, is on the border between Nepal and China.

As the mountains begin to level off in the north, the land becomes desert. Here one finds the Taklimakan Desert and the Gobi Desert. The **Taklimakan Desert** is over 600 miles in length, one of the longest deserts in the world. To the west and in the central part of China is the **Gobi Desert**, which can be one of the hottest and also one of the coldest places in the world. Much of the Gobi Desert is covered with sand and rocks.

China's fertile farming areas lay north and east of this great desert region. The **Huang He**, or **Yellow River**, begins in the mountainous plateau of Tibet. It flows toward the east and finally empties into the **Yellow Sea**. The yellow dust blowing out of the Gobi Desert is picked up by the Huang He and carried along as loess (another name for silt), giving both the river and the sea a yellowish color. Loess is also deposited along the river's path, creating rich soil for the farmers in the area. This river is also used for transporting people and goods, though sometimes annual floods make conditions along the river's path dangerous. The frequent flooding has led some to call the Huang He "China's Sorrow."

The **Yangtze River**, or Chang Jiang, also begins in the Tibetan Plateau. This river travels east until it reaches the East China Sea. Shanghai, one of China's most important ports, is located at the mouth of this river. The Yangtze River is over 3400 miles long making it China's longest river. This river goes through fertile farming land and is one of China's main transportation routes. The Yangtze River and Huang He River are connected by the Grand Canal, one of the world's oldest and longest canal systems. The oldest parts of the canal were built over 2000 years ago.

ASIA

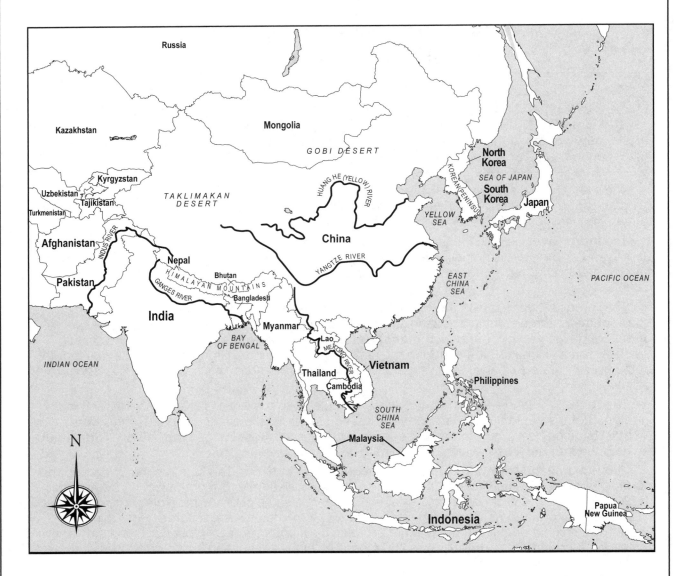

The **Mekong River** begins in the Tibetan Plateau. This river runs south from China through Myanmar, Thailand, Laos, Cambodia and finally Vietnam, where it empties into the **South China Sea**. The Mekong River delta has some of the richest farming land in the world.

The **Korean Peninsula** is a mountainous **peninsula** (a body of land that is surrounded by water on three sides). It is attached to China and bordered by the Yellow Sea and the Sea of Japan. Over half of the peninsula is made up of mountains. Even though so much of the country is mountainous, there is still plenty of rich farmland. Since the end of World War II Korea has been divided into two different countries, North Korea and South Korea.

The **Sea of Japan** is a small sea bound by Russia to the north, the Korean Peninsula to the west and Japan to the east.

Use the map on the next page to locate the geographic areas in questions 366-370.

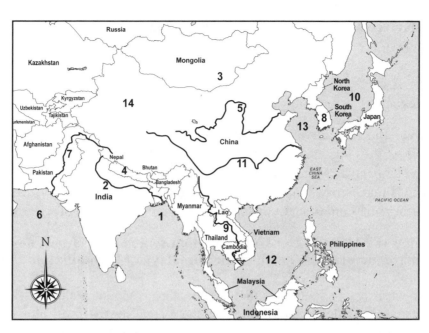

_____ **366. Which marks the Indus River?**
   A. 2
   B. 3
   C. 7
   D. 8

_____ **367. Which marks the Bay of Bengal?**
   A. 1
   B. 10
   C. 12
   D. 13

_____ **368. Which feature is marked by the "4"?**
   A. Gobi Desert
   B. Korean Peninsula
   C. Taklimakan Desert
   D. Himalayan Mountains

_____ **369. Which feature is marked by the "3"?**
   A. Gobi Desert
   B. Korean Peninsula
   C. Taklimakan Desert
   D. Himalayan Mountains

_____ **370. Which marks the Mekong River?**
   A. 2
   B. 5
   C. 9
   D. 11

ASIA

_____ **371. Which river flows through India and Bangladesh to the Bay of Bengal?**
   A. Indus
   B. Ganges
   C. Yangtze
   D. Mekong

_____ **372. Why are the Himalayas called the "roof of the world"?**
   A. The world's highest mountains are found in this area.
   B. The Himalayan Mountains are generally quite easy to travel.
   C. The Himalayan Mountains are so rugged that no people can live there.
   D. Little water comes out of this mountain range in the form of rivers or streams.

_____ **373. Which is the MOST LIKELY reason that some of the largest deserts in this world are found to the north of the Himalayan Mountains and the Tibetan Plateau?**
   A. No water can be found in either the Himalayan Mountains or the Tibetan Plateau.
   B. The year-round cold temperatures in these areas led to the creation of these deserts.
   C. Years of poor farming led to erosion of the soil and the gradual development of desert.
   D. These high mountains and plateau block rains and moisture that would come from the seas further to the south.

_____ **374. What are the two great deserts found in China?**
   A. Gobi and Ganges
   B. Gobi and Taklimakan
   C. Huang He and Yangtze
   D. Mekong and Taklimakan

_____ **375. Why is the Huang He River referred to as the Yellow River?**
   A. No one really knows where this name came from.
   B. The river was given this name by order of the Chinese government.
   C. Yellowish dust from the desert blows into the water and gives it a yellow color.
   D. Villagers living along this river are famous for producing cloth using a bright yellow dye.

_____ **376. What is loess?**
   A. silt that is carried in river water
   B. small fish that live in China's rivers
   C. another name for heavy seasonal rains
   D. name for the canals built along a river's path

_____ **377. Why is the Huang He sometimes called "China's Sorrow"?**
   A. The river often runs dry leaving farmers to starve.
   B. Floods along this river often cause great suffering.
   C. No one can drink the water from this river because of the pollution.
   D. The river has too many rapids and waterfalls for it to be used for transportation.

ASIA

_____ **378. Which river is the longest in China?**
    A. Ganges
    B. Mekong
    C. Yangtze
    D. Huang He

_____ **379. What is located at the mouth of the Yangtze River?**
    A. Beijing
    B. Shanghai
    C. Hong Kong
    D. Ho Chi Minh City

_____ **380. Which river runs south from Tibet to Vietnam and the South China Sea?**
    A. Indus
    B. Mekong
    C. Yangtze
    D. Huang He

_____ **381. What is the name for a body of land that is surrounded by water on three sides?**
    A. island
    B. swamp
    C. isthmus
    D. peninsula

_____ **382. Which country is a peninsula?**
    A. Japan
    B. China
    C. Korea
    D. Vietnam

ASIA

SS7G9 The student will locate selected features in Southern and Eastern Asia.

b. Locate on a world and regional political-physical map the countries of China, India, Indonesia, Japan, North Korea, South Korea, and Vietnam.

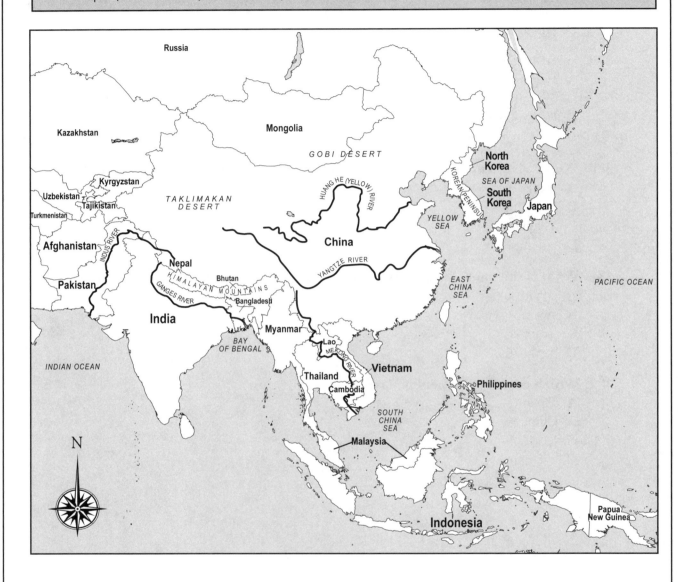

ASIA

Use the following map to answer questions 383-386.

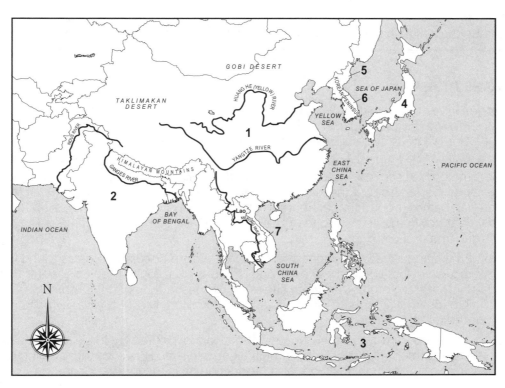

_____ **383. Which country is marked by a "1"?**
   A. China
   B. Japan
   C. Vietnam
   D. Indonesia

_____ **384. Which country is marked by a "7"?**
   A. China
   B. Japan
   C. Vietnam
   B. Indonesia

_____ **385. Which marks North Korea?**
   A. 2
   B. 3
   C. 5
   D. 6

_____ **386. Which marks Indonesia?**
   A. 2
   B. 3
   C. 5
   D. 6

ASIA

SS7G10 The student will discuss environmental issues across Southern and Eastern Asia

a. Describe the causes and effects of pollution on the Yangtze and Ganges Rivers.

THE GANGES RIVER

The **Ganges River** begins high in the Himalayan Mountains and flows 1600 miles through India and Bangladesh to the Bay of Bengal. This river provides water and transportation for the over 400 million people who live in its river valley. It is known as "Mother Ganges."

In spite of the river's importance and its place in the spiritual lives of Indians, the quality of the water has become poor. Chemicals used in fertilizer and industry are washed into the river every day. Human and animal waste also foul the river. The bodies of dead animals as well as the cremated remains of human beings (bodies that are burned after death and whose ashes are scattered in the river) regularly float down the river. In spite of this, many Indians bathe in the Ganges. They also use the water for drinking and cooking.

Cities along the Ganges have the highest rates of water-born diseases (diseases found in drinking water) of any who live in India. Still, these cities pour millions of gallons of sewage (water that contains waste products) into the river to be carried to cities and villages farther south. Outbreaks of such diseases as cholera, dysentery, typhoid, and hepatitis are common. Most officials say polluted river water is part of the reason.

India did begin a program called the Ganges Action Plan in 1985 to try to clean up the river. Many sewage and water treatment plants have been built along the river. However, the growing population of India and the run-off from industrial and farm production have meant that clean-up efforts fall short of what is needed.

_____ 387. **Into which country does the Ganges River flow after it leaves India?**
A. China
B. Pakistan
C. Bangladesh
D. Afghanistan

_____ 388. **Where does the Ganges River flow into the sea?**
A. Yellow Sea
B. Sea of Japan
C. Bay of Bengal
D. East China Sea

_____ 389. **Which is true about the Ganges River?**
A. The river is ignored by Indian religious rituals.
B. People do not drink the water because it is so polluted.
C. Many people use the river for transportation as well as a water supply.
D. Plant and animal life have not been affected by the poor quality of the river's water.

ASIA

_____ 390. **How has India's need to develop more industry ended up creating problems along the Ganges River?**

   A. Factories along the river dump industrial waste and chemicals into the river every day.

   B. No one is allowed to cremate dead bodies along the river since the large factories have been built.

   C. Industries located along the river use so much water that the Ganges is almost dry by the time it reaches the sea.

   D. Factory owners have refused to allow the Indians living along the river to bathe in the water or use the water for cooking.

_____ 391. **How has the Indian practice of cremating their dead been a problem for the river?**

   A. People are not allowed to go near the river when cremations are taking place.

   B. The banks along the river regularly catch fire and threaten Indian homes built there.

   C. Factory owners cannot use water once human ashes have been thrown into it upstream.

   D. The bodies of dead animals, as well as the ashes of human beings, have been placed in the river causing pollution.

_____ 392. **What was the purpose of the Ganges Action Plan begun in the 1980s?**

   A. to try and clean up the river

   B. to bring an end to the cremations

   C. to end using the river for drinking water

   D. to slow down the building of new factories

_____ 393. **Why has the Indian government had such a hard time making much progress in cleaning up the Ganges River?**

   A. Most people in India do not feel the river is polluted so they are not worried about it.

   B. The government of India has not made the cleaning up of the Ganges River one of its goals.

   C. Few people have gotten sick from the water in the Ganges River, so it is hard to get money for clean-up operations.

   D. India's combination of growing population and run-off from farming makes it hard to see much progress in controlling pollution.

THE YANGTZE RIVER

China's longest river, the **Yangtze River**, flows almost 4,000 miles from the northwestern part of the country to the East China Sea. The Yangtze River passes through over 185 towns where almost 400 million people live. Pumping stations along the river take water out to supply people with water for drinking, irrigation, and industrial uses. Millions of gallons of sewage are dumped into the river, along with chemicals from agricultural runoff and industrial wastes. Nitrogen from fertilizers and arsenic (poisonous chemical) from industrial uses are leading pollutants found in the Yangtze's waters.

The pollution in the river puts all of the cities along its banks at risk. Many species of plants and animals that once lived in the river are disappearing. The high levels of nitrogen and phosphates lead to the growth of blue-green algae. This growth reduces the oxygen in the water causing fish to die. Contaminated fish are caught and eaten by the Chinese people, leading to other health problems.

ASIA

China is building more water treatment facilities (process of removing contaminants from wastewater). It is encouraging cities along the river to build sanitary landfills (areas where waste is isolated from the environment until it is safe) for garbage rather than dumping the contaminants in the river. International organizations like the World Bank have worked with Chinese authorities to organize such programs. The massive Three Gorges Dam is being built along the Yangtze River in central China to provide hydroelectric power to millions of Chinese who have not had electricity. Some people feel the dam project was begun without taking into account the effects such a project would have on the environment. A number of species of plants and animals that live along the river where the dam has been built are now threatened with extinction. Another concern is that the dam has been built in an area prone to earthquakes.

_____ 394. **Why is the Yangtze River so important to the population and economy of China?**
   A. Water from the Yangtze River is used to irrigate the Gobi Desert.
   B. The Yangtze River is the international border between China and India.
   C. People can use the Yangtze River to get over the Himalayan Mountains.
   D. It supplies millions of people with water for drinking, irrigation, and industrial uses.

_____ 395. **Into what body of water does the Yangtze flow?**
   A. Indian Ocean
   B. Bay of Bengal
   C. East China Sea
   D. South China Sea

_____ 396. **What are some of the main causes of high levels of nitrogen in the waters of the Yangtze River?**
   A. The waste is from nuclear power plants.
   B. The bodies of dead animals are thrown into the river.
   C. The chemicals used in fertilizers run from the fields into the river.
   D. The exhaust fumes are from the millions of cars driven in this area of Asia.

_____ 397. **Which is one of the most common industrial pollutants found in the Yangtze River?**
   A. arsenic
   B. nitrogen
   C. nuclear waste
   D. human sewage

_____ 398. **What has been the effect of the rapid growth of algae in the Yangtze River?**
   A. The oxygen levels in the water go down and fish die.
   B. The river dolphins and porpoises can rely on the algae as a food source.
   C. The Yangtze River can no longer be used for shipping and transportation.
   D. The algae have provided a good source of fertilizer for those who live along the river.

_____ 399. **Why did the Chinese government decide to go ahead with the Three Gorges Dam project along the Yangtze River?**

    A. The dam would provide water for all of China's desert areas.

    B. China's people needed a reliable source of hydroelectric power.

    C. China needed to be able to store water because the Yangtze River often dried up in the summer.

    D. Careful study showed that there would be no environmental problems associated with the dam.

_____ 400. **How would building sanitary landfills along the Yangtze River help reduce pollution in the water?**

    A. The garbage could go into landfills instead of into the river.

    B. The landfills would reduce the general need for more electricity.

    C. The chemicals would no longer run into farmers' fields and into the river.

    D. All of the garbage would be recycled in landfills and there would be no waste.

SS7G10 The student will discuss environmental issues across Southern and Eastern Asia.

b. Describe the causes and effects of air pollution and flooding in India and China.

INDIA

Air pollution is one of India's most serious environmental problems. An enormous and growing population along with rapid growth of cities (urban areas) and development of industry have left many parts of India with some of the heaviest air pollution in the world. Indians living in several major cities have some of the highest rates of **respiratory disease** (diseases of the lungs, bronchial tubes, and trachea) in the world. In addition to industrial smoke, the growing number of automobiles and trucks in India contribute to the poor air quality. Some estimates say that **automobile emissions** (carbons and other chemicals that come from a car's engine) are responsible for almost 70 percent of the air pollution in some urban areas of India.

Many people in India are poor. They do not want to do anything that would slow down economic growth. For this reason, it has been difficult for the Indian government to enforce many of the laws on industry and transportation that might improve the country's air.

In rural areas, many families cook over open fires, using wood, animal dung, or coal as fuel. These fuel sources send carbon monoxide, soot, and many different chemicals into the air as well. The air inside the home is often as bad as the outside. This pollution can form **brown clouds** (haze of pollution) which reduce rainfall and temperatures.

_____ 401. **Why are India's urban areas having a problem with air pollution?**

    A. Few people in India feel that air pollution is a problem.

    B. There are no government efforts to control air pollution.

    C. There really is no effective way to control air pollution in the world today.

    D. The rapidly growing population, heavy industry, and thousands of automobiles have caused the problem.

_____ **402. How is air pollution a problem in rural areas?**

      A. Millions of people cook over wood or coal fires.

      B. Many heavy industries have relocated in rural areas because the land is cheap.

      C. People living in small villages drive a long distance to work in cars and trucks.

      D. Waste from nuclear power plants has made the air in rural areas dangerous to breathe.

_____ **403. What has been the effect of the heavily polluted "brown clouds" that are now common in some parts of India?**

      A. Rainfall has decreased and temperatures are cooler.

      B. Heavy rains have led to widespread flooding in India.

      C. There is an increase in the crops harvested, as they are not burned by the sun.

      D. The Indian government has decided to reduce the number of cars allowed on India's highways.

_____ **404. Why has the Indian government had problems reducing air pollution?**

      A. They do not want to slow economic growth.

      B. There are no effective ways to regulate air pollution in the world today.

      C. No one in India is concerned about the amount of air pollution in India.

      D. Health problems related to air pollution have shown up in the Indian population.

CHINA

When the Olympic Committee decided to have the 2008 Olympic Games in Beijing, one of the concerns among the athletes who were going to complete was the quality of the air in that Chinese city. Beijing, like many other major cities in China, has experienced tremendous growth in both population and industry during the past few decades. Much of China's energy is provided by burning coal, a process that sends tons of soot, ash, and chemicals into the atmosphere. In addition, millions of Chinese people now drive automobiles and trucks, whose exhaust is another source of massive air pollution.

According to the People's Republic of China's own statistics, the leading causes of death in that country are respiratory and heart diseases that can be tied to long exposure to air pollution. Airborne pollution also contributes to acid rain, a problem for at least a third of China's agricultural areas. Acid rain occurs when chemicals in the air, especially sulfur dioxide and nitrogen oxides that come from burning fossil fuels like coal, react with the moisture in the atmosphere and fall to the ground as rain containing sulfuric acid and nitric acid. Acid rain is harmful to plants, animals, and even buildings.

Before the 2008 Olympics, the Beijing Municipal Environmental Protection Bureau was established to work on the quality of the city's air. Automobile traffic was greatly reduced and many factories were temporarily closed. As a result, many major air pollutants were reduced by as much as 45 percent. Many of the people living in Beijing want the government to find ways to keep pollution down while still allowing for economic progress. Leaders at the World Bank make the argument that the expenses of health problems tied to air pollution are far greater than any economic profits tied to those industries and activities that contribute to the pollution. The impact of environmental and health problems related to air and water pollution take many years to show up in the general population. Often governments begin clean-up efforts long after the health of a country's population has begun to suffer. Because China and India have such enormous populations, almost one half of all the people on the planet, attention to health issues related to air and water pollution are of critical importance.

Copyright © Clairmont Press, Inc. DO NOT DUPLICATE. 1-800-874-8638

_____ **405. When Beijing, China was awarded the 2008 Olympics, which environmental issue was a big concern for many of the athletes?**

A. the city's air pollution

B. lack of fresh drinking water

C. temperatures would be too hot in the summer in China

D. heavy seasonal rains that come to China in the summer

_____ **406. Which contributes to air pollution problems in China?**

A. the shrinking population

B. use of coal-burning power plants for energy

C. the gradual drop in the number of new factories

D. the lack of automobiles and trucks in rural areas

_____ **407. Which is a leading cause of death in China?**

A. skin cancer

B. respiratory and heart disease

C. injuries from automobile accidents

D. injuries related to industrial and factory accidents

_____ **408. What was the job of the Beijing Municipal Environmental Protection Bureau in the months before the 2008 Olympics?**

A. improve the city's air quality

B. work to end the pollution in the countryside

C. begin building dams to provide fresh drinking water for the athletes

D. keep all automobiles and buses out of Beijing while the Olympics were in progress

_____ **409. Why is acid rain dangerous to the environment?**

A. may cause chemical fires

B. can harm plants and animals

C. often leads to massive flooding

D. it causes an increase in air temperature

_____ **410. What economic argument does the World Bank make to urge countries to do whatever they need to do to clean up serious environmental problems quickly?**

A. Health problems disappear very quickly once pollution problems are solved.

B. The process of cleaning up serious environmental problems is usually very easy to do.

C. Most serious pollution problems can be taken care of without spending a lot of money.

D. The long-term costs of pollution are often more expensive than the clean-up effort would be.

ASIA

The **climates** of most of the countries in Southern and Eastern Asia vary depending on each country's geography. Nearby oceans, mountains, deserts, latitude and wind patterns affect climate.

India has many types of climate. Snow and ice are in the northern mountains, hot dry plains are in the central plateau, and steamy tropical weather is along the southern coast. Along the mountain ranges to the north, the temperatures are like those in other high altitude locations. Some of the highest peaks are covered with glaciers and snow. A large desert area borders Pakistan, while the Ganges Plain is humid and almost tropical. The Deccan Plateau in the center of the country is more moderate, with a subtropical coastal plain along the Indian Ocean. Most of India's people rely on farming and other agricultural work, so most of the people live along the great rivers and in the fertile river valleys. Some of India's largest cities are located along the Ganges River or near the coast. Fewer people live in the Deccan Plain in the higher center of the country.

The climate of India is shaped by seasonal winds known as **monsoons**. These winds blow hot, dry air across the continent from the northeast during the winter. In the spring and summer, the winds come from the opposite direction and bring heavy rains from the ocean. These monsoon winds can be a blessing when they bring much needed rain. On the other hand, monsoon rains can cause destructive flooding. The monsoons are very unpredictable.

The people of India have had to live their lives around these seasonal winds and rains. When the shifts in the weather are moderate, the Indian people are able to farm the rich river valley soil and use the rivers for transportation and trade.

The same variety of climates is found in **China**. A country as large as China has nearly every type of climate. High mountain ranges to the south cut China off from India and the moisture that might come from the Indian Ocean. The Gobi and Taklimakan desert regions in the center of the country are harsh and dry. Mongolia to the north is semi-arid, and the areas to the east and south are humid and even tropical. Most of China's one billion people live in the areas of the country that have the milder climates. Here are found the great river valleys and the most fertile farmland.

Japan, an island nation on the far eastern edge of East Asia, has a climate affected by ocean currents. The Japan Current coming from the south brings warm water to the southern and eastern coasts of Japan, while the Oyashio Current coming from the north cools the northern coast. The warmer parts of the country are able to have longer growing seasons for farmers, while those living in the cooler north rely on fishing. Japan experiences monsoon rains and even tropical hurricanes called **typhoons**.

North Korea shares a border with China and has short summers and long, cold winters, much like that of the northeastern corner of China. The land is mountainous and not as heavily populated as South Korea.

South Korea has fewer mountains and a milder climate, due to the warm winds that come from the ocean. South Korea has a larger population than North Korea. Many South Koreans live in the country's largest city, Seoul. Farming is more widely practiced here than in the mountainous north.

Countries further to the southeast like **Vietnam** are warmer and tropical. Here climate and geography join to create rich farmlands where 90 percent of the world's rice is grown.

ASIA

_____ **411. The climate of India is affected by seasonal winds called**
    A. typhoons.
    B. tornadoes.
    C. hurricanes.
    D. monsoons.

_____ **412. Where do most of the people of India live?**
    A. southern coast
    B. center of the country
    C. northwest near Pakistan
    D. along the great rivers and fertile valleys

_____ **413. What is the best way to describe the climate of China?**
    A. hot and dry
    B. mild and temperate
    C. rainy and subtropical
    D. combination of all of these

_____ **414. Where do most Chinese live?**
    A. in Mongolia to the north
    B. in the central hilly plateau region
    C. area of the country with milder climates
    D. around the Gobi and Taklimakan deserts

_____ **415. Which has a major effect on the climate of Japan?**
    A. ocean currents
    B. monsoon rains from India
    C. winds coming off the desert
    D. cold air sweeping off large glaciers

_____ **416. What is the best way to describe the geography and climate of North Korea?**
    A. mountainous and cool
    B. large deserts, hot and dry
    C. mostly river delta and tropical
    D. mix of mountains and river valleys and mild

_____ **417. What is the best way to describe the geography and climate of South Korea?**
    A. mountainous and cool
    B. large desert, hot and dry
    C. mostly river delta and tropical
    D. mix of mountains and river valleys and mild temperatures

_____ **418. Which type of climate makes Vietnam ideal for growing rice?**
    A. warm and tropical
    B. dry and desert-like
    C. colder due to winds from glaciers
    D. bitter cold in winter, hot in summer

ASIA

India is separated from the rest of Asia by three ranges of mountains: the Hindu Kush, the Himalayas, and the Karakoram ranges. Because of this, India is often called a **subcontinent** (a division of a continent). Just south of the large mountain ranges, most of India is made up of a broad plain between the Indus River and the Ganges River. The land in this plain is very fertile, because the rivers provide tons of silt to enrich the soil. South of this great plain is an area of higher plateau called the Deccan Plateau. Even farther south, the land gives way to a narrow tropical strip along the coast of the Indian Ocean.

India's mountains have sometimes stopped invaders from the north who wanted India's fertile river valleys to the south. At other times, invaders have been able to use natural passes through the mountains to make their way into the heart of India and establish new rulers and customs.

Most Indians live in the major river valleys, particularly the Ganges. People are moving into cities from rural areas in large numbers looking for work and better opportunities for their families. The rivers provide transportation, trade routes, water for irrigation, and water to supply the people living in the cities. The rivers have become the easiest means of disposing of human, animal, and industrial waste. As a result, nearly all of India's large cities have problems with over-crowding and air and water pollution.

On the northern side of the Himalayan Mountains and across the Tibetan Plateau is the country of **China**. Its enormous size means there is a great variety of climates and terrain. Two great deserts are located in Northern China: the Gobi and the Taklimakan. Few people live in these regions, and many of those that do live as nomads and animal herders. Other parts of northern and western China have climates that are more moderate and some farming is possible. The northeast, along the route of the Huang He River, is China's most heavily populated region. Beijing is located here. While agriculture is still common, this region of the country is also China's industrial center. Farming is the most common occupation of the Chinese who live in the southeastern part of the country. Here the Yangtze River flows to Shanghai, China's largest port. This region of the country is the site of the Three Gorges Dam. This large hydroelectric project is designed to bring electricity to China's rural areas. For Chinese workers, rapid industrialization has meant many have left their rural homes and found work in overcrowded cities.

The mountains of **North Korea** have meant that it has had less success with agriculture than many others have in this region. There are fast-flowing rivers in the mountains where the North Koreans have developed hydroelectric power plants. The country earns a profit from mining coal and other minerals like iron and copper. Most of the people here live along the western half of the country where the mountains slope down to the sea and farming is more successful.

South Korea is less mountainous and a large part of the country has excellent farmland. The population is greater than that of North Korea, with about 25 percent of the people living in and around the capital city, Seoul. People living in or near Seoul have the advantages of markets, jobs, and education that are harder to find in rural areas. While there are cold winters and warm summers, the climate in South Korea is milder than that of North Korea because of the ocean winds.

BUDDHISM

Buddhism is a religion that also began in India. Siddhartha Gautama, a rich young man, founded the religion about 500 B.C. He had a life of luxury, but he was troubled by the poverty and suffering he saw in the world around him. He left his family and became a wandering monk for a number of years, hoping to learn why people had to suffer. Finally, he quit wandering and simply sat and thought, meditated, about the unhappiness of man. He felt he understood what needed to be done. He believed that people could find peace if they could reject greed and desire. He accepted the Hindu belief in reincarnation and karma, but he did not accept the caste system or the need for priests. He was called "**Buddha**," or "**The Enlightened One**," by his followers.

Buddha taught that there were **Four Noble Truths** in life. One was that life always brought pain. The second was that this suffering and sorrow were usually caused by greed and the desire for material things. The third was that by giving up these greedy desires, a person could end his suffering and reach **Nirvana**, a state of perfect peace. The fourth was that to achieve Nirvana, a person needed to follow **The Middle Way**.

The Middle Way was accomplished by following what Buddha called the **Eightfold Path** (eight rules for conduct):

- try to recognize the truth
- try to avoid evil actions and bad people
- do not say things that hurt others
- respect other people and their belongings
- choose a job that does no harm to others
- do not think evil thoughts
- avoid excitement or anger
- work at meditation, thinking carefully about what matters in life

Buddha believed that unselfishness was the key to everything. He did not recognize gods or see a need for priests. He felt man alone could change evil into good. If one followed the Middle Way, ones soul would eventually reach a state of perfect peace.

About 6 percent of the world's population today is Buddhist, making it the fourth largest religion in the world. Buddhism is practiced all over the world, though its largest numbers of followers are found in Southern and Eastern Asia.

ISLAM

Islam is another religion that is widely practiced in Southern and Eastern Asia. Islam began in the Arabian Peninsula in the 7th century AD with the teachings of the prophet Muhammad. Islam gained followers rapidly in Southwest Asia and North Africa in the years following Muhammad's death.

Islam came to India in the 1500s AD when Muslim armies swept into the country from the northwest. They established the Mogul Empire that ruled India for almost 200 years. Muslim conquerors treated the Hindus as conquered people and introduced Islam as a new religion.

Muslims practice what is known as the **Five Pillars of Islam**:

- profession of faith - there is only one god and Muhammad is his messenger
- pray five times a day facing the direction of Mecca
- charity to the poor
- fasting during the holy month of Ramadan
- pilgrimage to Mecca at least once in a person's lifetime

ASIA

Because **Muslims** believe in only one god, this religion is called a **monotheistic religion**. A religion that believes in more than one god is called a **polytheistic religion**. Muslims do not have an organized priesthood but they do gather in community mosques for prayer, and there are Muslim leaders for prayer as well as Muslim scholars. Muslims also have a holy book, The **Quran**, which they believe is the actual word of God handed down by the angel Gabriel. Muslims do not believe in the caste system, something that many of the Hindus in India have accepted. They also do not believe cows to be sacred, and they have no rules against eating beef. Few Muslims will eat pork, however, believing the meat to be unclean.

Today, many millions of Muslims live in Southern and Eastern Asia. Islam is the second largest religion in the world. Only Christianity has more followers.

SHINTO

The earliest religion of Japan was **Shintoism**, which literally means the "way of the gods." Shintoism centers on reverence for the **kami**, divine spirits that Shinto followers believe live in nature. The word kami means "superior." These spirits are believed to live in beautiful places, animals, and especially as a person's ancestors. Many Japanese people believe some of the mountains and rivers in Japan are the homes of these kami, and these places are considered sacred. Shintoism also stresses the virtue of cleanliness.

Those who practice Shintoism offer prayers and perform rituals to honor and please the kami, or spirits they feel are special. There is no elaborate philosophy in Shinto, and the religion does not stress life after death. Most Japanese households have a small altar where the family will offer prayers for the spirits they hope will bless and protect them. The worship of nature has also led the Japanese to perfect the art of creating small, beautiful gardens, areas of quiet and reflection in their crowded world. Shintoism was once the state religion of Japan. It is no longer the official state religion, but Shintoism is still widely honored among the Japanese. There are followers of Shintoism around the world, but they are relatively few in number when compared with other major religions.

CONFUCIANISM

Confucius was one of the most important scholars in Chinese history. He was born around 550 BC at a time when the government was having trouble keeping order and warlords controlled much of the countryside. He believed that the key to peace and social order was for people to behave with good character and virtue. Virtue is behaving fairly and with justice toward others. His **Golden Rule of Behavior** was "What you do not like when done unto yourself, do not unto others." He believed a good ruler was one who treated his people fairly and was kind to them. Confucius was not a religious prophet or even a religious leader. He saw himself as a teacher and Confucianism is thought of as a philosophy or ethical system based on good deeds and morality rather than a religion.

Confucius believed there were **five basic relationships** among men:

- ruler and subject
- father and son
- husband and wife
- older brother and younger brother
- friend and friend

He believed if each relationship were based on kindness, there would be peace and harmony in the country.

SS7G12 The student will analyze the diverse cultures of the people who live in Southern and Eastern Asia.

c. Evaluate how the literacy rate affects the standard of living.

Literacy, or the ability to read and write, has a big effect on the standard of living of a country. Those who cannot read or write have a very difficult time finding decent jobs. Lack of education also prevents many young people from becoming the engineers, doctors, scientists, or business managers that modern economies need in order to bring improvements to their countries. In many parts of the world, education is only available to those who can afford to pay for it themselves. In those countries, the literacy rate is often quite low. Countries that have stronger economics usually make money available so that anyone who wants an education can go to school.

One way to measure the standard of living is the **Gross Domestic Product**, or **GDP**. The GDP is the value of all final goods and services produced within a country in a given year and converted into United States dollars for comparison. When divided into a value **per capita** (or per person), it can be used as a measure of the living conditions in a country. The higher the GDP value, the better the living conditions in the country.

Southern and Eastern Asia offer some interesting contrasts. Many parts of Southern and Eastern Asia, especially those where there are fewer cities and towns, have lower literacy rates than found in Europe or the United States. Higher rates of literacy are usually found in countries that are the wealthy. In Southern and Eastern Asia, some countries have weak economies but very high literacy rates. Two of these, China and North Korea, have strong state-run education systems that require attendance through a certain age. Even though their economies lag behind the rest of the region in some areas, literacy is a national priority. China has some of the richest and poorest people in Eastern Asia. Even with the wide range of incomes, basic literacy is a primary goal for the Chinese government.

ASIA

Use these graphs to answer questions 453-457.

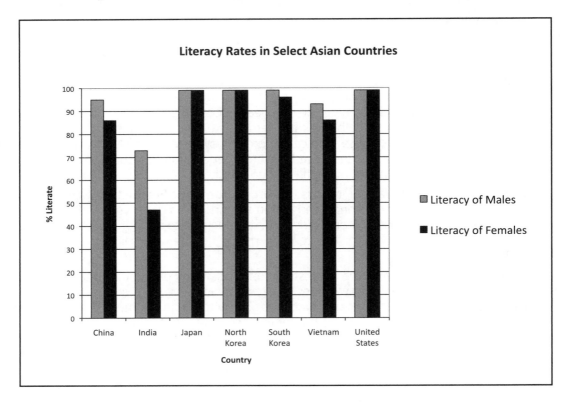

Literacy Rates in Select Asian Countries

% Literate

100
90
80
70
60
50
40
30
20
10
0

China India Japan North Korea South Korea Vietnam United States

Country

■ Literacy of Males
■ Literacy of Females

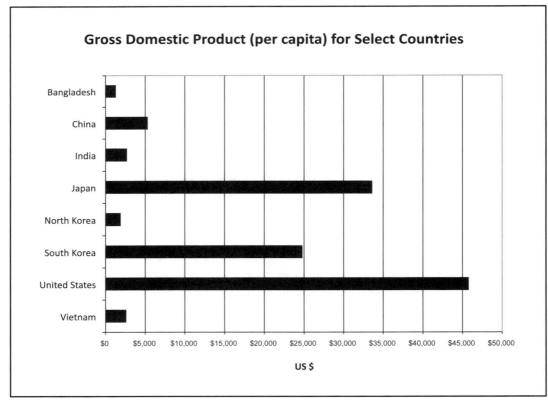

Gross Domestic Product (per capita) for Select Countries

Bangladesh
China
India
Japan
North Korea
South Korea
United States
Vietnam

$0 $5,000 $10,000 $15,000 $20,000 $25,000 $30,000 $35,000 $40,000 $45,000 $50,000

US $

ASIA

_____ **461. Which organization could be considered an example of a confederation form of government?**

    A. the Diet of Japan

    B. the Indian National Congress

    C. the Association of Southeast Asian Nations

    D. the Assembly of the People's Republic of China

_____ **462. How is government power handled in a federal form of government?**

    A. The king makes most of the important decisions.

    B. Power is shared among different levels of government.

    C. A central committee makes all of the political decisions.

    D. The local government has more power than the national government.

SS7CG6 The student will compare and contrast various forms of government.

b. Explain how governments determine citizen participation: autocratic, oligarchic, and democratic.

People who live under different kinds of governments often find there are great differences in the rights given to individual citizens.

An **autocratic government** is one in which the ruler has absolute power to do whatever he wishes and make and enforce whatever laws he chooses. Individuals who live under autocratic governments do not have any rights to choose leaders or vote on which laws are made and put into practice. Some autocratic governments may allow the people rights in certain areas like managing local affairs, but the central government keeps control of all the most important aspects of the country's life. In an autocratic system, people usually have little or no power to use against the government if they disagree with decisions that government or ruler has made. There are many different kinds of autocratic governments. The communist government of **North Korea** could be an example of an autocratic government. In North Korea, Kim Jong-il holds the office of premier and head of the National Defense Commission, the two most powerful positions in the government. He rules North Korea as an autocratic dictator.

An **oligarchy** means "government by the few." In this form of government, a political party or other small group takes over a government and makes all of the major decisions. The people of the country have little choice but to go along with the decisions they make. This sort of government can be very similar to an autocratic government. The government of the **People's Republic of China** could be considered an oligarchic government, as the leaders of the Chinese Communist Party control most of what goes on in the country.

In a **democratic government system**, the people play a much greater role in deciding who the rulers are and what decisions are made. **Democracy** comes from the Greek word "demos," which means "people." In this form of government, a great deal of power is left in the hands of the people themselves. People who live in a democracy generally recognize that there must be some rules to organized society, but the goal is to leave as much individual freedom as possible. Decisions are often made by majority votes, but there are also laws in place to protect individual rights. If a person living in a democracy feels his rights have been violated, he has the power to ask the government for help in correcting the situation. Among the countries of Southern and Eastern Asia, India, Japan, and South Korea are examples of democracies.

ASIA

_____ **463. Who makes most of the important governmental decisions in an autocracy?**
A. the ruler
B. the people
C. the court system
D. the elected legislature

_____ **464. Which Asian country could be described as an autocracy?**
A. India
B. Japan
C. South Korea
D. North Korea

_____ **465. Who makes most of the important governmental decisions in an oligarchy?**
A. the king
B. the people
C. the legislature
D. small group of powerful leaders

_____ **466. Which Asian country could be described as an oligarchy?**
A. India
B. Japan
C. China
D. South Korea

_____ **467. Why do the individual voters have more power in a democracy than they do in an autocracy or an oligarchy?**
A. Kings are always poor rulers.
B. The voters get to choose the people who make the laws.
C. All of the power stays in the hands of the local governments.
D. The voters in democratic countries always choose qualified leaders.

_____ **468. Which Asian countries have democratic systems of government?**
A. India and Japan
B. China and Vietnam
C. China and South Korea
D. North Korea and China

ASIA

In a **parliamentary form of democratic government**, the people vote for those who represent the political party they feel best represents their views of how the government should operate. The legislature they elect, **parliament**, makes and carries out (enforces) the laws for the country. The leader of a parliamentary form of government is usually chosen by the party that wins the majority of representatives in the legislature. This leader is often called a prime minister or premier and is recognized as the head of the government. The prime minister leads the executive branch of the government and must answer directly to the legislature for the actions and policies recommended. In many parliamentary governments, a head of state serves as ceremonial leader.

The actual work of the parliament is led by the **prime minister**, who represents the leading political party in the country. He rules with the help of a **cabinet**, or group of advisors. A prime minister holds power for whatever term of office the country's constitution allows. A prime minister may be voted out of office before the term runs out if the party he leads begins to lose power.

There are several countries in Southern and Eastern Asia that have parliamentary systems of government. **India** is the largest parliamentary democracy in the world. The people elect representatives to the Indian National Congress, and the majority party in the Congress chooses who will be the prime minister. **Japan** is also a good example of a parliamentary democracy. The Japanese two-house parliament is called the Diet. The Japanese Diet holds the real power in Japan, even if the government also includes an emperor. The Japanese emperor is a ceremonial figure who has no real power.

A **presidential form of democratic government** is sometimes called a **congressional form of government**. Here a **president**, or chief executive, is chosen separately from the legislature. The legislature passes the laws, and it is the duty of the president to see that the laws are enforced. The president holds power separately from the legislature, but he does not have the power to dismiss the legislature or force them to make particular laws. The president is the official head of the government. The legislature does not have the power to dismiss the president, except in extreme cases when the president has broken a law. The president is both the head of state and the head of the government.

One difference between a presidential and parliamentary system of government is that a prime minister is a member of a parliament while a president is in a separate branch of the government. In a presidential system, the president serves for a set period of time.

_____ 469. **Which branch of government is responsible for making and carrying out the laws in a parliamentary system of government?**
A. courts
B. monarch
C. president
D. legislature

_____ 470. **The leader of a parliamentary system is often called the**
A. king.
B. president.
C. prime minister.
D. constitutional monarch.

ASIA

_____ **471. The leader of a parliamentary system is chosen by**
   A. the monarch or king.
   B. a popular vote of the people.
   C. a decision by the national courts.
   D. the political party with the most representatives in the legislature.

_____ **472. Which branch of government makes the laws in a presidential system of government?**
   A. president
   B. legislature
   C. national courts
   D. both the president and the legislature together

_____ **473. In a presidential system of government, a president is chosen**
   A. by a decision of the national courts.
   B. by a majority vote of the legislature.
   C. in a separate vote from the one that chooses the legislature.
   D. by the political party with the most representatives in the legislature.

_____ **474. What is the role of the president regarding the laws passed by the legislature?**
   A. The president is supposed to enforce those laws.
   B. The president can change the laws he does not like.
   C. The president sends the laws to the states for approval.
   D. The president does not need to approve laws passed by the legislature.

_____ **475. What is one main difference between a president and a prime minister?**
   A. A prime minister has more power than a president.
   B. A president has to be elected while a prime minister does not.
   C. A prime minister does not belong to a particular political party while a president always does.
   D. A president is in a separate branch of government while a prime minister is a part of the legislature.

ASIA

Use the chart to answer questions 476-477.

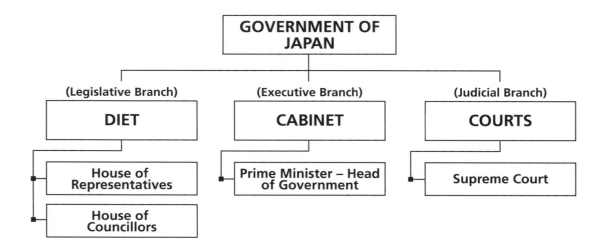

_____ 476. **What is the purpose of the chart?**
   A. to explain the role of the Emperor in Japanese government
   B. to explain how power is divided in the government of Japan
   C. to show that the prime minister controls all parts of the government
   D. to show that the three branches of government are not equally powerful

_____ 477. **Which part of the government leads the legislative branch?**
   A. the Diet
   B. the courts
   C. the cabinet
   D. the emperor

ASIA

THE REPUBLIC OF INDIA

The country of **India** came under British rule beginning in the 1700s. It was a colony of the British Empire until 1947. When India became independent in 1947, they modeled their government after Great Britain's government. India became the world's largest democracy. The Indian constitution was adopted in 1950. It guarantees all Indian citizens the same basic rights. Even the Untouchable caste was granted equal rights, and many among this group are elected officials of the government today. Women were granted voting rights as well. Several women have held the highest offices in India's government. Indira Gandhi was the first woman to be elected as India's prime minister in the 1990s.

Local power is in the hands of village councils in India. Each village council, known as a **panchayat**, is part of a larger group of villages. These larger groups belong to **district councils**. Indian law requires that women and Untouchables be allowed to run for positions in these three levels of councils. The national parliament of India is made up of two houses, and its representatives are elected from local districts. For this reason, India can be described as a **republic**, one in which elected individuals make decisions for the people. If the voters are unhappy with the way these representatives make decisions, they can choose different people in the next election. Elections for the Indian parliament are held every five years. The leader of the majority political party in the Indian parliament serves as **prime minister** and head of the government.

Because India is so large and has so many different languages, castes, and religions, the national government has had to work very hard to see that all groups feel included and are equally protected. The country is **secular**, meaning it favors no special religion, even though the majority of India's people are Hindu.

THE PEOPLE'S REPUBLIC OF CHINA

The **People's Republic of China** is a communist country. It is run as a one-party dictatorship. The Chinese Revolution in 1949 brought the communists to power under the leadership of **Communist Party Chairman Mao Tse-Tung**. Power was in the hands of Mao and a small committee called the **Political Bureau of the Communist Party**, a small group of men who made all of the decisions on how the Chinese government and life in that country would be organized. The Chinese communist government has some control over almost every aspect of Chinese life. People are put to work according to what the Party sees are the needs of the country. All children are expected to attend school. This is an improvement for the very poorest of the Chinese people. Property was taken from wealthy landowners and given to peasants who had no land before the revolution. When the communists took over the government, rural farmers were organized into communities and told to farm as the government saw they should. Chinese industries were organized and controlled by the government.

There was often great suffering in the years following the revolution, and starvation was widespread during some of the early years as officials tried to organize farming. While there were those in China who were more interested in having jobs, education, health care, and housing, most were not worried about losing their personal freedoms.

Today, the Chinese government is still run by the Chinese Communist Party. The government controls most aspects of Chinese life. The **National People's Congress** is elected every five years by a vote of the Chinese people. Every Chinese citizen over the age of 18 is eligible to vote; however, few candidates run for election if they are not approved by the Chinese Communist Party. The National People's Congress chooses a president and vice-president. The president then chooses a **premier** who serves the same five year term as the Congress.

There are signs that China is gradually opening itself up to the rest of the world. Demand for western goods and interest in western culture have become part of China's daily life. The Internet has made the Chinese people aware of life outside of China. The Beijing Olympics gave the rest of the world a look at China, including a look at how strong government control is of most things in that country. The role of the citizen, including what job and what education he or she will have, is determined by the state and there are no votes cast in Chinese elections for anyone other than candidates approved by the government.

THE CONSTITUTIONAL MONARCHY OF JAPAN

Before World War II, the country of Japan was a **monarchy**. It was ruled by a hereditary emperor named **Hirohito**. The people believed him to be descended from the Sun. He was thought to be a god, and few in the country had ever seen him. After Japan was defeated in World War II, the United States helped the Japanese reorganize their government as a constitutional monarchy. A **constitutional monarchy** is a government in which there is a king or emperor, who is limited to the power granted to him by the constitution or laws of the nation.

In 1947, Japan adopted their first constitution that created a **two-house parliament**. This parliament is called the **Diet**, and the government is led by a **prime minister** and a **cabinet** of advisors. The prime minister is chosen by an election of the members of the Diet. All Japanese citizens over the age of 20, including women, are guaranteed the right to vote for the members of the Diet. The constitution also includes a **Bill of Rights**, spelling out the basic freedoms that all Japanese citizens may enjoy. The **emperor** of Japan remains in his position, but he has no political power. The constitution also states that the emperor is no longer to be considered a god.

ASIA

Country	Type of Government	Who Votes	Role of Religion	Design of Government
Japan	Constitutional Monarchy	All citizens 20 years old or older	No direct role; the government is considered secular	Elected parliament (the Diet) and a prime minister chosen by the Diet members
China	Communist Party	All citizens over the age of 18	Religion is not encouraged by the Chinese government	National People's Congress with leaders chosen by the congress
India	Democratic Republic	All citizens over the age of 18	India is a secular government	Elected parliament with a prime minister chosen from the majority party

_____ 478. **Which best describes the Japanese government?**
A. monarchy
B. theocracy
C. federal democracy
D. constitutional monarchy

_____ 479. **The Japanese parliament is called the**
A. the Diet.
B. Knesset.
C. Congress.
D. House of Representatives.

_____ 480. **What role do religious leaders play in the Indian government?**
A. No religious leaders are allowed to run for political office in India.
B. Religious leaders choose the candidates that run from most rural areas.
C. They are guaranteed a certain number of representatives in each election.
D. The country has a secular government in order to avoid seeming to favor one group over another.

_____ 481. **Who is allowed to vote in Indian elections?**
A. All citizens who are over the age of 18.
B. All citizens who are 16 years of age or older.
C. Only men who can prove they are Indian citizens.
D. Only those who can prove they were born in India.

ASIA

_____ **482. Who is allowed to vote in Japan?**
  A. Only men can vote in Japanese elections.
  B. All citizens who are 20 years of age or older may vote.
  C. Only those who can read and write are allowed to vote.
  D. Voters who can prove they were born in Japan may vote.

_____ **483. What sort of government is the People's Republic of China?**
  A. monarchy
  B. federal democracy
  C. constitutional monarchy
  D. communist government

_____ **484. What is the name of the elected Chinese legislative assembly?**
  A. the Diet
  B. Political Bureau
  C. Chinese Communist Party
  D. National People's Congress

_____ **485. Who can vote in national elections in China?**
  A. only Chinese men
  B. only those who live in cities
  C. all citizens who are over the age of 18
  D. voters who have completed 12 years of school

_____ **486. How often are elections for the national government held in India?**
  A. Elections are held every six years.
  B. Party members are elected for life.
  C. Elections for national office are held every five years.
  D. Religious leaders can require new elections to be held if they think it is necessary.

_____ **487. Which country is the world's largest democracy?**
  A. India
  B. Japan
  C. China
  D. Korea

_____ **488. Who was Indira Gandhi?**
  A. mother of Mohandas Gandhi
  B. powerful religious leader in India
  C. first woman prime minister in India
  D. leader of the effort to end the Untouchable caste in India

ASIA

_____ 489. **What role do the people play in a government like that of Japan?**
  A. The people have the real power in Japan.
  B. They have the power to vote the Japanese emperor out of office.
  C. The people get to approve the laws made by the Japanese emperor.
  D. They have little power because the emperor makes most decisions.

_____ 490. **What was the position of the Japanese emperor before World War II?**
  A. His power was weakened by a powerful parliament.
  B. He was believed to be a god descended from the sun.
  C. The emperor played a part in selecting people to run for public office.
  D. The emperor was very involved running the government of the country on a daily basis.

_____ 491. **What group makes most of the important decisions in the government of the People's Republic of China today?**
  A. the wealthy landowners
  B. the Chinese Communist party
  C. Mao Tse-Tung and his advisors
  D. people in the local village councils

_____ 492. **Who chooses the president and vice-president of the National People's Congress in China?**
  A. People are chosen for these jobs by the king.
  B. The members of the National People's Congress choose them.
  C. The voters choose people for these jobs in the general election.
  D. These jobs are filled by the two oldest members of the National People's Congress.

_____ 493. **The premier of the National People's Congress in China is chosen by the**
  A. president.
  B. National People's Congress.
  C. president and the vice-president.
  D. Chinese voters in general election.

_____ 494. **Who was the first leader of the People's Republic of China?**
  A. Hirohito
  B. Mao Tse-Tung
  C. Indira Gandhi
  D. Mohandas Gandhi

ASIA

ECONOMIC UNDERSTANDINGS

> **SS7E8 The student will analyze different economic systems.**
> a. Compare how traditional, command, and market economies answer the economic questions of (1) what to produce, (2) how to produce, and (3) for whom to produce.

Every society must deal with providing goods and services for its people. Each society must also develop an economic system that can decide how to use the limited resources of that society as well. Three basic questions must be answered:

1. What goods and services will be produced?
2. How will goods and services be produced?
3. Who uses the goods and services that are produced?

TRADITIONAL ECONOMY

In a **traditional economy**, most of the economic decisions are made based on **custom** and on the **habit** of how such decisions were made in the past. The word tradition means something that has been passed down in a culture from one generation to the next. Goods and services are exchanged instead of using cash as a payment in a traditional economy. This is also known as **bartering**. In very rural areas of India and China, bartering still plays a role in local economies. As areas become more urbanized, however, bartering gives way to cash as payment. No country today can be described as having a traditional economy. Japan still produces fine traditional crafts, but there are many other types of economic activities going on in Japan as well.

_____ **495. In a traditional economy, how are economic decisions made?**
   A. custom and habit
   B. government planners
   C. consumers and the market
   D. combination of consumers and government planners

_____ **496. Which would be a problem for a country with a traditional economy?**
   A. the supply of cash runs short in times of economic crises
   B. people find they can trade services more easily than goods
   C. a farmer having an especially good year with lots of grain to trade
   D. people need things and are unable to barter to obtain them

COMMAND ECONOMY

A **command economy** is one in which government planning groups make most of the economic decisions for the workers. This group decides which goods and services should be produced, as well as prices for the goods and wages paid to the workers. No individual could decide to start a new business. The government decides what and where to produce the goods. The government decides what jobs the workers do and how and where the goods produced would be sold. The best example of a command economy in Southern and Eastern Asia today is **North Korea**. In that country, the government makes all economic decisions. The government owns nearly all the important factories and industries. China was set up along a command economic system in the 1950s after the communist revolution, but now the country is beginning to make exceptions to the rule of total government control.

ASIA

_____ **497. In a command economy, how are economic decisions made?**

    A. custom and habit

    B. government planners

    C. consumers and the market

    D. combination of consumers and government planners

A MARKET ECONOMY

The third basic type of economic system is a market economy. In a market economy, economic decisions are made by individuals who decide what to produce and what to buy. Other names for a market economy are **capitalism**, **free enterprise**, or **laissez-faire** (French phrase that means to allow them to do as they please). In a market economy, individuals who want to begin their own business may do so. They take economic risk as they invest in their new business. If the new businesses are successful, the people who organized and funded it will be successful and make a profit. If the businesses fail, the investors will lose money. Japan and South Korea have a market economy, or free enterprise economic systems.

_____ **498. In a market economy, how are economic decisions made?**

    A. individuals

    B. custom and habit

    C. government planners

    D. consumers and the market

_____ **499. Who takes on the financial risk in starting a new business in a market economy?**

    A. consumers

    B. government planners

    C. individual business people

    D. combination of government planners and individual investors

A MIXED ECONOMY

Today, no countries in the world have economic systems that are purely traditional, purely command, or purely market systems. **India** is a good example of a mixed economy in Southern and Eastern Asia. The government makes some decisions about agriculture and industry, but free enterprise and entrepreneurship are very common. The economy of a country like **China** is a good example of one that is similar to a command system, although in recent years many business entrepreneurs have begun operating in China as well. Nearly all countries today have mixed economies. In other words, they have the characteristics of a free market and free enterprise as well as some government planning and control.

_____ 500. **Why do most economies in the world today operate somewhere in between a market economy and a command economy?**

    A. Government control makes a market economy more profitable.

    B. Most consumers prefer government control to a free market system.

    C. Government control of some aspects of the economy has never been successful in the modern world.

    D. Most economies have found they need a mix of free market and some government control to be successful and protect consumers.

THE ECONOMY OF CHINA

The government of **The People's Republic of China** was originally designed as a command economy. The government had control over nearly all of the major parts of the economy, including large industries and banks. The government also made the decisions about what was to be produced, what goods would cost, and what workers were to be paid.

When the Chinese Communists came to power in 1949, nearly all of China was agricultural. The leader of the Chinese Revolution was a man who called himself **Chairman Mao Zedong**. He was the chairman of the Chinese Communist party and he ruled China until his death in 1976. The leader of the Communist Party decided how much of the country would remain in farming and how much would switch to industrial production. Traditional farms were reorganized into **collective farms**, where people worked together and shared whatever they produced. The government tried to reorganize the economy in the late 1950s, during a period known as the **Great Leap Forward**. Conditions did not improve fast enough, and another program, the **Cultural Revolution**, came about in the 1960s. This program tried to do away with all previous programs, and reorganized farms, businesses, and most of society. The people in charge of the Cultural Revolution wanted China to do away with everything old - to have a new approach to all aspects of their life. This program was also a failure.

ASIA

In the 1970s China's leader, Deng Xiaoping, began to reorganize the Chinese economy with what he called the **Four Modernizations**. Farmers were given more control over what they decided to produce and they were allowed to sell surplus products and keep the profits. Industry shifted from heavy industries like iron and steel to the production of more consumer goods. Factory workers and managers were allowed to make more of the decisions in the running of the factories. **Special Economic Zones** were set up along the coastal areas to try to encourage foreign companies to do business with China. Defense industries were also built up and made more productive. The results of all these efforts were mixed. The coastal areas of the country began to grow economically. But some of the farm areas in the countryside fell behind. People began to leave and come to cities looking for work. The rapid growth of cities created new problems for the Chinese government.

Many Chinese people today have small businesses of their own, even though the Chinese government still has final authority in most matters. There are many more examples of a market economy at work in China than in the years since the revolution. Although China does not have an unlimited supply of farmland, especially in light of the country's huge population, the country still manages to feed itself. At least half of China's workers remain in agriculture.

Today China's economy continues to be growing and strong, and many Chinese enjoy a higher standard of living than ever before. Cities along the southeastern part of China are experiencing tremendous growth, especially places like Shanghai and Hong Kong.

_____ **501. The economy of China can best be described as**
 A. mixed.
 B. autocratic.
 C. command.
 D. free market.

_____ **502. In the years after the communist revolution, the Chinese government organized farmers into**
 A. free markets.
 B. collective farms.
 C. economic zones.
 D. mixed economies.

_____ **503. The Great Leap Forward and the Cultural Revolution were examples of China's attempt to**
 A. end communist rule.
 B. improve the economy.
 C. sell more goods overseas.
 D. control population growth.

_____ **504. The purpose of China creating Special Economic Zones was to**
 A. spread communist teachings.
 B. improve agricultural harvests.
 C. increase trade with foreign countries.
 D. keep foreign workers out of the country.

ASIA

Not every country can produce all of the goods and services it needs. Because of this, countries **specialize** in producing those goods and services they can provide best and most efficiently. They look for others who may need these goods and services so they can sell their products. The money earned by such sales then allows the purchase of goods and services the first country is unable to produce. In international trade, no country can be completely **self-sufficient** (produce all the goods and services it needs). Specialization creates a way to build a profitable economy and to earn money to buy items that cannot be made locally.

The countries in Southern and Eastern Asia are very different in terms of how their economies are organized. **India** has a lot of farm land, but the population is so large it is often difficult to grow enough food for everyone. India has a booming industrial and technological economy. This specialization makes it possible for an economy as enormous as that of India to focus on those businesses that are the most profitable. **China** is much the same. Some areas of the country are almost all agricultural. Others have large cities and modern industries. **Japan** is a country with very few natural resources, so specialized industries have been developed to earn money needed to buy food and raw materials from other countries. **North Korea** has had many problems in their attempts to improve the harvests on their farms. As a result, the North Korean government has had to turn to industries that use the country's natural resources like iron and coal in order to keep the economy going. Specialization allows countries to produce what they do best and generate income to buy what they still need.

_____ 520. **What is the definition of "economic specialization"?**
   A. trying to avoid investing in industry and technology because of the high costs
   B. directly swapping goods from one country to another without having to use money
   C. producing all goods and services needed for a country's growth so that trade with other countries is not needed
   D. producing those goods a country can make most easily so they can trade them for goods made by others that cannot be produced locally

_____ 521. **Why does economic specialization make trade between countries easier?**
   A. The competition between countries will no longer exist.
   B. There will always be a steady supply of manufactured goods on the market.
   C. Countries can produce those things they make best and trade with others for what they need.
   D. A country's economy will never go through a difficult time or a depression if economic specialization is practiced.

ASIA

SS7E9 The student will explain how voluntary trade benefits buyers and sellers in Southern and Eastern Asia.

b. Compare and contrast different types of trade barriers such as tariffs, quotas, and embargos.

Trade barriers are anything that slows down or prevents one country from exchanging goods with another. Some trade barriers are put in place to protect local industries from lower priced goods made in other countries. Other times trade barriers are created due to political problems between countries. Trade is stopped until the political issues are settled. The countries in Southwest Asia, as in most parts of the world, have experienced trade barriers at one time or another.

A **tariff** is a tax placed on goods when they are brought into (**imported**) from one country to another country. The purpose of a tariff is usually to make the imported item more expensive than a similar item made locally. This sort of a tariff is called a **protective tariff** because it protects local manufacturers from competition coming from cheaper goods made in other countries.

A **quota** is a different way of limiting the amount of foreign goods that can come into a country. A quota sets a specific amount or number of a particular product that can be imported or acquired in a given period of time.

A third type of trade barrier is called an **embargo**. An embargo is when one country announces that it will no longer trade with another country in order to isolate the country and cause problems with that country's economy. Embargos usually come about when two countries are having political disputes. Embargos often cause problems for all countries involved.

_____ **522. What is the definition of a tariff?**
   A. a tax paid by the purchaser when goods are sold
   B. a tax placed on goods coming into one country from another
   C. a tax placed on goods made by local craftsmen or manufacturers
   D. a fee paid when goods are shipped from one state to another in the United States

_____ **523. What is a quota?**
   A. a tax placed on imported goods when they enter the country
   B. a decision to prevent certain goods from being imported at all
   C. a tax placed on goods when they are purchased in the market place
   D. a limit to the number of foreign-produced goods that are allowed into the country

_____ **524 What is an embargo?**
   A. a tax placed on goods coming into the country from overseas
   B. a limit to the amount of a certain good allowed into the country
   C. a tax paid by the producer before he can sell his goods in another country
   D. a halt to trade with a particular country for economic or political reasons

ASIA

Most of the countries in Southern and Eastern Asia have their own type of **currency** (money). In order for them to pay for goods as they trade with each other, they have to establish a system of changing from one type of currency to another. This system is known as an **exchange rate**. They also have to be able to exchange their currencies with those used by other countries around the world. The currency of the United States is based on the dollar. Much of the currency used in Western Europe is called the Euro. In Southern and Eastern Asia, there are many different types of currency. In order for them to trade with each other, they have to be able to figure out what goods cost in each currency.

Use this chart to answer questions 525-526.

Country	Currency	Equivalent in US Dollars
United States	Dollar ($)	$1.00
India	Rupee	41.5 per dollar
China	Yuan	7.61 per dollar
Japan	Yen	117 per dollar
North Korea	Won	140 per dollar
Vietnam	Dong	16,000 per dollar

_____ 525. **If a shirt costs 415 Rupees in India, how much would it cost in US dollars?**
   A. $0.41
   B. $4.15
   C. $10.00
   D. $100.00

_____ 526. **If a gallon of gas cost $4.00 in the United States, what would it cost in China?**
   A. 0.34 Yuan
   B. 3.40 Yuan
   C. 6.80 Yuan
   D. 30.44 Yuan

_____ 527. **Why is it important for nations to have a system to convert from one currency to another?**
   A. The dollar is the most valuable currency in the world today.
   B. The conversion to different currencies makes goods cost less.
   C. The banks are not able to handle different kinds of currencies.
   D. Converting currency makes it possible to buy and sell goods between nations with different types of money.

ASIA

> **SS7E10 The student will describe factors that influence economic growth and examine their presence or absence in India, China, and Japan.**
> a. Explain the relationship between investment in human capital (education and training) and gross domestic product (GDP).

Human capital means the knowledge and skills that make it possible for workers to earn a living producing goods or services. The more skills and education workers have, the better they are able to work without mistakes and to learn new jobs as technology changes. Companies that invest in better training and education for their workers generally earn more profits. Good companies also try to make sure working conditions are safe and efficient, so their workers can do their jobs without risk.

Gross domestic product, or **GDP**, is determined by taking the total value of all goods and services produced by a country in a single year. Wealthy countries have a much higher **per capita GDP** (amount of goods and services produced compared to the number of people) than do developing or underdeveloped countries.

Companies that have invested in human capital through training and education are most likely to have profitable businesses and more satisfied workers than companies that do not make these investments. Countries where training and education are easily available often have higher production levels of goods and services, therefore higher gross domestic product, than countries that do not offer these opportunities. Many of the countries in Southern and Eastern Asia have great differences in their GDP. Those countries that have made the decision to invest in human capital have stronger economies than those that have not. The countries of **India**, **China**, and **Japan** are very different in terms of the challenges each faces as they try to improve their economies, and the ways each country has chosen to meet those challenges.

INDIA

India is a country that presents a wide variety of economic activities. Over half of India's population still works in agriculture of some type, either farming or raising animals. Most of these farms are very small, and those who live there usually produce only enough food for their own families. These people live in a very traditional economy, and they produce about 25 percent of India's GDP.

In the 1960s, the Indian government announced the beginning of a program called the **Green Revolution**, which was a national project aimed at helping farmers use more modern methods and technologies to improve crop production. Many farmers also learned new techniques for building irrigation systems to bring water to their fields. This program was an example of the Indian government investing in the country's human capital. Crop production did increase, and many Indian farmers began to grow new and improved types of rice and wheat, two of the country's leading agricultural products. Even with these improvements, India still has to struggle to produce enough food for the ever increasing population.

While many of the people in India still work in agriculture, this country is also one of the world's top ten industrial nations. The Indian government has stressed education during the past decades. As a result many Indians, particularly those living in the cities, are highly educated and have jobs in the sciences, computer and information technology, arts and literature, and industrial production and research. India is now one of the leading software producers in the world. Because so many in India speak English, this country has become a leader in technology support for people in other parts of the world.

India also has a rich traditional arts history, as well as one of the largest film industries in the world. The Indian middle class is growing rapidly. These are people who are well educated and who play an active part in the country's industrial growth. The country's GDP has been growing at a rate of about 8.5% (percent) per year. The challenge for India is for the economy to keep up with the rapidly growing population and the strains that population puts on both the economy and the environment.

CHINA

China is also a country where the investment in human capital is very important, as about one-quarter of all the people on earth live in this country. Because most of the major economic decisions in China are made by the central government, they are able to make investments in both training and technology that might be more difficult for privately owned businesses. Though there is a lot more private decision making in Chinese business today, the country still remains in many ways a command economy.

In the 1970s, the Chinese government announced that the country would begin a program called the **Four Modernizations**, an effort to improve all aspects of Chinese production including farming, military defense, heavy and light industry, and scientific and technical research and production. Money was made available for newer and better farming equipment and seed, and new quotas were set for higher production. In addition, farmers were allowed to sell crops produced above the quota for their own profit. Industrial production was shifted to making more consumer goods that would sell on the world market. Though the government planners retained most of the control, factory managers and workers were encouraged to make suggestions about how their companies could be reorganized to be more efficient. New methods of production required new training, all of which meant investment in the human capital of China. Four **Special Economic Zones** were established in provinces along the eastern coast of China to act as trade centers for global trade in these new consumer goods.

These changes in the Chinese economy have had both positive and negative results. The gross domestic product of China continues to go up about 8 percent every year, and China has become a leader in exporting consumer goods to the world market. The United States imports about 20 percent of the goods produced in China for foreign sale today.

Many Chinese people have benefitted from earning more money and having better training and education. On the other hand, while the areas in the eastern part of the country in and around the Special Economic Zones have prospered, many parts of the rural interior of the country have not done as well. Millions of workers have left farms and moved to cities, hoping to find better work there, but often jobs have been scarce because these workers do not have the skills they need for the jobs that are available. The Chinese government is looking for ways to bring industrial development to other parts of the country, to help those areas where the economy is not as strong. As the Chinese economy moves more toward industrial and service industries, the investment in human capital is going to become even more important to keep the GDP growing at a rate that will keep up with China's rapidly growing population.

JAPAN

The country of Japan is one of the most powerful industrial nations in the world. Japan has achieved this status in the years following that country's complete devastation after World War II. One of the greatest resources Japan has is its population. The Japanese are among the most highly educated people in the world. The literacy rate in Japan is consistently 99 percent, with most Japanese people completing high school and at least one-third going on to college. This investment in human capital through education is among the highest in the world. The Japanese also have a solid work ethic as a part of their culture, a dedication to whatever job is put before them. Japanese workers are known to work longer hours than many workers in other parts of the world. Most Japanese workers stay with the companies they work for their entire careers, and many describe their co-workers as a part of their extended family. Japanese companies also go to a great deal of effort to provide benefits for their workers, like health insurance, recreational programs, and financial planning help. This corporate investment in human capital pays off in dedicated workers who give their best efforts to their employers.

ASIA

The Japanese government also cooperates with the Japanese business community to be sure companies are tuned into the demands of the world market and are producing those products that will have the best chance of selling well and earning profits. The **Ministry of International Trade and Industry (MITI)** brings government leaders and business leaders together so they can keep track of how the Japanese economy is responding to changes in the world market. Because Japan has almost no raw materials, the country must be able to get what they need from other countries as well as sell the finished products in the same markets. Careful planning is needed from both government and industry to be able to balance all the things Japan's economy needs to be successful. The job of these government and industry leaders is also helped by the fact that Japan spends very little of its GDP on the military or defense. (Treaties signed at the end of World War II limited Japan's military development). A benefit of this restriction is that the country has had more money to invest in other areas of their economy.

Japan is one of the world leaders in the production of motor vehicles and electronic equipment, two types of products that require constant updates in production methods and use of new technologies. An educated workforce is essential to remain successful and keep up with world demand. Industrial production and work in providing services account for almost 98% of Japan's GDP.

_____ **528. What is the definition of human capital?**
    A. skills and education the workers have
    B. taxes collected from a country's workers
    C. money paid to workers for producing goods
    D. amount of goods sold in foreign trade in a year

_____ **529. What is the definition of gross domestic product (GDP)?**
    A. the total value of goods and services a country produces in a year
    B. the amount collected in taxes from the people of a country in a given year
    C. the value of all the products a country buys from overseas nations in a year
    D. the value of all goods and services produced by small shops and individually owned businesses in a country

_____ **530 If a country does not invest in its human capital, how can it affect the country's gross domestic product (GDP)?**
    A. Investment in human capital has little effect on a country's GDP.
    B. GDP is only affected if workers pay for the investment out of their own pockets.
    C. Most workers want to keep their jobs just as they are and do not care about GDP.
    D. GDP may go down because poorly trained workers will not be able to do their jobs as well.

_____ **531. What percentage of India's population work in agriculture?**
    A. 25 percent
    B. 75 percent
    C. over 50 percent
    D. nearly 100 percent

_____ 532. **Which best describes the majority of the farms in India?**
   A. small, family-owned farms
   B. collective farms owned and worked by entire villages
   C. large cooperatives owned and operated by the government
   D. corporate farms owned by India's major agricultural industries

_____ 533. **How much of India's GDP comes from farming?**
   A. 10 percent
   B. 25 percent
   C. 50 percent
   D. 75 percent

_____ 534. **How was the Green Revolution an example of investment in human capital in India?**
   A. Farmers were given training and new technology.
   B. Money was provided to build new houses for Indian farmers.
   C. Farmers were encouraged to move into the cities and find better work.
   D. Rural children were sent to government schools so they would not have to farm.

_____ 535. **How does India rank in the world in terms of industrial production?**
   A. India is one of the world's leading industrial countries.
   B. Industry is growing in India, but it is not comparable to agriculture.
   C. India was once an industrial leader, but has fallen behind in recent years.
   D. Industrial production is low because so many Indians work in agriculture.

_____ 536. **What role does the Chinese government play in decisions made about investing in human capital?**
   A. The government was once important in such decisions, but not anymore.
   B. The Chinese government only gets involved if military issues are included.
   C. The government only plays a role in investments in human capital in agriculture.
   D. The government involvement is important because China is still very much a command economy.

_____ 537. **How did the Four Modernizations affect Chinese agriculture?**
   A. The farmers were given better seed and equipment.
   B. Many farmers were forced off the land and had to move to cities.
   C. Factories involved in heavy industry were moved to rural areas to provide jobs.
   D. Farmers were forced to sell all surplus agricultural products to the government.

_____ 538. **How did the Four Modernizations affect Chinese industry?**
   A. Most factories shifted to the production of weapons and military supplies.
   B. The Chinese government gave up all control of decision making for the factories.
   C. Little money was invested in worker training and went instead into improving agriculture.
   D. Many factories began to increase the production of consumer goods that were easier to sell.

ASIA

_____ **539. What was the purpose of China's setting up the four Special Economic Zones?**
   A. to act as trade centers for global trade
   B. to improve agricultural production in rural areas
   C. to keep all foreign competition out of local markets
   D. to create places where workers could get special discounts on food and housing

_____ **540. What is one of the most important ways Japan has invested in human capital?**
   A. education
   B. tax breaks for workers
   C. unemployment insurance
   D. early retirement programs

_____ **541. How do Japanese companies invest in human capital in dealing with their workers?**
   A. Japanese companies often bring in and train foreign workers.
   B. Japanese companies are not interested in investing in human capital.
   C. Companies provide benefits like health care and recreation facilities.
   D. Most Japanese workers have shorter working hours than workers in other countries.

_____ **542. The Japanese government promotes the country's industrial growth and development by**
   A. keeping foreign goods out of Japan with high tariffs.
   B. preventing Japanese workers from moving to other countries to take jobs.
   C. ending Japanese dependence of foreign countries for supplies of raw materials.
   D. working with industry to be sure they are keeping up with world markets and trends.

_____ **543. Which is the source of nearly all of Japan's GDP?**
   A. agriculture
   B. public education
   C. military production
   D. industry and services

SS7E10 The student will describe factors that influence economic growth and examine their presence or absence in India, China, and Japan.

b. Explain the relationship between the investment in capital (factories, machinery, and technology) and gross domestic product (GDP).

Capital goods (the factories, machines, and technology that people use to make products to sell) are important to economic growth. Advanced technology and the organization of this technology into factories where many workers can work together increases production and makes the production more efficient. Producing more goods for sale in a quicker and more efficient way leads to economic growth and greater profit. This greater profit leads to a higher gross domestic product (GDP).

INDIA

India is a country that has invested heavily in the factories, modern machinery and advanced technology that make up what is known as capital goods. Even though a large portion of the country and its people are still engaged in agriculture, India is a leader among the world's industrial countries. Modern agricultural techniques have become more widely used in India since the **Green Revolution** in the 1990s. India's cities are home to some of the most advanced communications and computer technology in that part of the world. Enormous amounts of money have been poured into Indian industry in recent years, put to good use by India's increasingly well-educated middle class. Although poverty and over-population remain constant problems for India, progress in the modernization of farming techniques and industry have enabled the country to boast of a growing GDP every year for the past decade.

CHINA

China has had many of the same experiences as India in terms of rapid growth and change in recent years. Because China's government has more control over spending and planning in both agriculture and industry, China has been able to establish programs and make changes more quickly than a country where power is more widely shared among regions, communities, and individuals. China's **Four Modernizations** program is a clear example of government decisions to increase the country's investment in capital goods. More modern equipment and technology was brought into nearly every area of Chinese production, including agriculture, industry and the military. One big change has been that new technology and planning have allowed China to increase the production of smaller consumer goods that have sold well in the world market. The **Special Economic Zones** created places in China that were convenient for foreign trade so the goods produced by the newly improved industries could find foreign buyers.

JAPAN

Few countries in the world have made the investments in capital goods that the country of Japan has made. Japan is a country with few natural resources; therefore, nearly all of Japan's GDP comes from industry and services. Technology and up-to-date training in the uses of that technology are essential for the Japanese economy to continue to grow. Japanese industry leads most countries in the world in the use of **robotics** (assembling goods using mechanical techniques like robots). Many electronics and software products are put together with robotics in Japanese factories. Japanese businessmen are always looking for more efficient technology to keep their production levels high. Japanese workers are encouraged by their employers to make suggestions for ways they feel products can be made and businesses can be run more efficiently. Continuing investment in capital goods makes Japan a world leader in industrial production and in providing the wide range of services demanded by the world market.

ASIA

_____ 544. **What are capital goods?**
   A. factories and machines used to make the goods
   B. workers who make the goods and perform services
   C. money spent to train workers to use new technology
   D. goods and services that are produced for a country's economy

_____ 545. **Why is investment in capital goods important for a country like Japan?**
   A. Investment in capital goods makes overseas trade unnecessary.
   B. Investment in capital goods makes up for a poor literacy rate in Japan.
   C. Japan needs investment in capital goods to develop its rich natural resources.
   D. Japan's economy depends heavily on industry and must be modern to be competitive.

_____ 546. **India must invest in capital goods to help overcome which problems?**
   A. GDP that has not grown
   B. overpopulation and poverty
   C. lack of a strong middle class
   D. expense of maintaining a large military

_____ 547. **Investment in capital goods has helped China do well in which world markets?**
   A. fashion design
   B. consumer goods
   C. educational software
   D. communications services

SS7E10 The student will describe factors that influence economic growth and examine their presence or absence in India, China, and Japan.
c. Describe the role of natural resources in a country's economy.

Distribution of natural resources throughout Southern and Eastern Asia plays a major part in determining the type of work people do and how comfortably they are able to live. A **natural resource** is something that is found in the environment that people need. Water, trees, rich soil, minerals, and oil are all examples of natural resources. One of the most valuable resources in this part of the world is rich farmland. All of the countries, with the exception of Japan, in Southern and Eastern Asia depend on agriculture to feed rapidly growing populations. India and China have large, rich areas of farmland which is most important for their rapidly expanding populations.

India and China have good supplies of coal. While this is an important fuel and energy source for all of the economies of these countries, coal burning is a major contributor of air pollution.

Japan has very little in the way of natural resources. For this reason, the country must rely on industry and trade to supply its population with what it needs.

_____ 548. **Which is an example of a natural resource?**
   A. factory
   B. deposit of coal
   C. irrigation canal
   D. hydroelectric dam

Entrepreneurs are creative, original thinkers who are willing to take risks to create new businesses and products. Entrepreneurs think of new ways to combine **productive resources** (natural, human, and capital) to produce goods and services that they expect to sell for a price high enough to cover production costs. They are willing to risk their own money to produce these new goods and services in the hope that they will earn a profit. Because no one can tell how popular their new products and services will be, not all entrepreneurs can count on making a profit. Many businesses are not successful. Only about 50 percent of all new businesses are still operating three years after they begin.

India has many stories of entrepreneurship in its history. Some of the world's largest and most successful companies were founded by Indian entrepreneurs. In addition to these large financial empires, India is also a land of smaller entrepreneurs in what is known as the **micro-credit industry**. Thousands of Indian men and women have been able to borrow small amounts of money to start little local businesses. Entrepreneurship through micro-credit is changing the quality of life in many rural Indian villages.

Entrepreneurship in **China** is relatively new, as the Chinese government has only allowed individual business ventures since the late 1970s. Even so, many have taken advantage of the new openness, and China now may have as many as 100 people who could qualify as billionaires. The Chinese government realizes that the country has to be more competitive in the world market, and they have decided to let their own entrepreneurs help lead the way. The Chinese government is still working out what its relationship will be to these new companies. China can never go back to the old total command economy it once had if it is to be competitive in the modern global marketplace.

Japan is a land of entrepreneurs. The need for business development, the availability of good education, and the Japanese work ethic have combined to make Japan an ideal place for someone who has a good idea and the energy to see if it can work.

_____ **549. Which is an entrepreneur?**
   A. someone who is willing to take a risk to begin a new business
   B. someone who is always successful in whatever he or she attempts
   C. a businessman who relies on money from the government to finance a new business
   D. a businessman who is able to guarantee investors will make a profit if they support his project

_____ **550. What has been the role of entrepreneurship in India?**
   A. Indian entrepreneurs have been successful in agriculture but not in industry.
   B. The only successful entrepreneurs have been foreigners who have moved to India.
   C. The Indian government has discouraged entrepreneurs because business is too risky.
   D. The country has all sorts of entrepreneurs, both wealthy and those with modest incomes.

_____ **551. Who has benefitted from the micro-credit industry in India?**
   A. those working to set up new computer industries
   B. the failed businessman who has had a hard time getting traditional loans
   C. the international businessmen who want to expand small parts of their production
   D. rural village men and women who wish to set up small businesses to help their families

ASIA

_____ 552. How has China's attitude toward entrepreneurship changed in the past several decades?

A. Entrepreneurs are allowed to operate but only with overseas businesses.

B. The government has become more open to the idea of allowing some free enterprise.

C. The Chinese government was more open to entrepreneurship in the years before 1970.

D. Entrepreneurs are encouraged but only in the areas of making weapons and military equipment.

_____ 553. What is the attitude of the Japanese toward entrepreneurship?

A Japan's economic development depends on the creative ideas of the country's entrepreneurs.

B. The Japanese government only allows a certain number of entrepreneurs to do business within Japan.

C. Entrepreneurs in Japan are focused mainly on the development of the country's natural resources.

D. Most of Japan's successful entrepreneurs have made their fortunes in improving the country's agriculture.

ASIA

HISTORICAL UNDERSTANDINGS

SS7H3 The student will analyze continuity and change in Southern and Eastern Asia leading to the 21st century.
a. Describe how nationalism led to independence in India and Vietnam.

Nationalism is the belief that people should be loyal to those with whom they share common history, customs, origins, and sometimes language or religion. People who share these things often think of themselves as a distinct nation, although not all of these characteristics may be the same from one nation to another.

INDIA

A feeling of nationalism began to surface in **India** in the 1800s. People began to be upset that their country was a part of the British colonial empire. They were second-class citizens in their own country. The best jobs and best education were reserved for the British. Indian craftsmen were not allowed to run their traditional businesses if that meant competition for the British. One example was the production of cloth. Indians grew fine cotton and weaving was a traditional craft. Indians were forced to send all of their cotton to Britain and then had to buy the finished cloth from the British factories.

The first two groups to form work for the rights of Indians were the **Indian National Congress**, organized in 1885 and the **Muslim League**, begun in 1906. The Indian National Congress attracted mainly Indian Hindus, and the Muslim League attracted Indians who followed Islam. As they gathered more members and became better organized, they began to call for Indian independence from British colonial control. Years of contact with the British had taught Indians about western ideas of democracy and self-government. However, the British did not want to share these two ideals with their colonies.

During World War I, millions of Indians joined forces with the British, hoping that their service would be rewarded with more control of their government. The British Parliament even promised that when the war ended, India would be able to work toward self-government. Unfortunately, after the war, nothing changed. Indians were still second-class citizens. Those who began to protest were arrested under the new **Rowlatt Act**, which gave the British the power to send Indians to jail for up to two years without a trial. In 1919, British authorities opened fire on a large gathering of Indians in the town of Amritsar, claiming they were gathering illegally. Over 400 people were killed and another 1200 wounded. This massacre made Indians all over the country furious, and almost overnight they were united in a call for complete independence.

Following the slaughter at Amritsar, **Mohandas Gandhi** began to urge Indians to refuse to cooperate with British laws they felt were unjust. He also urged them to be sure they did nothing violent in their protests. His goal was to show the world the injustice of British colonial rule in India. Gandhi's plan was one of what he called **civil disobedience** (the non-violent refusal to obey an unfair law). Indians all over the country began to follow Gandhi's lead, boycotting British-made goods, refusing to attend second-class schools, and refusing to pay unfair taxes. In time, these efforts began to hurt the British economy, which was dependent on colonial markets. Though the British authorities often responded with arrests and beatings, Gandhi and his followers refused to do the same. The world watched as the British Empire found itself unable to stop the protests and Indian refusal to obey British laws.

ASIA

In 1935, the British government gave up. Britain passed the **Government of India Act** that gave India some self-government. This was a start but not the independence most Indians wanted. When World War II broke out, Great Britain offered India **dominion** (control or the exercise of control) status in the British Empire if they would help the war effort. This would mean more independence, but not the complete independence India wanted. Gandhi and the Indian National Congress refused the offer. They announced that they would not take sides in Britain's war with Japan and Germany. The Muslim League, however, had begun to worry that Indian independence might mean rule by the more numerous Hindus, and they supported the British war effort. They hoped they would be rewarded after the war ended. While many Indians did help the British war effort, support for the war became tangled up in India's desire for independence.

When World War II ended, the British decided to grant India independence. However, by this time disputes had begun between Indian Hindus and Indian Muslims about how power in the new country should be organized. The British colonial leader, Lord Louis Mountbatten, decided that the only way to grant independence and avoid fighting was to divide the country into Hindu and Muslim sections. Feelings of nationalism in each group were more strongly influenced by religion than by any of the other factors the people had in common. The country would be partitioned into three new countries. **Hindu India** would be in the center, the largest because there were many more Hindus than any other religion. The Muslims would be moved to smaller countries created in both the east and the west along the borders of India. The areas were to be named **East** and **West Pakistan**. Muslims living here would have to move to the newly created India. Through 1947, millions of people left homes they had lived in for generations to make the moves ordered by the creation of the new governments. There was much fighting and many people lost their lives. In the end, the three new countries were created. On August 15, 1947, British rule in India came to an end and the independent countries of India, West Pakistan, and East Pakistan were created. Religion became the one factor that had the most important role in determining the nationalism of the people who chose to live in these new countries.

VIETNAM

Vietnam was another Southeastern Asian country controlled by a European country. In the early 1900s, the French gained control of an area of Southeast Asia known as Indochina. Later, this became the modern country of Vietnam. The French wanted control in Indochina because they used the seaports and the area was a rich source of agricultural products and natural resources.

Nationalism was a factor in the area known as French Indochina. The people who lived there had worked hard to maintain independence from China, their powerful northern neighbor. They saw themselves as a separate people among the many groups on Southeast Asia. That nationalist energy was directed at the French colonial rulers.

A young man, **Ho Chi Minh**, began to work for Vietnamese independence from the French. He thought the Communist Party might be the best route to take because the communists were outspoken critics of European colonialism. In the 1930s, he organized an Indochinese Communist Party. They began to stage protests against French rule. His efforts landed his followers in jail and he had to leave the country to avoid a death penalty.

When World War II began, Ho Chi Minh hoped it would mean the end of French rule in his country. He helped to found a new group, the **Vietminh League**, a group that had Vietnamese independence as its goal. Unfortunately, when the war ended, the French moved to regain control of its colonial possession, which they still called French Indochina.

For the next nine years, Ho Chi Minh and his Vietminh fought with the French colonial forces. While the French were able to maintain control of most of the cities, particularly in the south, the people in the countryside worked with Ho Chi Minh. They wanted control of their own country. In 1954, the French decided to surrender control of the country to Ho Chi Minh.

All parties to the conflict went to Geneva, Switzerland for a conference to end French involvement in Vietnam.

At this **Geneva Conference** in 1954, the United States became alarmed at the prospect of Ho Chi Minh ruling Vietnam. The United States saw him as a communist rather than a nationalist leader. The U.S. feared that a communist Vietnam would lead other countries in the area to become communist as well. The United States used its influence to have Vietnam temporarily divided into two parts. Ho Chi Minh was in charge in the north and the United States was in control in the south. The plan was to stabilize the country and then let the people vote on what sort of government they wanted. The United States hoped to find someone they could put up as a democratic alternative to Ho Chi Minh, so the country could be reunited, but as a democracy rather than as a communist state.

The Geneva Conference in 1954 began the United States' long involvement in the politics of Vietnam. Northern and southern zones were drawn into which opposing troops were to withdraw. The northern and southern parts were to be reunited after free elections to be held in July 1956. As the years stretched out, the Vietnamese became more and more anxious to have independence. Many in the southern part of the country sympathized with those in the north, seeing them as fellow countrymen rather than the enemy. Feelings of nationalism were more important than ideas about what political system they should have. After many years of fighting and the loss of many thousands of lives among the Vietnamese as well as the American soldiers, the United States decided to withdraw its forces from Vietnam. The last American helicopters left Vietnam in April 1975. The forces of the North Vietnamese army took over the country and unified it the next day as the **Republic of Vietnam**. While the new country was communist, most of the other countries in the region did not become communist.

_____ 554. **What is nationalism?**
   A. loyalty based on geographic location
   B. a feeling of belonging to a group that is highly educated and wealthy
   C. a sense of belonging that is based on a written document like a constitution
   D. loyalty to a group with whom one shares a common history, culture, and/or religion

_____ 555. **Indian nationalism in the 1800s began as a reaction to**
   A. British rule.
   B. religious conflict.
   C. communist-led revolution.
   D. long period of drought and famine.

_____ 556. **Which was one of the early goals of the Indian National Congress?**
   A. working to modernize Indian farming
   B. trying to bring more industry to India
   C. greater independence from British control
   D. ending the religious wars being fought all over India

_____ 557. **Indians helped the British in World War I because they believed it would**
   A. end unemployment in India.
   B. help Indians that were eager to go to war.
   C. encourage the British to grant India greater freedom after the war.
   D. develop a strong Indian military that could later force the British to leave.

ASIA

_____ **558. People in India were angry about the Rowlatt Act passed by the British in 1919 because it**

A. ended public schooling for Indian children.

B. prohibited Indians from working in government jobs.

C. stated that only Indian Hindus could apply for British citizenship.

D. allowed the government to send Indians to jail without giving them a trial.

_____ **559. Which was an effect of the massacre at Amritsar?**

A. Indians were afraid to ask for more rights because they thought they might be killed.

B. The Amritsar massacre got little press coverage so it had very little effect on Indian feelings.

C. Most people were so angry about the killings they became more united against the British.

D. Most Indians felt the people gathered at Amritsar were breaking the law anyway and deserved punishment.

_____ **560. What was Mohandas Gandhi's plan of civil disobedience?**

A. people should refuse to obey a law they felt was unfair

B. violent demonstrations were needed in India until the British left

C. it was best to go along with British laws to avoid making the colonial authorities angry

D. the best way to change the laws was through passing legislation in the Indian National Congress

_____ **561. Why did the Indians turn down dominion status when it was offered to them in the 1930s?**

A. They wanted total freedom from Great Britain.

B. Gandhi was going to be asked to leave the country.

C. They thought dominion status would be temporary.

D. This arrangement would only have been offered to Indian Hindus.

_____ **562. What did Gandhi urge Indians to do during World War II?**

A. Gandhi took no position on World War II.

B. Gandhi urged Indians to work for the Japanese.

C. Gandhi felt everyone should help the British war effort.

D. Gandhi did not want Indians to take sides during the war.

_____ **563. When independence finally came in 1947, what was it about the decision that made many Indians unhappy?**

A. The country was divided along religious lines.

B. India was not allowed to have its own military.

C. Indians still had to depend on Britain for food and protection.

D. Most people in India wanted to turn down the offer of independence.

Use the passage to answer the following question.

> *"Be the change that you want to see in the world."*
> *— Mohandas Gandhi*

_____ **581. Which is the BEST meaning of this quote by Gandhi?**

    A. It is not good just to change things without a reason.

    B. Change is not going to happen as long as people do not complain.

    C. People must act in a way that causes change to improve the world.

    D. The world will not change for the better when people do not see any problems.

SS7H3 The student will analyze continuity and change in Southern and Eastern Asia leading to the 21st century.
c. Explain the role of the United States in the rebuilding of Japan after World War II.

After Japan's surrender in September 1945, the country was reduced to rubble. Industries and farms were destroyed, the government was in shambles, the people were demoralized, and the emperor had been exposed as an ordinary mortal rather than the god the Japanese people had believed him to be. The American commander of the occupation forces was **General Douglas MacArthur**. He was given the job of putting Japan back on its feet, in a way that would guarantee that Japan would not pose a military threat to other countries in the future.

General MacArthur wanted Japan to have a democratic government, but he also appreciated the important place the Japanese emperor occupied in the Japanese culture. He decided Japan would be a constitutional monarchy. He wrote a constitution for the country, still referred to as **The MacArthur Constitution** that created a two-house parliament called a **Diet**. The emperor remained as a symbol of the country. The Japanese people were granted universal suffrage, and everyone over the age of 20 was allowed to vote for members of the Diet. The new constitution designed by MacArthur contained a **Bill of Rights** and guaranteed basic freedoms. One clause in this constitution prevents Japan from declaring war. They are allowed to fight only if they are attacked first.

The Japanese signed all peace treaties ending the war and pledged to pay war **reparations** (damages) to the countries they had harmed during World War II. American troops were allowed to remain in Japan, and the Japanese were not permitted to rebuild their military in any major way.

_____ **582. What U.S. General was given the job of rebuilding Japan after the end of World War II?**

    A. Louis Mountbatten

    B. Douglas MacArthur

    C. Dwight Eisenhower

    D. George C. Marshall

_____ **583. What type of government was created for Japan in the years following the war?**

    A. autocratic state

    B. communist state

    C. traditional monarchy

    D. constitutional monarchy

ASIA

_____ **584. What was the role of the Japanese emperor in the new government?**

    A. His role was mainly ceremonial.

    B. He was a powerful political figure.

    C. The office of emperor was eliminated.

    D. He served in the parliament as the presiding officer.

_____ **585. What is the name of the Japanese parliament?**

    A. the Diet

    B. Congress

    C. House of Lords

    D. Constitutional League

_____ **586. Which requirement is written into the Japanese constitution?**

    A. to restrict voting to men only

    B. to end the position of emperor

    C. to never declare war on another country

    D. to maintain a strong military for their protection

> **SS7H3 The student will analyze continuity and change in Southern and Eastern Asia leading to the 21st century.**
>
> d. Describe the impact of communism in China in terms of Mao Zedong, the Great Leap Forward, the Cultural Revolution, and Tiananmen Square.

Nationalism was also a powerful influence in China at the end of World War I. Chinese nationalists were able to overthrow the Qing Dynasty in 1912, a dynasty that had ruled China since the 1600s. The new government was called the **Republic of China**, which declared that one of its aims would be an end to foreign control in China's affairs. The leading political party was called the Kuomintang, or the Nationalist Party, led by a man named Sun Yixian. Unfortunately, the new government was not able to either bring order to China or help the Chinese people. Many people were killed as robbers and thieves roamed the countryside. Agriculture was wrecked and many Chinese faced famine. World War I took the attention of most people away from the problems of China, and at the end of the war, European politicians signed the Treaty of Versailles, restoring the government of Sun Yixian and giving Japan control of some Chinese territory.

Many young Chinese were angry about the treaty and wanted an end to what they felt was the failed government of Sun Yixian and the Kuomintang. They were disillusioned with western style democracy and looked to Russia and their Communist Revolution as an alternative. In 1921 a group of young Chinese men, including a young teacher, **Mao Zedong**, met in Shanghai to form the first **Chinese Communist Party**.

After Sun Yixian died, the new head of the Kuomintang, Jiang Jieshi, tried to make alliances with the new Chinese Communist Party, and for some years the two groups worked together to try and bring order to China. Eventually though, Jiang Jieshi and the Kuomintang government turned on the communists and many of them were killed. In 1929, Jiang Jieshi announced the formation of his new government, the **Nationalist Republic of China**.

Mao Zedong survived the attack on the communists by Jiang Jieshi's government and he decided that his future and the future of the communist party in China would be found in the countryside with support from the peasants. A civil war began between Mao and his communist followers and the Nationalist government of Jiang Jieshi. In 1933 Mao led his followers, over 600,000 people, into the

Copyright © Clairmont Press, Inc. DO NOT DUPLICATE. 1-800-874-8638

mountains to escape being defeated by the nationalist government. They walked nearly 6,000 miles to avoid capture. This journey is known as the **Long March**, and Chinese communists today look back at this time as a sign of Mao's dedication to his cause and to what he felt was the cause of the Chinese people.

The Chinese communists and the Nationalist forces had to call a temporary truce during World War II as both groups fought to keep the Japanese from taking over China. At the war's end the truce ended. Civil war between the two groups raged from 1946 until 1949, when Mao's communists, now called the **Red Army**, swept the Nationalist government from power. In October 1949, Mao proclaimed the creation of the **People's Republic of China**, a communist government that now led one of the largest countries in the world.

Mao tried to reorganize all of China along communist lines of collective ownership of farms and factories. Private ownership was eliminated and production quotas were set for agriculture and industry. He decided in 1958 to organize all farms into large **collectives**, where all ownership and decision making would be in the hands of the government. This program was known as the **Great Leap Forward** because Mao thought tremendous positive changes would follow. In fact, many Chinese farmers did not like the large farms. They missed their own land and because they no longer owned anything themselves, they had little reason to work very hard. A series of crop failures in the late 1950s made everything even worse, and China went through a period of famine. The Great Leap Forward was abandoned in 1960.

After the failure of this program, some in China began to suggest that private ownership might not be a bad idea. Farmers and factory workers began to do some work for themselves and Mao saw his ideal of a classless society, one where everyone was treated exactly the same and no one had more than anyone else, drifting away. His response was to announce the **Cultural Revolution** in 1966. He urged students to leave school and make war on anything in Chinese society that looked like it was encouraging class differences. Many students were organized into an army known as the **Red Guards**. It was their job to single out and remove anyone who was preventing China from becoming a really classless society. Mao wanted China to become a nation of farmers and workers, all of whom would be equal. Leaders in the Chinese community who seemed to be in higher positions were attacked. Business managers, college professors, even government officials who were not in step with the Cultural Revolution were thrown out. Some were put into prison; others were actually killed. The result was chaos. The Cultural Revolution raged on for almost ten years, at which time even Mao himself had to admit it had been a mistake. In 1976 the Red Guard was ended and gradually order returned to China.

Mao died in 1976 and by 1980 **Deng Xiaoping** was named the leader of China. Though Deng had been with Mao since the days of the Long March, he was more moderate in his ideas about the path China should follow. He began to allow farmers to own some of their own land and make decisions about what they would grow. He allowed some private businesses to organize, and he opened China to foreign investment and technological advances. He found that openness to western business also meant that the Chinese people were also exposed to western ideas. In 1989, when communist governments were under siege in a number of places around the world, China went through a period of student protests that resulted in a huge demonstration in **Beijing's Tiananmen Square**. Over 10,000 students gathered to protest what they felt was corruption in the Chinese government. They called for a move toward democracy. The world watched as Deng Xiaoping ordered thousands of soldiers into Beijing to end the protest. The students even went so far as to raise a statue they called the **Goddess of Democracy**, modeled on America's Statue of Liberty. On June 4, 1989, the Chinese government ordered the soldiers in Tiananmen Square to break up the demonstration. They fired on the students, destroyed the statue of the Goddess of Democracy, and arrested thousands of people. The brief pro-democracy movement was destroyed as well, and Deng Xiaoping was left in control. He held power until his death in 1997.

ASIA

One place where this struggle was clearly seen was in the Korean Peninsula. At the end of World War II, the Soviet Union was in control of the northern half of the peninsula and the United States controlled the southern half. Though the peace treaty called for elections to be held to unify Korea into one country, the Soviet Union wanted a communist government, and the United States wanted a western style democracy. Because they could never agree on how to hold elections, the country was simply divided into two countries. North Korea became a communist state allied with the Soviet Union. South Korea became a western style democracy allied with the United States. The United States insisted on supporting a free South Korea. They believed that if any additional countries in Southeast Asia went to a communist form of government, others would quickly follow. This idea was called the **Domino Theory**. If one country fell to communism, all the others nearby would fall as well.

War broke out between the two countries in 1950 and after three years of fighting a truce redrew the original boundary, where it remains today. Today North Korea remains a communist country under the autocratic rule of the premiere. The country has heavy industry and a well-armed military, but there are many other problems, including poor farm production and frequent problems with famine. The country remains the ally of other communist countries including the People's Republic of China. However, most other communist countries have moved away from the strict type of rule North Korea maintains. South Korea, with free elections and a democratic constitution, has been more prosperous because they have had trade and foreign aid from the United States and other wealthy western countries.

VIETNAM

Vietnam was also caught in the same western worry about the Domino Theory and the spread of communism. At the end of World War II, many in Vietnam wanted to reorganize the country under the leadership of a popular nationalist, Ho Chi Minh, who had spent many years fighting French colonialism in that country. Ho Chi Minh was **communist**, and the United States did not want any new communist countries formed in Southeast Asia. The United States supported French efforts to reclaim colonial control of Vietnam in the years after the war ended.

In 1954, when the French decided to give up the fight, the United States stepped in. Decisions were made at an international conference in Geneva, Switzerland to temporarily divide the country into North Vietnam and South Vietnam. The plan was that within a year, nationwide elections would be held to let the Vietnamese people decide what kind of government they wanted. However, the United States worried that they would choose Ho Chi Minh and the communists, so the elections were never held and the country remained divided until 1975. Many years and billions of dollars were spent by the United States, and thousands of lives were lost fighting in Vietnam to prevent that country from becoming communist. In the end, the country did reunite after the United States ended the war. The People's Republic of Vietnam was declared a communist country.

_____ 597. **At the end of World War II, one of Russia's main goals was to**
   A. avoid having to join the United Nations.
   B. redesign their government as a democracy.
   C. build a friendly alliance with the United States.
   D. be sure they would never be attacked again by a Western European country.

_____ 598. **What did the leaders of the Soviet Union feel would provide the most protection for their country?**
   A. if all weapons were to be removed from Europe
   B. having free trade with all the countries in Europe and Asia
   C. having friendly, pro-communist countries along all their borders
   D. receiving a declaration from the United Nations condemning war

_____ **599. What was the name given to the disagreements between the United States and the Soviet Union at the end of World War II?**

A. the Cold War

B. the Dual Alliance

C. the Great Depression

D. the Cultural Revolution

_____ **600 How was the country of Korea divided at the end of World War II?**

A. The country was entirely under Soviet control.

B. Koreans had control of their own country at that time.

C. Soviet control in the north; United States control in the south.

D. The Japanese controlled much of the country when the war ended.

_____ **601. What was the fear of the United States about both Korea and Vietnam at the end of World War II?**

A. They feared the two countries would become communist.

B. They were afraid the two countries would threaten the new government of China.

C. They worried that the war-damaged economies would not be able to recover in time to prevent famine.

D. They were afraid both countries would be taken over by the French as they tried to rebuild their colonial empire.

_____ **602. What was the meaning of the Domino Theory?**

A. Political decisions have to be built slowly, like a game of dominoes.

B. International politics is a game, and there are always winners and losers.

C. If one country in a region became communist, others would quickly follow.

D. Few countries would really be interested in communism if they knew what it was like.

_____ **603. What has become of the political division of Korea made in 1954?**

A. Korea was reunited by the United Nations several years ago.

B. Korea is still divided between a communist north and a democratic south.

C. The two parts of Korea were reunited soon after the war ended in the 1950s.

D. Both parts of Korea are communist today, even though they are separate countries.

_____ **604. What were the objections the United States had to Ho Chi Minh's leadership on Vietnam?**

A. He seemed too inexperienced to lead a country.

B. Most of the Vietnamese people did not like him or his politics.

C. He was a communist and a threat to the United States interests.

D. He had been educated in Europe and had no connection with the Vietnamese people.

ASIA

_____ **605. What became of United States efforts to prevent Ho Chi Minh from taking over the country of Vietnam and reuniting it as one country?**

    A. The United States is still working to prevent Vietnam from becoming a communist country.

    B. Vietnam became a western style democracy under a government designed by the United States.

    C. Vietnam remains permanently divided, with the North communist and the South democratic.

    D. American efforts ended in 1975 and Vietnam was united under the government designed by Ho Chi Minh.

Use the map below to answer questions 606-609.

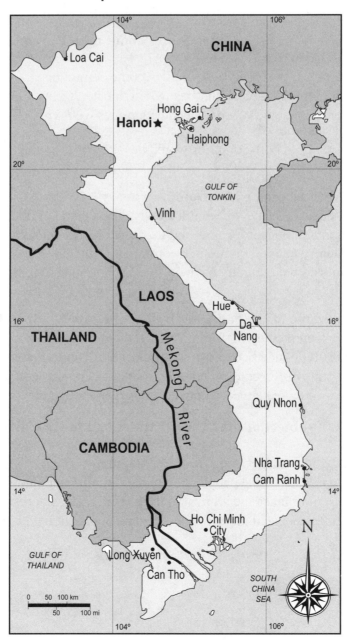

ASIA

_____ **606. What is the approximate distance (in miles) from Ho Chi Minh City to Hanoi?**
   A. 200
   B. 700
   C. 1,100
   D. 1,200

_____ **607. Which country is located at 17°N, 103°E?**
   A. Laos
   B. China
   C. Thailand
   D. Cambodia

_____ **608. In which direction does the Mekong River generally flow?**
   A. east to west
   B. west to east
   C. north to south
   D. south to north

_____ **609. Which geographic feature is east of Vinh?**
   A. Mekong River
   B. Gulf of Tonkin
   C. South China Sea
   D. Gulf of Thailand

ASIA

Use this information to answer questions 610-612.

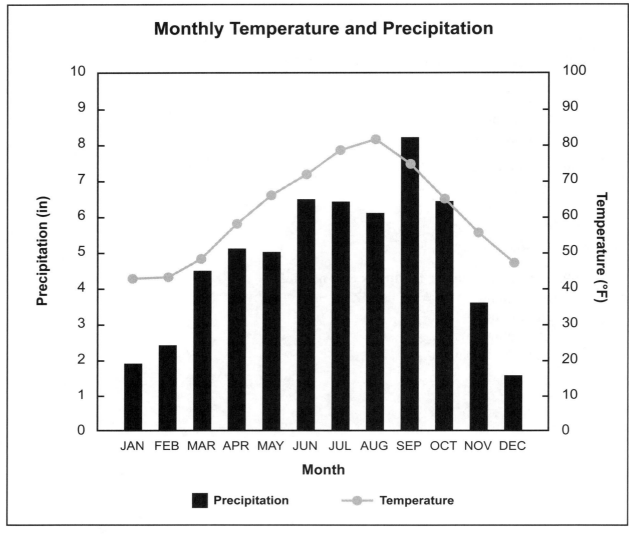

Tokyo, Japan Climograph

Monthly Temperature and Precipitation

_____ **610. Which month is usually the driest in Tokyo, Japan?**
A. January
B. October
C. December
D. September

_____ **611. Which is TRUE about the climate in Tokyo, Japan?**
A. Winter is the wettest and coldest time of year.
B. Late summer is the hottest and among the wettest times of year.
C. Spring is driest and temperatures are about the same as in winter.
D. Autumn begins a period of dryness, and temperatures are the hottest.

ASIA

Table 1

Month	Mean
January	0.7
February	0.9
March	1.3
April	1.9
May	4.0
June	10.2
July	13.1
August	12.9
September	11.6
October	6.0
November	0.7
December	0.3

Table 2

Month	Mean
January	0.6
February	0.7
March	0.8
April	1.6
May	2.7
June	3.7
July	3.2
August	3.0
September	1.6
October	1.2
November	0.6
December	0.7

Table 3

Month	Mean
January	2.3
February	2.2
March	1.9
April	1.5
May	0.9
June	0.4
July	0.1
August	0.3
September	1.3
October	2.6
November	2.2
December	2.6

Table 4

Month	Mean
January	1.9
February	2.4
March	4.5
April	5.1
May	5.0
June	6.5
July	6.4
August	6.1
September	8.2
October	6.4
November	3.6
December	1.6

_____ **612. Which table matches the precipitation data on the graph?**
   A. Table 1
   B. Table 2
   C. Table 3
   D. Table 4

ASIA

SOCIAL STUDIES

SKILLS TEST

Country	Total Literacy Rate	Literacy of Males	Literacy of Females	GDP – Gross Domestic Product, per capita*
Burkina Faso	21%	21.8%	15%	$1,300
Congo	67%	80.9%	54.1%	$300
Egypt	71.4%	83%	59.45%	$5,500
Ghana	51.9%	66.4%	49.8%	$1,400
Kenya	85.1%	90.6%	79.7%	$1,700
South Africa	86.4%	87%	85%	$9,800
United States (for comparison)	99%	99%	99%	$45,800

*Gross Domestic Product is the value of all goods and services produced within a country in a given year (converted into US dollars for comparison). When divided into a value per capita (or per person) it can be used as a measure of the wealth or living conditions in the country. The higher the GDP value, the better the living conditions in the country.

Use the chart above to answer questions 1-3.

1. Which African country has the highest literacy rates and GDP?

   A. Kenya

   B. Ghana

   C. South Africa

   D. Burkina Faso

2. Which African country has the lowest literacy rate for females?

   A. Kenya

   B. Ghana

   C. South Africa

   D. Burkina Faso

3. How do the literacy rates for men and women compare in most of the countries represented on this chart?

   A. It costs more for a country to educate women.

   B. The chart proves that most women do not want to go to school.

   C There is very little difference in the literacy rates for men and women.

   D. In nearly all the countries, women have a lower literacy rate than men.

SOCIAL STUDIES

SKILLS TEST

Use the diagram to answer questions 4-6.

Government of Iran

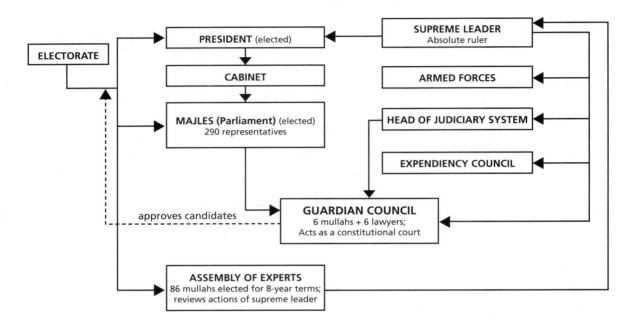

4. What is the purpose of this diagram?

   A. to identify the people in Iran who can vote

   B. to show the types of leaders that a country can have

   C. to show how the government of Iran is organized

   D. to identify the people in Iran who hold elected office

5. Who is the most powerful elected official in Iran?

   A. president

   B. electorate

   C. Supreme Leader

   D. head of the judiciary

6. How does the Guardian Council affect elections?

   A. The mullahs tell people who to vote for.

   B. The mullahs and lawyers must agree on the Supreme Leader.

   C. They approve candidates that will be placed on the ballots in elections.

   D. They cannot affect elections since they are appointed by the Majles and Supreme Leader.

SOCIAL STUDIES

SKILLS TEST

Use the chart below to answer questions 7-8.

Area of Comparison	South Africa	Nigeria
Type of economy	A technologically advanced market economy with some government control; one of the strongest economies in the region	Poorly organized economy after a long period of military dictatorship and corruption; now trying to reorganize with more private enterprise allowed; want to be able to take advantage of strong world oil market
Goods produced	Mining (platinum, diamonds, and gold), automobile assembly, machinery, textiles, iron and steel chemicals, fertilizer	Oil and petrochemicals are the primary market goods; Nigeria once exported food and other agricultural products but now must import them.
Leading Exports	Gold, diamonds, platinum, other minerals, machinery and equipment	Oil and petrochemical products
GDP per capita	$9,800	$2,000
Labor Force	Agriculture – 9% Industry – 26% Services – 65%	Agriculture – 17% Industry – 52% Services – 30%
Unemployment Rate	24%	4.9%

7. What are among South Africa's main exports?

A. oil

B. textiles

C. gold and diamonds

D. agricultural products

8. Which of the two countries has the largest per capita GDP?

A. Nigeria

B South Africa

C. GDP information not available

D GDP is almost the same in both countries

SOCIAL STUDIES

SKILLS TEST

Use this chart to answer questions 9-10.

Country	Type of Government	Who Votes	Role of Religion	Design of Government
Israel	Parliamentary Democracy	All citizens 18 years old or older	No direct role, other than religious leaders elected to parliament	Elected parliament (the Knesset) and a prime minister chosen by the leading party
Saudi Arabia	Hereditary Monarchy	Citizens do not vote	Religious leaders advise the king but decisions are his	King chooses his advisors. No parliament
Iran	Theocracy or Theocratic Republic	All citizens 16 years old or older	Religious leaders are very influential in government decisions	Elected parliament with powerful religious leaders as advisors

9. Who rules Saudi Arabia?

   A. a king

   B. a popularly elected president

   C. the representative government

   D. a small group of leading religious leaders

10. What is the name of the parliament in Israel?

   A. Senate

   B. Knesset

   C. Congress

   D. House of Representatives

SOCIAL STUDIES

SKILLS TEST

Use the graph to answer questions 11-13.

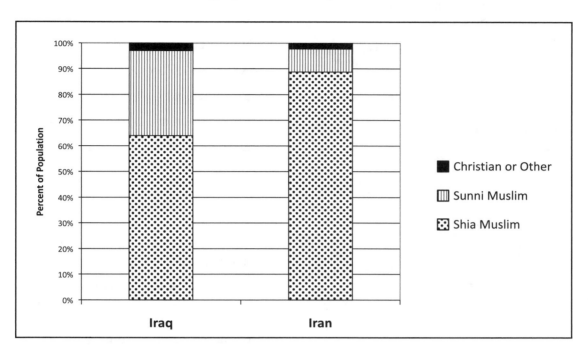

11. What part of the population of Iran is Sunni Muslim?

    A. 9%

    B. 33%

    C. 64%

    D. 89 %

12. Which would be the BEST alternative for showing these data in another way?

    A. use two line graphs

    B. use one circle graph

    C. use two circle graphs

    D. use a line graph with two lines of different colors

13. Which question could be answered using information from the graph?

    A. Which country has the most Shia Muslims?

    B. What part of the population of Iran is Hindu?

    C. What part of the population of Iraq is Christian?

    D. Which country has the highest proportion of its population as Shia Muslim?

14. Which reference book would be most useful for finding the location and population of several towns in North America?

    A. almanac

    B. gazetteer

    C. thesaurus

    D dictionary

SOCIAL STUDIES

SKILLS TEST

Use the map below to answer questions 15-17.

15. Which countries border the Gaza Strip?

    A. Iraq and Jordan

    B. Israel and Egypt

    C. Lebanon and Syria

    D. Israel and the West Bank

16. What is the approximate location of the Dead Sea from Jerusalem?

    A. nearly 35 miles east

    B. nearly 35 miles west

    C. about 15 miles southeast

    D. about 15 miles southwest

17. What country is found at 32° N, 36° E?

    A. Egypt

    B. Israel

    C. Syria

    D. Jordan

PLEASE GO ON TO THE NEXT PAGE.

SOCIAL STUDIES

SKILLS TEST

Use the graph to answer questions 18-20.

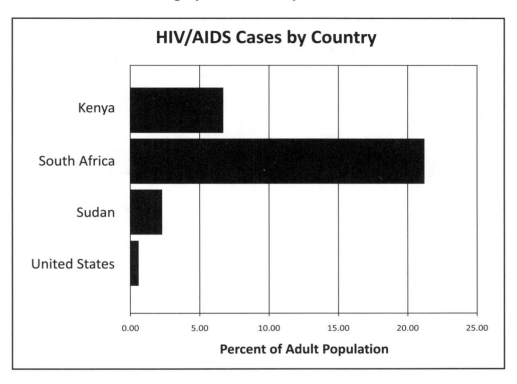

HIV/AIDS Cases by Country

Kenya

South Africa

Sudan

United States

0.00   5.00   10.00   15.00   20.00   25.00

Percent of Adult Population

18. What part of the adult population of South Africa has HIV/AIDS?

    A. about 7%

    B. over 10%

    C. nearly 22%

    D. less than 5%

19. Which question can be answered using the graph?

    A. How many people in Africa have HIV/AIDS?

    B. What part of the population of Sudan has HIV/AIDS?

    C. Which of the countries listed have the most adults with HIV/AIDS?

    D. Which African country has the highest percentage of adults with HIV/AIDS?

20. What is the BEST reason for including data from the United States on the graph?

    A. only three African countries have adults with HIV/AIDS

    B. many people in the U.S. have ancestors that came from Africa

    C. to compare data from African countries with data from our own

    D. the U.S. has assisted people from many countries in fighting HIV/AIDS

SOCIAL STUDIES

SKILLS TEST

Use the information from the timeline to answer questions 21-23.

Events in the Life of Nelson Mandela

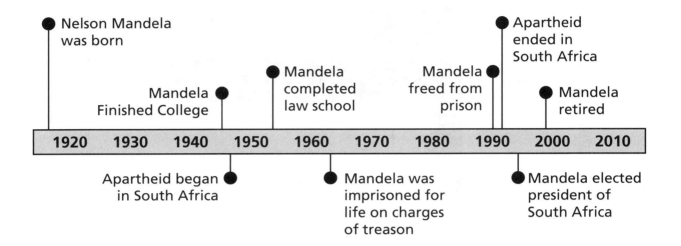

21. In what year was Nelson Mandela born?

    A. 1918

    B. 1945

    C. 1962

    D. 1999

22. About how long after Mandela was imprisoned did he become president of South Africa?

    A. about 30 years

    B. nearly 20 years

    C. less than 10 years

    D. more than 40 years

23. Which event in Mandela's life happened before the official beginning of apartheid?

    A. Mandela completed college.

    B. Mandela finished law school.

    C. Mandela was convicted of treason.

    D. Mandela retired as president of South Africa.

SOCIAL STUDIES

SKILLS TEST

Use information from the map to answer questions 24-26

24. Which body of water extends southeast from Khartoum?

    A. Red Sea

    B. Blue Nile

    C. Nile River

    D. White Nile

25. Which is located at about 8° N latitude and 31° E longitude?

    A. Waw

    B. Nyala

    C. Darfur

    D. Malakāi

26. About how far (in miles) is it from Khartoum to Port Sudan?

    A. 300

    B. 400

    C. 650

    D. 900

PLEASE GO ON TO THE NEXT PAGE.

SOCIAL STUDIES

SKILLS TEST

Use the graph below to answer questions 27-30.

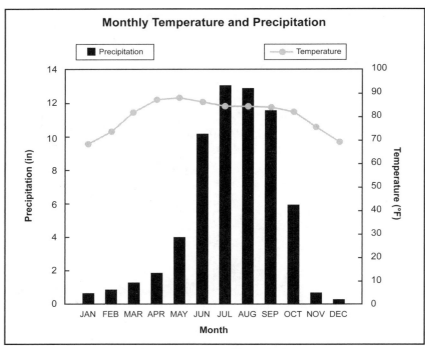

Climograph on Calcutta, India

27. What is the average temperature in Calcutta in December?

    A. 2° F

    B. 44° F

    C. 69° F

    D. 75° F

28. What is generally true of Calcutta's average temperatures from May to December?

    A. They are increasing.

    B. They are decreasing.

    C. They are staying the same.

    D. They increase for the first few months then go down the last few months.

29. Which is TRUE about the climate in Calcutta, India?

    A. Summers are the driest and hottest times of the year.

    B. Winters are very cold with a little less rainfall than summers.

    C. Summers are the wettest and nearly the hottest times of the year.

    D. Winters are cooler than summer but they have about same amount of precipitation.

30. About how much precipitation falls on Calcutta from December to January?

    A. about 80 inches

    B. about two inches

    C. close to 140 inches

    D. less than two inches

SOCIAL STUDIES

SKILLS TEST

Table 1

Month	Mean
January	0.7
February	0.9
March	1.3
April	1.9
May	4.0
June	10.2
July	13.1
August	12.9
September	11.6
October	6.0
November	0.7
December	0.3

Table 2

Month	Mean
January	0.6
February	0.7
March	0.8
April	1.6
May	2.7
June	3.7
July	3.2
August	3.0
September	1.6
October	1.2
November	0.6
December	0.7

Table 3

Month	Mean
January	2.3
February	2.2
March	1.9
April	1.5
May	0.9
June	0.4
July	0.1
August	0.3
September	1.3
October	2.6
November	2.2
December	2.6

Table 4

Month	Mean
January	1.9
February	2.4
March	4.5
April	5.1
May	5.0
June	6.5
July	6.4
August	6.1
September	8.2
October	6.4
November	3.6
December	1.6

31. Which table matches the precipitation data on the graph?

    A. Table 1

    B. Table 2

    C. Table 3

    D. Table 4

32. Which would be the BEST research question for a seventh grader's report on China?

    A. Who are China's neighbors?

    B. What is the capital of China?

    C. What was the history of China?

    D. How have Chinese-Americans adapted to life in the U.S?

SOCIAL STUDIES

SKILLS TEST

Use the Venn diagram to answer questions 33-36.

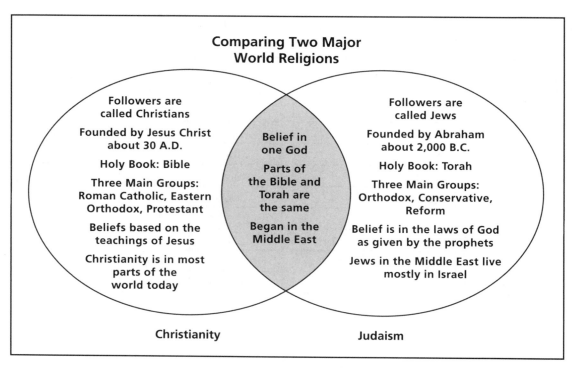

Comparing Two Major World Religions

Followers are called Christians

Founded by Jesus Christ about 30 A.D.

Holy Book: Bible

Three Main Groups: Roman Catholic, Eastern Orthodox, Protestant

Beliefs based on the teachings of Jesus

Christianity is in most parts of the world today

Belief in one God

Parts of the Bible and Torah are the same

Began in the Middle East

Followers are called Jews

Founded by Abraham about 2,000 B.C.

Holy Book: Torah

Three Main Groups: Orthodox, Conservative, Reform

Belief is in the laws of God as given by the prophets

Jews in the Middle East live mostly in Israel

Christianity   Judaism

33. Which religion began in the Middle East?

   A. Judaism

   B. Christianity

   C. both of them

   D. neither of them

34. What is a similarity between the two religions?

   A. belief in one God

   B. holy writings are the same

   C. beliefs are based on the teachings of Jesus

   D. Orthodox, Conservative, and Reform are the main groups

35. What is one difference between the two religions?

   A. belief in one God

   B. began in the Middle East

   C. some holy writings are the same

   D. beliefs are based on the teachings of Jesus

36. Which question can be answered using this diagram?

   A. What are the major religions in the Middle East?

   B. Who were the founders of Christianity and Judaism?

   C. Which religion has the most followers in the Middle East?

   D. What cities are considered "holy" to Christians and Jews?

37. Which is an opinion about two of the world's religions?

  A. Judaism is the older of the two religions.

  B. Christians and Jews each believe that there is only one God.

  C. Christians base their beliefs on the teachings of Jesus.

  D. The Jewish synagogues are the most beautiful churches in the world.

38. Which is required on a bar graph for it to be useful for sharing information?

  A. a data table

  B. graph paper

  C. labels for each axis

  D. different colored bars

39. Which reference book would be best to locate a map of Indonesia?

  A. atlas

  B. almanac

  C. thesaurus

  D. dictionary

40. Which BEST describes the purpose of an almanac?

  A. to be a source of maps for locations in the world

  B. to suggest synonyms and antonyms of given words

  C. to give definitions and origins of a language's words

  D. to provide an annual update of useful facts and statistical information

41. Which model gives the BEST representation of the location of places on the earth's surface?

  A. globe

  B. atlas map

  C. foldable map

  D. highway map

SOCIAL STUDIES

SKILLS TEST

Use the graph to answer questions 42-44.

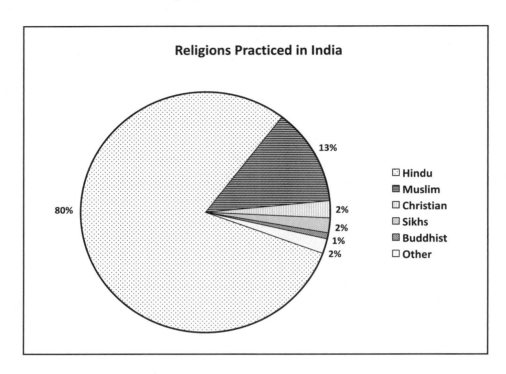

Religions Practiced in India

80%

13%

2%

2%

1%

2%

- ⊡ Hindu
- ▤ Muslim
- ▢ Christian
- ▨ Sikhs
- ▩ Buddhist
- ▢ Other

42. What is the purpose of this circle graph?

    A. to show how many different religions are practiced in India

    B. to show the number of people who practice different religions in India

    C. to represent the percent of the population practicing different religions in India

    D. to represent the changes in number of people practicing different religions in India

43. Which question could be answered using the graph?

    A. Which is the fastest growing religion in India?

    B. Which religion has the most followers in India?

    C. How are the religious groups in India different?

    D. Which religious groups have the most power in India?

44. What part of the Indian population is Christian?

    A. 1%

    B. 2%

    C. 7%

    D. not enough information

SOCIAL STUDIES

SKILLS TEST

Use the graph to answer questions 45-47.

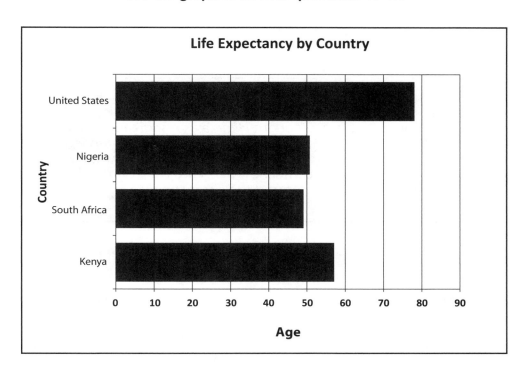

Life Expectancy by Country

45. What is the average life expectancy of a person living in South Africa?

   A. 49

   B. 50

   C. 57

   D. 78

46. How much longer would a typical American live than a citizen of Nigeria?

   A. 20 years

   B. 27 years

   C. 78 years

   D. 21/2 years

47. Which country's citizens have a life expectancy of about 57 years?

   A. Kenya

   B. Nigeria

   C. South Africa

   D. United States

48. Which would be the best source of information about a recent terrorist attack?

   A. almanac

   B. dictionary

   C. encyclopedia

   D. news Web site

SOCIAL STUDIES

SKILLS TEST

Use information from the passage to answer questions 49-50.

> *Jake was completing his research project on the country of Nigeria. He used an encyclopedia and a book about Nigeria as resources. Before he finished, he found that a neighbor had lived in Nigeria. He interviewed the neighbor and gathered a lot of useful information. Jake was able to include information from the interview in his project along with information from the encyclopedia and the library book.*

49. Which BEST describes the sources Jake used for his research project?

  A. tertiary sources

  B. primary sources

  C. secondary sources

  D. primary and secondary sources

50. Which would be the best source for Jake to get information on Nigeria's climate for his research project?

  A. almanac

  B. gazetteer

  C. thesaurus

  D. dictionary

PLEASE STOP! STOP!

Student Name: _____

Assignment: _____

Period: _____

Marking Instructions:

- Use a No. 2 pencil (no ink or ballpoint pens)
- Fill the circles in completely
- Erase completely to change your answer
- Make no stray marks

Example:

A   B   C   D

1 ○ ● ○ ○

Score:

Student ID Number

0○	0○	0○	0○	0○	0○	0○	0○	0○
1○	1○	1○	1○	1○	1○	1○	1○	1○
2○	2○	2○	2○	2○	2○	2○	2○	2○
3○	3○	3○	3○	3○	3○	3○	3○	3○
4○	4○	4○	4○	4○	4○	4○	4○	4○
5○	5○	5○	5○	5○	5○	5○	5○	5○
6○	6○	6○	6○	6○	6○	6○	6○	6○
7○	7○	7○	7○	7○	7○	7○	7○	7○
8○	8○	8○	8○	8○	8○	8○	8○	8○
9○	9○	9○	9○	9○	9○	9○	9○	9○

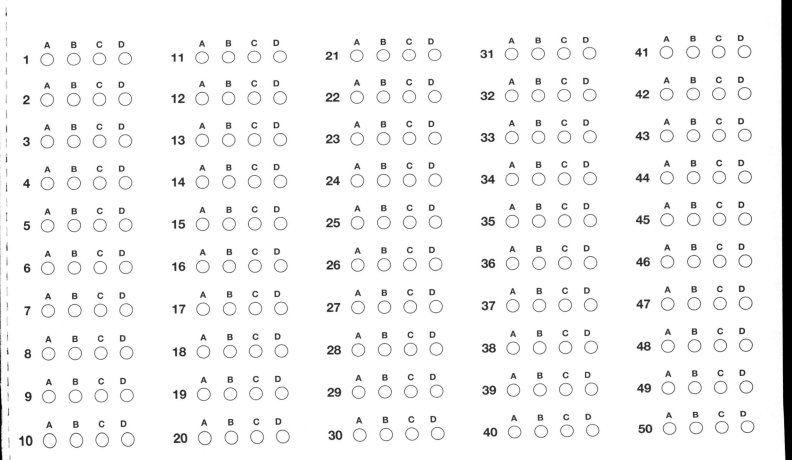

17

SOCIAL STUDIES

AFRICA UNIT TEST

**Use the map to answer
questions 1-3.**

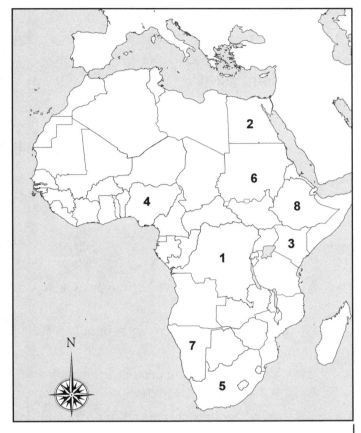

1. Which country is marked by the "2"?

   A. Egypt

   B. Kenya

   C. Nigeria

   D. Democratic Republic of the Congo

2. Which number marks South Africa?

   A. 1

   B. 3

   C. 5

   D. 8

3. What country is marked by the "4"?

   A. Kenya

   B. Nigeria

   C. Namibia

   D. South Africa

4. Which BEST describes the Sahara Desert?

   A. perfectly flat and sandy

   B. the largest desert in the world

   C. impossible for people to go across

   D. located only in the northwest corner of
   Africa

5. Why is farming so difficult in the African
   Sahel?

   A. little rain falls in this region

   B. no rain falls in the Sahel at all

   C. thick grass makes farming difficult

   D. farm animals in the Sahel eat up all the
   crops

6. What is causing the Sahel to expand in recent
   years?

   A. several years of heavy rains and flooding

   B. damming rivers and preventing irrigation

   C. over-grazing and cutting down trees for fuel

   D. government programs that have moved too
   many people into the area

7. Which would be typical of what one would find in a savanna?

A. desert

B. grasslands

C. coastal plains

D. high mountain ranges

8. Which phrase BEST describes the rainforest?

A. hot and dry desert

B. semi-arid farmland

C. rolling grassy plains

D. humid and warm with thick vegetation

9. Which is the biggest threat to African rainforests today?

A. overpopulation

B. war and political unrest

C. extended periods of drought

D. pollution from nuclear power plants

10. What is one of the major problems facing those who depend on the Nile River for their water?

A. The river has no fish in it.

B. The river is too shallow to be used for transportation.

C. The river always dries up during the summer months.

D. The water is contaminated with human and industrial waste.

11. What do some people believe might lead to "water wars" in Africa in the future?

A. end of farming as Africa moves to heavy industry

B. demands to reroute rivers to supply water to the rain forests

C. competition among countries that compete for scarce water resources

D. United Nations decrees telling African nations how to share their water

12. Why do some governments ignore industrial pollution of major rivers and waterways?

A. The people of most countries do not care about pollution.

B. Industries always have plans in place to clean up polluting wastes.

C. Most government officials do not recognize that pollution is a problem.

D. Leaders want the industries to be profitable and believe that controlling pollution is too costly.

SOCIAL STUDIES

AFRICA UNIT TEST

Use this chart to answer questions 21-23.

Country	Total Literacy Rate	Literacy of Males	Literacy of Females	GDP – Gross Domestic Product, per capita*
Burkina Faso	21%	21.8%	15%	$1,300
Congo	67%	80.9%	54.1%	$300
Egypt	71.4%	83%	59.45%	$5,500
Ghana	51.9%	66.4%	49.8%	$1,400
Kenya	85.1%	90.6%	79.7%	$1,700
South Africa	86.4%	87%	85%	$9,800
United States (for comparison)	99%	99%	99%	$45,800

21. Which African country has the highest literacy rates?

A. Kenya

B. Ghana

C. South Africa

D. Burkina Faso

22. Which African country has the highest GDP?

A. Kenya

B. Ghana

C. Burkina Faso

D. South Africa

23. How do the literacy rates for men and women compare in most of the countries represented on this chart?

A. It costs more for a country to educate women.

B. The chart shows that most women do not want to go to school.

C. There is very little difference in the literacy rates for men and women.

D. In nearly all the countries, women have a lower literacy rate than men.

24. In a unitary government system, who holds most of the power?

    A. individual voters

    B. local governments

    C. central government

    D. central and local governments

25. Who makes most of the important governmental decisions in an oligarchy?

    A. the people

    B. the monarch

    C. the legislature

    D. small group of powerful leaders

26. Which branch of government is responsible for making and carrying out the laws in a parliamentary system of government?

    A. courts

    B. monarch

    C. president

    D. legislature

27. Which branch of government passes the laws in a presidential system of government?

    A. the president

    B. the legislature

    C. the national courts

    D. both the president and the legislature together

28. Why is the literacy rate for girls in Kenya, Sudan, and South Sudan lower than it is for boys?

    A. Girls have shown they cannot do schoolwork as easily as boys.

    B. Traditional views say girls should be married rather than educated.

    C. Most girls in these countries say they have no interest in going to school.

    D. Very few schools have been opened for girls in either of these countries.

29. South Sudan became a separate country from Sudan in 2011 due to

    A. the civil war in Sudan.

    B. better highways in southern Sudan.

    C. better educational opportunities in the south.

    D. economic difficulties along the Nile River Basin.

SOCIAL STUDIES

AFRICA UNIT TEST

Use information from the map to answer questions 30-32.

Sudan 2010

30. Which body of water flows north from Khartoum?

   A. Red Sea

   B. Blue Nile

   C. Nile River

   D. White Nile

31. Which is located at about 12° N latitude and 23° E longitude?

   A. Libya

   B. Darfur

   C. Al Fashir

   D. Khartoum

32. About how far (in kilometers) is it from Khartoum to Port Sudan?

   A. 300

   B. 450

   C. 650

   D. 900

33. Which describes the rate of HIV/AIDS infection in Sub-Saharan Africa?

   A. infection is rapidly decreasing

   B. among the highest in the world

   C. not a real concern for most people

   D. information is not available on infection rates

SOCIAL STUDIES

AFRICA UNIT TEST

34. In a traditional economy, how are economic decisions made?

    A. custom and habit

    B. government planners

    C. consumers and the market

    D. combination of consumers and government planners

35. Why are most modern economies referred to as "mixed" economies?

    A. Poverty is always highest in countries with market economies.

    B. Most countries have aspects of all three types in their economies.

    C. Government planners do not know how to handle economic problems.

    D. Products made by traditional economies have no markets in the modern world.

36. Why is specialization so valuable in international trade today?

    A. Most countries only make one product very well.

    B. Specialization limits the amount of agriculture a country allows.

    C. Specialization keeps the prices low on goods that are imported into a country.

    D. Specialization allows people to do a more efficient job at producing what they make best and trade for the things they need.

37. In which area has South Africa begun to specialize?

    A. oil production

    B. grain production

    C. textile manufacturing

    D. gold and diamond mining

38. In which area has Nigeria worked to specialize?

    A. oil production

    B. gold and salt trade

    C. corn and wheat production

    D. iron and steel manufacturing

39. Why is a system of currency exchange necessary for international trade?

    A. Nearly all world currencies are really worthless on the world market.

    B. Those buying goods on the world market want to be paid in gold and silver.

    C. Most goods bought on the international market must be paid for in US dollars.

    D. There must be a way to pay for goods purchased from countries with different types of currencies.

PLEASE GO ON TO THE NEXT PAGE.

40. What is the definition of human capital?

    A. skills and knowledge workers have

    B. taxes collected from a country's workers

    C. money paid to workers for producing goods

    D. the amount of goods sold in foreign trade in a year

41. Why has the country of South Africa made a big investment in human capital?

    A. They were forced to provide training and education by the United Nations.

    B. Most schools and universities are free because of foreign investment in the country.

    C. South Africa has no natural resources to develop, so they have to depend on humans.

    D. Some of the country's most important industries need workers with specialized skills.

42. What is the definition of gross domestic product (GDP)?

    A. The total value of goods and services a country produces in a year.

    B. The value of all the products a country buys from overseas nations in a year.

    C. The amount collected in taxes from the people of a country in any given year.

    D. The value of all goods and services produced by small shops and individually owned businesses in a country.

43. If a country does not invest in its human capital, how can it affect the country's gross domestic product (GDP)?

    A. Investment in human capital has little effect on a country's GDP.

    B. GDP is only affected if workers pay for the investment out of their own pockets.

    C. Most workers want to keep their jobs just as they are and do not care about GDP.

    D. GDP may go down because poorly trained workers will not be able to do needed jobs.

44. In what areas has South Africa invested heavily in capital goods?

    A. agriculture

    B. space technology

    C. mining and heavy industry

    D. constructing new government buildings

SOCIAL STUDIES

AFRICA UNIT TEST

Use the graph to answer questions 45-47.

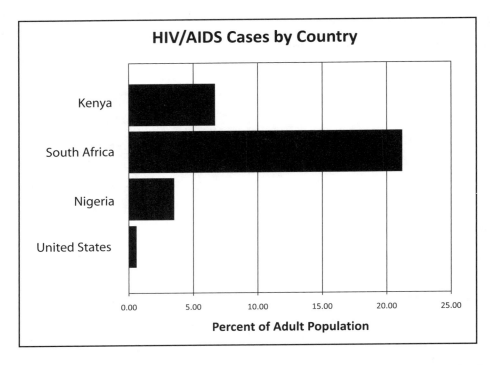

HIV/AIDS Cases by Country

Kenya
South Africa
Nigeria
United States

0.00   5.00   10.00   15.00   20.00   25.00

Percent of Adult Population

45. What part of the adult population of Kenya has HIV/AIDS?

   A. about 7%

   B. over 10%

   C. nearly 22%

   D. less than 5%

46. Which question can be answered using the graph?

   A. How many people in Africa have HIV/AIDS?

   B. What part of the population of Nigeria has HIV/AIDS?

   C. Which country has the most adults with HIV/AIDS?

   D. Which country has the highest percentage of adults with HIV/AIDS?

47. What is the BEST reason for including data from the United States on the graph?

   A. only three African countries have adults with HIV/AIDS

   B. many people in the U.S. have ancestors that came from Africa

   C. to compare data from African countries with data from our own

   D. the U.S. has assisted people from many countries in fighting HIV/AIDS

SOCIAL STUDIES

AFRICA UNIT TEST

Use information from the timeline to answer questions 48-50.

Events in the LIfe of Nelson Mandela

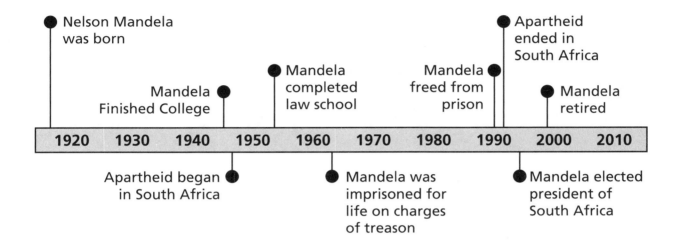

48. In what year was Nelson Mandela born?

    A. 1918

    B. 1945

    C. 1962

    D. 1999

49. About how long after Mandela was imprisoned did he become president of South Africa?

    A. about 30 years

    B. nearly 20 years

    C. less than 10 years

    D. more than 40 years

50. Which event in Mandela's life happened before the official beginning of apartheid?

    A. Mandela completed college.

    B. Mandela finished law school.

    C. Mandela was convicted of treason.

    D. Mandela retired as president of South Africa.

PLEASE STOP! STOP!

Student Name: _____

Assignment: _____

Period: _____

Example:

	A	B	C	D
1	○	●	○	○

Score:

Student ID Number

0○	0○	0○	0○	0○	0○	0○	0○	0○
1○	1○	1○	1○	1○	1○	1○	1○	1○
2○	2○	2○	2○	2○	2○	2○	2○	2○
3○	3○	3○	3○	3○	3○	3○	3○	3○
4○	4○	4○	4○	4○	4○	4○	4○	4○
5○	5○	5○	5○	5○	5○	5○	5○	5○
6○	6○	6○	6○	6○	6○	6○	6○	6○
7○	7○	7○	7○	7○	7○	7○	7○	7○
8○	8○	8○	8○	8○	8○	8○	8○	8○
9○	9○	9○	9○	9○	9○	9○	9○	9○

#	A	B	C	D		#	A	B	C	D		#	A	B	C	D		#	A	B	C	D		#	A	B	C	D
1	○	○	○	○		11	○	○	○	○		21	○	○	○	○		31	○	○	○	○		41	○	○	○	○
2	○	○	○	○		12	○	○	○	○		22	○	○	○	○		32	○	○	○	○		42	○	○	○	○
3	○	○	○	○		13	○	○	○	○		23	○	○	○	○		33	○	○	○	○		43	○	○	○	○
4	○	○	○	○		14	○	○	○	○		24	○	○	○	○		34	○	○	○	○		44	○	○	○	○
5	○	○	○	○		15	○	○	○	○		25	○	○	○	○		35	○	○	○	○		45	○	○	○	○
6	○	○	○	○		16	○	○	○	○		26	○	○	○	○		36	○	○	○	○		46	○	○	○	○
7	○	○	○	○		17	○	○	○	○		27	○	○	○	○		37	○	○	○	○		47	○	○	○	○
8	○	○	○	○		18	○	○	○	○		28	○	○	○	○		38	○	○	○	○		48	○	○	○	○
9	○	○	○	○		19	○	○	○	○		29	○	○	○	○		39	○	○	○	○		49	○	○	○	○
10	○	○	○	○		20	○	○	○	○		30	○	○	○	○		40	○	○	○	○		50	○	○	○	○

SOCIAL STUDIES

SOUTHWEST ASIA (MIDDLE EAST) UNIT TEST

Use the chart to answer questions 1-2.

Country	Total Literacy	Literacy of males	Literacy of Females	GDP – Gross Domestic Product, per capita*
Bahrain	86.5%	88.6%	83.6%	$32,000
Gaza/West Bank	92.4%	96%	88%	$ 1,100
Iran	77%	83.5%	70.4%	$10,600
Iraq	74.1%	84.5%	64.2%	$ 3,600
Israel	97.1%	98.5%	95.9%	$25,800
Jordan	89.9%	95.1%	84.7%	$ 4,900
Kuwait	93.3%	94.4%	91%	$39,300
Lebanon	87.4%	93.1%	82.2%	$11,300
Oman	81.4%	86.8%	73.5%	$24,000
Qatar	89%	89.1%	88.6%	$80,900
Saudi Arabia	78.8%	84.7%	70.8%	$23,200
Syria	79.6%	86%	73.6%	$ 4,500
Turkey	87.4%	95.3%	79.6%	$12,900
United Arab Emirates	77.9%	76.1%	81.7%	$37,300
Yemen	50.2%	70.5%	30%	$ 2,300
United States (for comparison)	99%	99%	99%	$45,800

1. Which two Southwest Asian countries have the highest literacy rates?

   A. Turkey and Qatar

   B. Israel and Kuwait

   C. United States and Yemen

   D. Gaza/West Bank and Israel

2. What generalization can be made about the relationship between GDP and literacy?

   A. Literacy is always lower in countries with a higher GDP.

   B. Literacy is usually higher in countries with a higher GDP.

   C. Countries with oil wealth always have the highest literacy rates.

   D. There is no relationship between a country's GDP and its literacy rate.

SOCIAL STUDIES

SOUTHWEST ASIA (MIDDLE EAST) UNIT TEST

Use information in the passage to answer questions 3-4.

> *The Saudi royal family controls the national government of Saudi Arabia. The king is the son of the previous king, and his son will rule after him. All government leaders serve by appointment from the king. The king appoints the governors of the provinces, as well. The king has the ability to remove any government official from a village, town, or province. The governments of the provinces and towns have no rights or authority*

3. Which type of government is described in the passage?

    A. unitary

    B. federation

    C. confederation

    D. parliamentary

4. Which BEST describes the government of Saudi Arabia?

    A. oligarchy

    B. monarchy

    C. democracy

    D. dictatorship

5. Which branch of government is responsible for making and carrying out the laws in a parliamentary system of government?

    A. the courts

    B. the monarch

    C. the president

    D. the legislature

6. In a presidential system of government, how is a president chosen?

    A. by a decision of the national courts

    B. by a majority vote of the legislature

    C. in a separate vote from the one that chooses the legislature

    D. by the political party with the most representatives in the legislature

7. What are the Five Pillars?

    A. the first five books of the Quran

    B. the five columns that support the roof of the Ka'aba

    C. five beliefs shared by Judaism, Christianity, and Islam

    D. five basic obligations that Muslims are supposed to do in their lives

PLEASE GO ON TO THE NEXT PAGE.

SOCIAL STUDIES

SOUTHWEST ASIA (MIDDLE EAST) UNIT TEST

Use the chart to answer questions 8-9.

Country	Type of Government	Who Votes	Role of Religion	Design of Government
Israel	Parliamentary Democracy	All citizens 18 years old or older	No direct role other than religious leaders elected to parliament	Elected parliament (the Knesset) and a Prime Minister chosen by the leading party
Saudi Arabia	Absolute Monarchy	Citizens do not vote	Religious leaders advise the king but decisions are the king's – the Quran is the official constitution	King chooses his advisors and no parliament
Iran	Theocracy or Theocratic Republic	All citizens 16 years old or older	Religious leaders are very influential in government decisions	Elected parliament (Majlis) with powerful religious leaders as advisors

8. Iran is to Majlis as Israel is to:

   A. Senate

   B. Congress

   C. the Knesset

   D. House of Representatives

9. Which country's government is LEAST controlled by religion or religious leaders?

   A. Iran

   B. Israel

   C. Saudi Arabia

   D. none are influenced by religion

10. Why is Iran sometimes called a theocratic republic?

   A. Iran's religious leaders make all the laws for the country.

   B. Religious leaders decide which Iranian citizens can vote.

   C. The people of Iran have no say in choosing their government leaders.

   D. Both an elected parliament and powerful religious leaders lead Iran's government.

11. Who takes on the financial risk in starting a new business in a market economy?

   A. economists

   B. entrepreneurs

   C. government planners

   D. combination of government planners and economists

SOCIAL STUDIES

SOUTHWEST ASIA (MIDDLE EAST) UNIT TEST

Use the diagram to answer questions 12-13.

Government of Iran

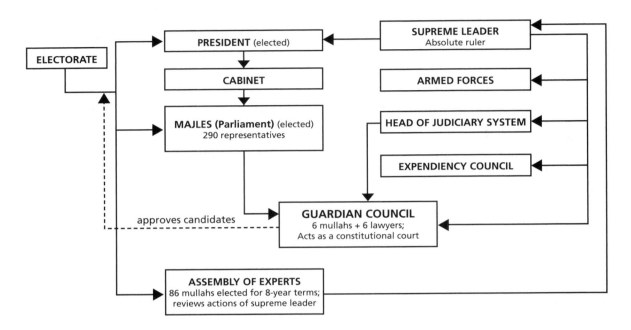

12. Who is the most powerful elected official in Iran?

    A. president

    B. electorate

    C. Supreme Leader

    D. head of the judiciary

13. How does the Guardian Council affect elections?

    A. The mullahs tell people who to vote for.

    B. The mullahs and lawyers must agree on the Supreme Leader.

    C. They approve candidates that will be placed on the ballots in elections.

    D. They cannot affect elections since they are appointed by the Majles and Supreme Leader.

14. Why do most economies in the world today operate somewhere in between a market economy and a command economy?

   A. Most consumers prefer government control to a free market system.

   B. Government control always makes a market economy more profitable.

   C. Government control of some aspects of the economy has never been successful in the modern world.

   D. Most countries have found they need a mix of free market and government control to be successful and protect consumers.

15. How has Israel made up for its lack of natural resources?

   A. They have put everyone to work and have no unemployment.

   B. They have developed a strong technology sector of their economy.

   C. They have relied primarily on farming to keep their economy going.

   D. Israelis have refused to import oil, saving huge amounts of money each year.

16. What is the definition of economic specialization?

   A. directly swapping goods from one country to another without having to use money

   B. trying to avoid investing in industry and technology because of the expense involved

   C. producing all goods and services needed for a country's growth, so that trade with other countries is not needed

   D. producing those goods a country can make most easily so they can trade them for goods made by others that cannot be produced locally

SOCIAL STUDIES

SOUTHWEST ASIA (MIDDLE EAST) UNIT TEST

Use information in the passage to answer questions 17-18.

> The OPEC nations control about 40% of the world's oil output. The OPEC countries work together to control prices for oil and to keep profits flowing to their countries. One way that they control prices is to limit production. Each member country is given a maximum amount of oil that they can sell in a given time.

17. What describes the limit that OPEC puts on its members' production of oil?

   A. tax

   B. tariff

   C. quota

   D. embargo

18. What happens to the price of oil when OPEC countries decide to reduce production of oil?

   A. prices rise

   B. prices drop

   C. prices stay the same

   D. oil stops being sold

19. Why is it important for nations to have a system to convert from one currency to another?

   A. Banks are not able to handle different kinds of currencies.

   B. Converting to different currencies makes goods cost less.

   C. The dollar is the most valuable currency in the world today.

   D. Converting to different currencies makes it possible to buy and sell goods between nations with different types of money.

20. Israel has made heavy investment in capital goods in all of the following EXCEPT

   A. defense.

   B. oil industry.

   C. communications.

   D. farming and agriculture.

21. The economy of Saudi Arabia is based on which of the following?

   A. agriculture

   B. manufacturing

   C. oil and natural gas

   D. computer design and technology

PLEASE GO ON TO THE NEXT PAGE.

SOCIAL STUDIES

SOUTHWEST ASIA (MIDDLE EAST) UNIT TEST

Use the map below to answer questions 22-24.

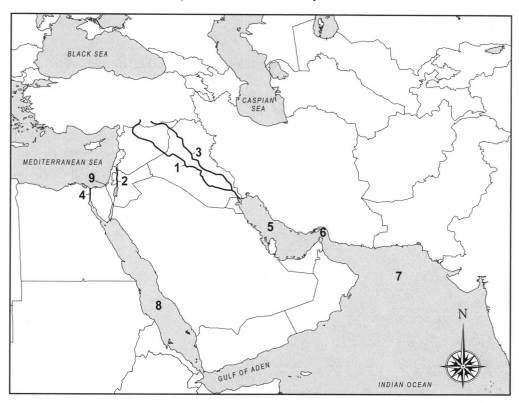

22. Which feature is marked by the "6"?

    A. Suez Canal

    B. Arabian Sea

    C. Persian Gulf

    D. Strait of Hormuz

24. Which number marks the Gaza Strip?

    A. 3

    B. 6

    C. 8

    D. 9

23. Which number marks the Euphrates?

    A. 1

    B. 2

    C. 3

    D. 4

SOCIAL STUDIES

SOUTHWEST ASIA (MIDDLE EAST) UNIT TEST

25. When the Ottoman Empire ended and new countries were created, what problems did the new boundaries cause as people found themselves living in newly created countries?

    A. All of the new countries were very poor.

    B. People in the new countries were no longer allowed to practice their religion.

    C. Most of the new countries were all desert and people could not make a living.

    D. The new countries often included people who did not have very much in common.

26. Which describes "anti-Semitism"?

    A. denying women the right to vote

    B. refusal to allow immigrants into your country

    C. hatred of Jews simply because they practice Judaism

    D. refusal to allow the practice of religion of any kind

27. Why did so many countries in the United Nations feel it was right to create the state of Israel in 1948?

    A. There was no one else living on the land at that time.

    B. Many felt the Jews deserved help because they had suffered so much in the Holocaust.

    C. Arab countries in the area supported the creation of a homeland for the Jews in Palestine.

    D. All national groups in the former Ottoman Empire were being given homelands at the same time.

28. What was the outcome of the 1948 War between the new state of Israel and the Arabs living in and around Palestine?

    A. The conflict ended and all Palestinian Arabs became citizens in the new State of Israel.

    B. Israel won the war and the new State of Israel was even larger than originally planned.

    C. Almost no Jewish people were willing to go to Israel because of the country's Arab neighbors.

    D. The United Nations decided to withdraw the proposal to create a State of Israel because of all the problems it caused in the area.

SOCIAL STUDIES

SOUTHWEST ASIA (MIDDLE EAST) UNIT TEST

29. Why did the United Nations form a coalition to stop Iraq from taking over the country of Kuwait in 1990?

    A. The United Nations wanted to completely destroy the country of Iraq.

    B. The only job of the United Nations is military action around the world.

    C. The economies of many countries depend on oil and Iraq's actions threatened that supply.

    D. The United Nations has to intervene whenever any member nation has a conflict with another country.

30. What led the United States to bomb and invade the country of Afghanistan in 2001?

    A. Afghanistan invaded the country of Kuwait and threatened the United States' oil supply.

    B. Nations asked the United States to overthrow the Taliban government of Afghanistan.

    C. The United States was afraid that Afghanistan was working to develop nuclear weapons and they wanted to put a stop to that program.

    D. The U.S. believed the government of Afghanistan was offering safety to al-Qaeda, the organization that led attacks on the United States on September 11, 2001.

31. Why did the United States go to war against Iraq in 2003?

    A. Iraq was threatening Afghanistan with nuclear weapons.

    B. The United Nations believed Iraq was about to invade Kuwait a second time.

    C. Iraqi troops launched an attack on Saudi Arabia, a close ally of the United States.

    D. The United States believed Iraq was developing nuclear weapons and offering aid to groups like al-Qaeda.

32. What is one of the reasons Iraqis had difficulty forming a new government after the fall of Saddam Hussein?

    A. Most Iraqis wanted Saddam Hussein to stay in power.

    B. Iraq is a poor country because they have no oil reserves.

    C. There are many religious and ethnic groups in Iraq who want power.

    D. The Iraqis have not tried to form a government of their own.

SOCIAL STUDIES

SOUTHWEST ASIA (MIDDLE EAST) UNIT TEST

Use the map below to answer questions 33-35.

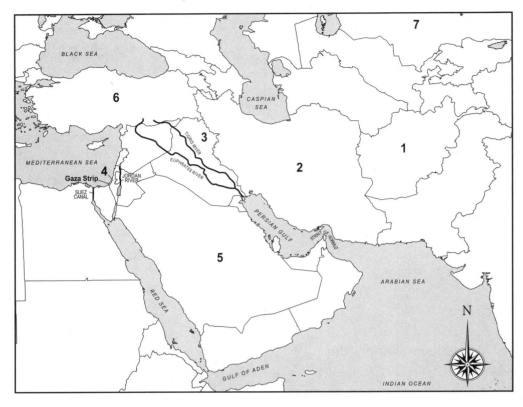

33. What number marks Afghanistan?

    A. 1

    B. 2

    C. 7

    D. 8

34. Which country is marked by the "3"?

    A. Iran

    B. Iraq

    C. Turkey

    D. Saudi Arabia

35. What number marks Israel?

    A. 2

    B. 4

    C. 5

    D. 6

36. Why is the Suez Canal so important to international shipping?

    A. The Suez Canal is the only way for ships to get out of the Persian Gulf.

    B. The Suez Canal is Iraq's only waterway leading into the Persian Gulf.

    C. The Suez Canal makes it possible to get from the Mediterranean to the Red Sea without sailing all the way around Africa.

    D. The Suez Canal connects the Jordan River to the Persian Gulf, making it less expensive to ship oil to other parts of Southwest Asia.

37. Which are connected by the Strait of Hormuz?

    A. the Red Sea and the Arabian Sea

    B. the Persian Gulf and the Arabian Sea

    C. the Mediterranean Sea and the Red Sea

    D. the Mediterranean Sea and the Persian Gulf

11

PLEASE STOP! STOP!

SOCIAL STUDIES

SOUTHWEST ASIA (MIDDLE EAST) UNIT TEST

Use the map below to answer questions 38-40.

ISRAEL

38. Which countries border the Gaza Strip?

   A. Iraq and Jordan

   B. Israel and Egypt

   C. Lebanon and Syria

   D. Israel and the West Bank

39. What is the approximate distance of the Dead Sea from Jerusalem?

   A. nearly 35 miles east

   B. nearly 35 miles west

   C. about 15 miles southeast

   D. about 15 miles southwest

40. What country is found at 31° N, 34° E?

   A. Egypt

   B. Israel

   C. Jordan

   D. Saudi Arabia

41. Why are technologies like desalinization and drip irrigation not more widely used to reduce water shortages in Southwest Asia?

   A. The technologies are too expensive.

   B. Drip irrigation is not very effective in a hot, dry climate.

   C. Most countries do not know about these technologies.

   D. Few countries in Southwest Asia have access to seawater.

PLEASE GO ON TO THE NEXT PAGE.

SOCIAL STUDIES

SOUTHWEST ASIA (MIDDLE EAST) UNIT TEST

42. Many of the largest cities in Southwest Asia are located on or near

    A. deserts

    B. major rivers

    C. large grasslands

    D. mountain ranges

43. Which best describes the climate of much of Southwest Asia?

    A. hot and dry

    B. windy and cold

    C. tropical and rainy

    D. moderate and cool

44. Which best describes the religion of those who call themselves Arabs?

    A. All Arabs are Sunni Muslims.

    B. Most Arabs are either Muslims or Jews.

    C. The majority of Arabs are Shia Muslims.

    D. Most are Muslim though there are also many Christians and those of other faiths.

45. Which are connected by the Suez Canal?

    A. the Red Sea and the Arabian Sea

    B. the Persian Gulf and the Arabian Sea

    C. the Mediterranean Sea and the Red Sea

    D. the Mediterranean Sea and the Persian Gulf

46. Which is TRUE of the difference between an ethnic group and a religious group?

    A. An ethnic group can have members of different races, but a religious group cannot.

    B. All members of a religious group worship the same god; members of an ethnic group may have different religions.

    C. Members of religious groups may have different religious beliefs; ethnic group members have the same religious beliefs.

    D. An ethnic group has a common race or culture but not a common religion; religious groups have a common race or culture and religion.

47. Which person is a common figure in the origins of Judaism, Christianity, and Islam?

    A. Jesus

    B. Abraham

    C. Confucius

    D. Muhammad

SOCIAL STUDIES

SOUTHWEST ASIA (MIDDLE EAST) UNIT TEST

Use the graph to answer questions 48-50.

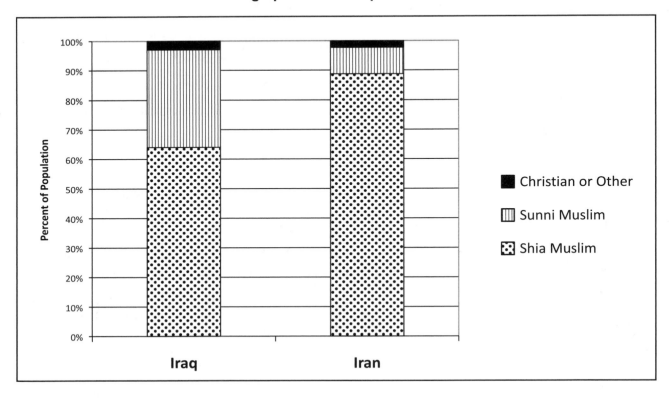

48. What part of the population of Iran is Sunni Muslim?

    A. 9%

    B. 33%

    C. 64%

    D. 89 %

49. Which would be the BEST alternative for showing these data in another way?

    A. use two line graphs

    B. use one circle graph

    C. use two circle graphs

    D. use a line graph with two lines of different colors

50. Which question could be answered using information from the graph?

    A. Which country has the most Shia Muslims?

    B. What part of the population of Iran is Hindu?

    C. What part of the population of Iraq is Christian?

    D. Which country has the highest proportion of its population as Shia Muslim?

14

PLEASE STOP! STOP!

Student Name:_____

Assignment: _____

Period:_____

Marking Instructions:
- Use a No. 2 pencil (no ink or ballpoint pens)
- Fill the circles in completely
- Erase completely to change your answer
- Make no stray marks

Example:

   A   B   C   D
1 ○ ● ○ ○

Score:

Student ID Number

0○	0○	0○	0○	0○	0○	0○	0○	0○
1○	1○	1○	1○	1○	1○	1○	1○	1○
2○	2○	2○	2○	2○	2○	2○	2○	2○
3○	3○	3○	3○	3○	3○	3○	3○	3○
4○	4○	4○	4○	4○	4○	4○	4○	4○
5○	5○	5○	5○	5○	5○	5○	5○	5○
6○	6○	6○	6○	6○	6○	6○	6○	6○
7○	7○	7○	7○	7○	7○	7○	7○	7○
8○	8○	8○	8○	8○	8○	8○	8○	8○
9○	9○	9○	9○	9○	9○	9○	9○	9○

Answer grid (each with columns A B C D):

1 ○○○○   11 ○○○○   21 ○○○○   31 ○○○○   41 ○○○○
2 ○○○○   12 ○○○○   22 ○○○○   32 ○○○○   42 ○○○○
3 ○○○○   13 ○○○○   23 ○○○○   33 ○○○○   43 ○○○○
4 ○○○○   14 ○○○○   24 ○○○○   34 ○○○○   44 ○○○○
5 ○○○○   15 ○○○○   25 ○○○○   35 ○○○○   45 ○○○○
6 ○○○○   16 ○○○○   26 ○○○○   36 ○○○○   46 ○○○○
7 ○○○○   17 ○○○○   27 ○○○○   37 ○○○○   47 ○○○○
8 ○○○○   18 ○○○○   28 ○○○○   38 ○○○○   48 ○○○○
9 ○○○○   19 ○○○○   29 ○○○○   39 ○○○○   49 ○○○○
10 ○○○○   20 ○○○○   30 ○○○○   40 ○○○○   50 ○○○○

SOCIAL STUDIES

SOUTHERN AND EASTERN ASIA UNIT TEST

1. How has the Indian practice of cremating their dead on the banks of the Ganges River and development of more industry been a problem for other people who use the river?

   A. People are not allowed to go near the river when cremations are taking place.

   B. The banks along the river regularly catch fire and threaten Indian homes built there.

   C. Factory owners cannot use water once human ashes have been thrown into it upstream.

   D. The ashes of the dead, as well as partially burned bodies, constantly float down the river, along with industrial waste from factories.

2. What is the source of the air pollution that causes problems in India's urban areas?

   A. Few people in India feel air pollution is a problem.

   B. No government efforts have been made to control air pollution.

   C. There really is no effective way to control air pollution in the world today.

   D. It is due to a rapidly growing population, heavy industry and thousands of automobiles.

Olympics, what environmental issue was a big concern for many of the athletes?

   A. the city's terrible air pollution

   B. heavy seasonal rains that come to China in the summer

   C. temperatures would be too hot in the summer in China

   D. lack of fresh drinking water was the main concern before the games

4. What generalization can be made about the climate and geography of Southern and Eastern Asia?

   A. Most of this area is covered with desert and has very few people.

   B. This large area has many different types of both climate and geography.

   C. Eastern Asia has fewer mountains and therefore has a milder climate than Southeastern Asia.

   D. The climate of Southern Asia is cold and dry because of the large number of mountains and deserts.

1 **PLEASE GO ON TO THE NEXT PAGE.**

SOCIAL STUDIES

SOUTHERN AND EASTERN ASIA UNIT TEST

Use the map below to answer questions 5-7.

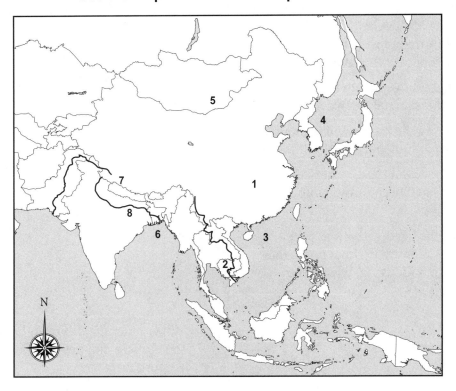

5. What number marks the location of the Himalayan Mountains?

   A. 1

   B. 2

   C. 7

   D. 8

6. Which feature is marked by the "6"?

   A. Huang He

   B. Sea of Japan

   C. Bay of Bengal

   D. South China Sea

7. Which feature is marked by the "5"?

   A. Gobi Desert

   B. Ganges River

   C. Korean Peninsula

   D. Taklimakan Desert

SOCIAL STUDIES

SOUTHERN AND EASTERN ASIA UNIT TEST

Use the map below to answer questions 8-9.

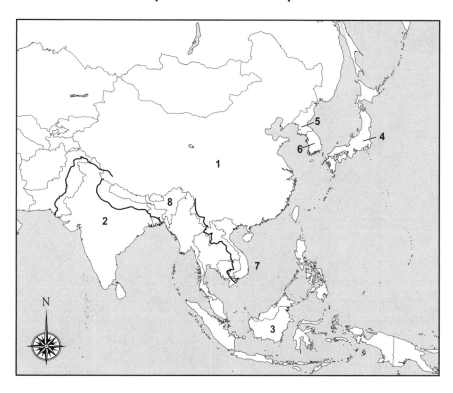

8. Which country is marked by the "4"?

   A. Japan

   B. Indonesia

   C. North Korea

   D. South Korea

9. Which country is marked by the "1"?

   A. India

   B. China

   C. Vietnam

   D. Bangladesh

PLEASE GO ON TO THE NEXT PAGE.

SOCIAL STUDIES

SOUTHERN AND EASTERN ASIA UNIT TEST

Use the chart to answer questions 10-12.

Religion or Philosophy	Country of Origin	Important People	Important Literature or Sacred Text	Basic Beliefs	Where Found Today
Buddhism	India	Siddhartha Gautmam (Buddha)	Works containing the collected teachings of Buddha	The Four Noble Truths and The Middle Way	Primarily in Southern and Eastern Asia
Confucianism	China	Confucius	The Four Books, including the writings of Confucius	Honesty, love of family, kindness to others, honest work, respect for the state	Important in China and other places in East Asia
Hinduism	India	Brahman	The Vedas	Reincarnation, the Caste System, Karma	Primarily in India, although Hinduism is practiced worldwide
Islam	Arabia	Muhammad	The Quran	The Five Pillars	Worldwide
Shintoism	Japan	No individual founder	Follow the code of Confucius as well as its own moral code; honor kami	Life and nature are sacred and must be protected	Primarily in Japan

10. What is the name of the Hindu sacred text?

   A. the Vedas

   B. the Quran

   C. the Middle Way

   D. the Four Noble Truths

11. Where was the religion of Buddhism founded?

   A. India

   B. Japan

   C. China

   D. Vietnam

12. In which country did Shintoism begin?

   A. India

   B. Japan

   C. China

   D. Vietnam

SOUTHERN AND EASTERN ASIA UNIT TEST

13. What is the caste system?

    A. the name of the Hindu priesthood

    B. a voting system used in Asian elections

    C. the name for the way labor in India is divided between men and women

    D. the division of all the people in a society into categories that are hereditary

14. What did Confucius believe were the keys to social order and peace?

    A. strict caste system

    B. worship of one god

    C. good behavior and virtue

    D. ruler who could keep order

15. Which country has a federal system of government?

    A. Japan

    B. India

    C. North Korea

    D. People's Republic of China

16. How do the Japanese feed their people with so little good farmland?

    A. Many of the Japanese people starve every year.

    B. The Japanese depend on fishing and imported food.

    C. The Japanese sell oil to earn money to buy food from other countries.

    D. Tourists coming to see Japanese volcanoes provide most of the money the country needs.

SOCIAL STUDIES

SOUTHERN AND EASTERN ASIA UNIT TEST

Use the graph below to answer questions 17-18.

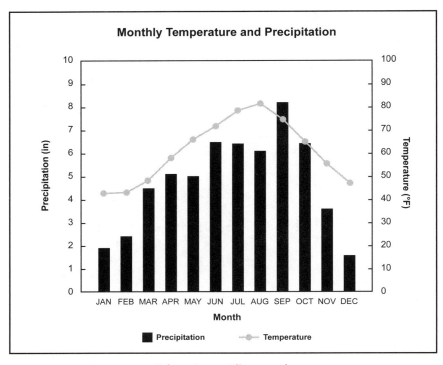

Tokyo, Japan Climograph

17. Which is TRUE about the climate in Tokyo, Japan?

   A. Winter is the wettest and coldest time of year.

   B. Spring is driest and temperatures are about the same as in winter.

   C. Late summer is the hottest and among the wettest times of year.

   D. Autumn begins a period of dryness, and temperatures are the hottest.

18. Which month is usually the driest in Tokyo, Japan?

   A. January

   B. October

   C. December

   D. September

SOCIAL STUDIES

SOUTHERN AND EASTERN ASIA UNIT TEST

Use the tables below to answer question 19.

Table 1

Month	Mean
January	0.7
February	0.9
March	1.3
April	1.9
May	4.0
June	10.2
July	13.1
August	12.9
September	11.6
October	6.0
November	0.7
December	0.3

Table 2

Month	Mean
January	0.6
February	0.7
March	0.8
April	1.6
May	2.7
June	3.7
July	3.2
August	3.0
September	1.6
October	1.2
November	0.6
December	0.7

Table 3

Month	Mean
January	2.3
February	2.2
March	1.9
April	1.5
May	0.9
June	0.4
July	0.1
August	0.3
September	1.3
October	2.6
November	2.2
December	2.6

Table 4

Month	Mean
January	1.9
February	2.4
March	4.5
April	5.1
May	5.0
June	6.5
July	6.4
August	6.1
September	8.2
October	6.4
November	3.6
December	1.6

19 Which table matches the precipitation data on the graph?

A. Table 1

B. Table 2

C. Table 3

D. Table 4

20. Which Asian country could be described as an autocracy?

A. India

B. Japan

C. South Korea

D. North Korea

21. Which Asian countries have a democratic system of government?

A. India and Japan

B. China and Vietnam

C. China and South Korea

D. North Korea and China

SOCIAL STUDIES

SOUTHERN AND EASTERN ASIA UNIT TEST

Use the chart below to answer questions 22-23.

Country	Type of Government	Who Votes	Role of Religion	Design of Government
Japan	Constitutional Monarchy	All citizens 20 years old or older	No direct role; the government is considered secular	Elected parliament (the Diet) and a prime minister chosen by the Diet members
China	Communist Party	All citizens over the age of 18	Religion is not encouraged by the Chinese government	National People's Congress with leaders chosen by the congress
India	Democratic Republic	All citizens over the age of 18	India is a secular government	Elected parliament with a prime minister chosen from the majority party

22. Which best describes the Japanese government?

A. theocracy

B. monarchy

C. federal democracy

D. constitutional monarchy

23. What sort of government is the People's Republic of China?

A. a monarchy

B. a federal democracy

C. a communist oligarchy

D. a constitutional monarchy

SOCIAL STUDIES

SOUTHERN AND EASTERN ASIA UNIT TEST

Use the chart to answer questions 24-25.

Country	Total Literacy	Literacy of Males	Literacy of Females	GDP – Gross Domestic Product, per capita*
Bangladesh	43%	53%	31%	$1,300
China	91%	95%	86%	$5,300
India	61%	73%	47%	$2,700
Japan	99%	99%	99%	$33,600
North Korea	99%	99%	99%	$1,900
South Korea	98%	99%	96%	$24,800
Vietnam	90%	93%	86%	$2,600

*By or for each individual person

24. Which countries have the greatest percent difference in literacy rates between men and women?

   A. China and Japan

   B. India and Vietnam

   C. Bangladesh and India

   D. Vietnam and Bangladesh

25. Which country is unusual in that almost every man and woman can read and write but the GDP is among the lowest in the world?

   A. India

   B. China

   C. Bangladesh

   D. North Korea

SOCIAL STUDIES

SOUTHERN AND EASTERN ASIA UNIT TEST

26. What role do the people play in the government of Japan?

    A. The people have ultimate power through elections.

    B. They have the power to vote the emperor out of office.

    C. The people get to approve the laws made by the emperor.

    D. They have little influence since the emperor makes most decisions.

27. What group makes most of the important decisions in the government of the People's Republic of China today?

    A. the wealthy landowners

    B. advisers and Mao Tse-Tung

    C. the Chinese Communist Party

    D. people in the local village councils

28 The Great Leap Forward and the Cultural Revolution were examples of China's attempt to

    A. end communist rule.

    B. improve the economy.

    C. sell more goods overseas.

    D. control population growth.

29. In the 1970s, China tried to improve the country's economy by announcing which of the following programs?

    A. the Cultural Revolution

    B. the Great Leap Forward

    C. the Four Modernizations

    D. the People's Economic Congress

30. Which area was targeted for improvement by India's Green Revolution?

    A. education

    B. air quality

    C. agriculture

    D. iron and steel manufacturing

31. Which country's economy is a command economy?

    A. China

    B. Japan

    C. North Korea

    D. South Korea

32. Which is an area that India is a world economic leader?

    A. health care

    B. military weapons production

    C. modern farming and agriculture

    D. technology and service industries

33. Why has Japan specialized in the area of technology?

    A. Japan has few natural resources and little farming.

    B. Japan has a very poorly educated population.

    C. The country has little in the way of fishing and shipping.

    D. The country uses the money earned to support a large military.

34. How has Japan used tariffs to help the country's economy?

    A. The tariffs have provided money for health care.

    B. The tariffs have kept cheap foreign-made goods off the Japanese market.

    C. The tariffs have made it easier for Japanese people to buy foreign imported goods.

    D. The tariffs have made little difference in what Japanese people pay for imported goods.

35. Why is it important for nations to have a system to convert from one currency to another?

    A. The dollar is the most valuable currency in the world today.

    B. Most banks are not able to handle different kinds of currencies.

    C. The conversion to different currencies makes goods cost less.

    D. This makes it possible to buy and sell goods between nations with different types of money.

36. How did the Four Modernizations affect Chinese agriculture and industry?

    A. Many farmers were forced off the land and had to move to cities.

    B. Factories involved in heavy industry were moved to rural areas to provide jobs.

    C. Farmers were forced to sell all surplus agricultural products to the government.

    D. Farmers were given better seeds and equipment; factories increased production of smaller consumer goods that were easier to sell.

37. Why is investment in capital goods so important for the economy of a country like Japan?

   A. The investment in capital goods makes overseas trade unnecessary.

   B. The investment in capital goods makes up for a poor literacy rate in Japan.

   C. Japan needs investment in capital goods to develop its rich natural resources.

   D. Japan's economy depends heavily on industry and must be modern to be competitive.

38. Which has been a persistent problem for India's economy?

   A. a lack of a strong middle class

   B. the expense of maintaining a large military

   C. a GDP that has not grown in the past ten years

   D. overpopulation and poverty found throughout the country

39. How has China's attitude toward entrepreneurship changed in the past several decades?

   A. Entrepreneurs are allowed to operate, but not with overseas businesses.

   B. The government has become more open to the idea of allowing some free enterprise.

   C. The Chinese government was more open to entrepreneurship in the years before 1970.

   D. Entrepreneurs are encouraged, but only in the areas of making weapons and military equipment.

40. Nationalism is defined as

   A. loyalty based on geographic location only.

   B. a feeling of belonging to a group that is highly educated and wealthy.

   C. a sense of belonging that is based on a written document like a constitution.

   D. loyalty to a group with whom one shares a common history, culture, and/or religion.

41. Which was one of the goals of the Indian National Congress and the Muslim League in India?

   A. working to modernize Indian farming

   B. trying to bring more industry to India

   C. greater independence from British control

   D. ending the religious wars being fought all over India

SOCIAL STUDIES

SOUTHERN AND EASTERN ASIA UNIT TEST

42. What was involved in Mohandas Gandhi's plan of civil disobedience?

   A. He wanted violent demonstrations all over the country until the British left.

   B. The people should refuse to obey a law they felt was unfair, but do it with non-violence.

   C. Gandhi felt it was best to go along with British laws to avoid making the colonial authorities angry.

   D. He thought the best way to change the laws was through passing legislation in the Indian National Congress.

43. What was the political party of Ho Chi Minh in Vietnam?

   A. Green Party

   B. Socialist Party

   C. Communist Party

   D. Democratic Party

44. Which explains one way the Korean War and Vietnam War were alike?

   A. American troops fought against Russian and Chinese forces.

   B. American troops were under the direction of the United Nations.

   C. The United States entered the wars to stop the spread of communism.

   D. The United States supported the wars with money and supplies but not with troops.

45. What was the role of the Japanese emperor in the new government after World War II?

   A. His role was mainly ceremonial.

   B. He was a powerful political figure.

   C. The office of emperor was eliminated.

   D. He served in the parliament as the presiding officer.

46. What was Mao's attempt to organize small farms into larger farms where ownership of everything was shared?

   A. the Long March

   B. the Kuomintang

   C. the Great Leap Forward

   D. the Collective Movement

47. Which was Mao's attempt to silence anyone who criticized his government in China?

   A. the Long March

   B. the Middle Way

   C. the Cultural Revolution

   D. the Great Leap Forward

48. In 1989, what happened to students protesting for greater political freedom in Tiananmen Square in the city of Beijing?

    A. They were attacked by Chinese troops and many were killed or arrested.

    B. Most students lost interest in the demonstration and returned quietly to classes.

    C. They were able to hold meetings with the Chinese government and present their demands.

    D. They got so much positive publicity that the Chinese government had to give into their demands.

49. Which describes the Domino Theory as related to communism?

    A. Political decisions must be made slowly, like a game of dominoes.

    B. International politics is a game, and there are always winners and losers.

    C. Few countries would really be interested in communism if they knew what it was like.

    D. If one country in a region became communist then others would quickly follow.

50. What became of American efforts to prevent Ho Chi Minh from taking over the country of Vietnam and reuniting it as one country?

    A. Vietnam became a western-style democracy under a government designed by the United States.

    B. The United States is still working to prevent Vietnam from becoming a communist country.

    C. Vietnam remains permanently divided with the north communist and the south democratic.

    D. American efforts ended in 1975 and Vietnam was united under the government designed by Ho Chi Minh.

PLEASE STOP! STOP!

Student Name:_____

Assignment: _____

Period:_____

Marking Instructions:
- Use a No. 2 pencil (no ink or ballpoint pens)
- Fill the circles in completely
- Erase completely to change your answer
- Make no stray marks

Example:

Score:

1 A ○ B ● C ○ D ○

Student ID Number

SOCIAL STUDIES

CRCT PRACTICE TEST

Use the timeline to answer the next three questions.

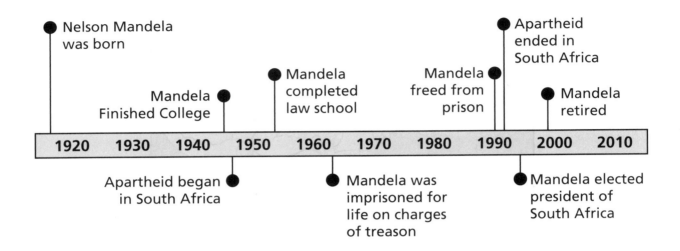

5. How long was Nelson Mandela in prison?

   A. life

   B. 10 years

   C. over 25 years

   D. can't determine from this time line

6. Which sentence is TRUE based on information in the time line?

   A. Racial prejudice did not exist in South Africa after 1990.

   B. Nelson Mandela lived to see the end of apartheid in South Africa.

   C. The South African government freed Nelson Mandela in the 21st century.

   D. The people of South Africa did not trust Nelson Mandela after he was imprisoned.

7. Which would be the BEST title for this time line?

   A. 21st Century South Africa

   B. Africa in the 20th Century

   C. The Life of Nelson Mandela

   D. Important Events in South Africa

SOCIAL STUDIES

CRCT PRACTICE TEST

8. Why do some governments in Africa ignore industrial pollution of major rivers and waterways?

   A. They want the industries to be profitable.

   B. The people of most countries do not care about pollution.

   C. Industries always have plans in place to clean up polluting wastes.

   D. Most government officials do not recognize that pollution is a problem.

9. Which is the BEST example of an ethnic group?

   A. people who grow similar food

   B. people who like to read similar books

   C. people who share a belief in a god or gods

   D. people who share a culture, national origin, or religion

10. In a unitary government system, who holds most of the power?

    A. individual voters

    B. local governments

    C. central government

    D. central and local governments share power

11. Which branch of government is responsible for making and carrying out the laws in a parliamentary system of government?

    A. judicial

    B. executive

    C. monarchy

    D. legislative

12. Which country is known for its history of apartheid?

    A. China

    B. India

    C. Sudan

    D. South Africa

13. Which country is LEAST likely to have people using a traditional economy?

    A. Japan

    B. Sudan

    C. Kenya

    D. Nigeria

14. Which are MOST important in a command economy?

    A. custom and habit

    B. government planners

    C. consumers and the market

    D. a combination of consumers and government planners

SOCIAL STUDIES

CRCT PRACTICE TEST

Use the diagram to answer question 15.

Economic Systems

Command Economy ←――↑――――――↑――――――↑――――↑――→ Market Economy

North Korea   China   India   Japan

15. Which country's businesses are under the most government control?

   A. China

   B. India

   C. Japan

   D. North Korea

16. Why are most modern economies referred to as "mixed" economies?

   A. Poverty is always highest in countries with market economies.

   B. Government planners do not know how to handle economic problems.

   C. Products made by traditional economies have no markets in the modern world.

   D. Most countries have all aspects of three economic types at work in their economies.

17. Why is specialization so valuable in international trade today?

   A. Most countries can only make one product very well.

   B. Specialization limits the amount of agriculture a country allows.

   C. Specialization always keeps the prices low on goods that are imported into a country.

   D. Specialization allows people to do a more efficient job at producing what they make best and trade for the things they need.

SOCIAL STUDIES

CRCT PRACTICE TEST

**Use the information in the box
to answer question 18.**

> *Fishermen in Japan were worried. Fish
> from the United States were being
> imported at a lower price than Japanese
> fish. Japanese consumers began buying
> more of the American fish and less of
> the Japanese fish. The only way for the
> Japanese fishermen to sell their fish
> was to lower the price and reduce their
> profits. The fishermen asked the Japanese
> government to create a special tax on
> fish imported from the United States.
> The extra tax would make the American
> fish cost more. The Japanese fishermen
> believed that if the American fish cost
> more, consumers in Japan would buy
> Japanese fish instead of American fish.*

18. What type of action did the Japanese
    fishermen want from their government?

    A. tariff

    B. subsidy

    C. boycott

    D. embargo

19. What is a "quota"?

    A. a tax placed on imported goods when they
       enter the country

    B. a decision to prevent certain goods from
       being imported at all

    C. a tax placed on goods when they are
       purchased in the market place

    D. a limit to the number or amount of a
       foreign-produced good that is allowed into
       the country

20. What is an "embargo"?

    A. a tax placed on goods coming into the
       country from overseas

    B. a limit to the amount of a certain good
       allowed into the country

    C. a tax paid by the producer before he can sell
       his goods in another country

    D. a formal halt to trade with a particular
       country for economic or political reasons

21. What is the definition of human capital?

    A. skills and education workers have

    B. taxes collected from a country's workers

    C. money paid to workers for producing goods

    D. the amount of goods sold in foreign trade in
       a year

22. Which is associated with a high gross
    domestic product (GDP)?

    A. extreme poverty

    B. a low literacy rate

    C. a high standard of living

    D. low productivity of workers

23. Which are a part of a business's capital resources?

    A. factories used to make goods

    B. money for scholarships to graduate schools

    C. workers who make the goods and perform services

    D. money spent to train workers to use new technology

24. Why were the boundaries of the new African states created after World War II the cause of problems?

    A. The boundaries carefully followed the paths of rivers.

    B. All of the new countries were too large to rule effectively.

    C. The boundaries ignored where different cultural and tribal groups lived.

    D. Europeans drew the boundaries so they could keep all the mineral wealth for themselves.

25. What was significant about Nelson Mandela's election to political office in South Africa in 1994?

    A. He was the first black president of South Africa.

    B. He was elected as a representative of the Zulu nation.

    C. He united the Zulu and Ashanti people in order to win the election.

    D. He was the overwhelming choice of British citizens living in South Africa.

SOCIAL STUDIES

Use the graph below to answer questions 26-27.

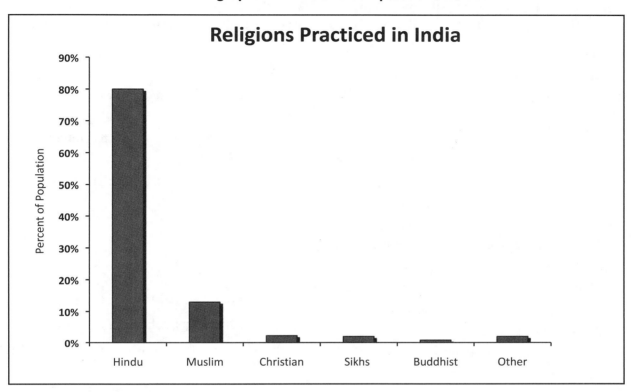

Religions Practiced in India

26. Which can be answered using information in the graph?

    A. How many Hindus live in India?

    B. How many people in India are Muslim?

    C. What part of the Indian population is Jewish?

    D. What percentage of people in India practice Christianity?

27. Which BEST describes which part of the people in India are Hindu?

    A. nearly half

    B. about 8 out of 10

    C. more than Muslim, less than Sikh

    D. less than all other religions combined

28. Why are such technologies like desalinization and drip irrigation not more widely used in Southwest Asia?

    A. These technologies are very expensive.

    B. Drip irrigation is not very effective in a hot, dry climate.

    C. Most countries do not know about these technologies.

    D. Few countries in Southwest Asia have access to sea water.

29. Which countries have the largest deposits of oil in Southwest Asia today?

    A. Iran and Kuwait

    B. Israel and Jordan

    C. Turkey and Oman

    D. Saudi Arabia and Iraq

30. Why does the organization OPEC play such a powerful role in the world economy today?

    A. This organization is a part of the United Nations.

    B. It builds dams along rivers shared by several countries.

    C. The group controls both the supply and price of a majority of the world's oil.

    D. Membership includes many oil companies owned by firms in the United States.

31. Which BEST describes the religion of those who call themselves Arabs?

    A. All Arabs are Sunni Muslims.

    B. Most Arabs are either Muslims or Jews.

    C. The majority of Arabs are Shia Muslims.

    D. Though most are Muslim, there are also many Christians and those of other faiths.

32. What is the main belief that distinguished the Jewish faith from the others in the ancient world?

    A. the belief in life after death

    B. the organization of believers into a separate state

    C. the worship of a single god rather than many gods

    D. the offering of sacrifices during religious ceremonies

33. What are the "Five Pillars"?

    A. the first five books of the Quran

    B. the five columns that support the roof of the Ka'aba

    C. five beliefs shared by Judaism, Christianity, and Islam

    D. five basic obligations that Muslims are supposed to do in their lives

34. Which Southwest Asian country is an autocracy?

    A. Iraq

    B. Israel

    C. Turkey

    D. Saudi Arabia

SOCIAL STUDIES

CRCT PRACTICE TEST

Use the map below to answer questions 35-36.

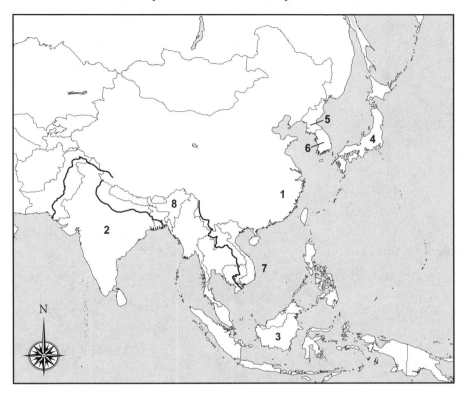

35. What country is marked by the "3" on the map?

    A. China

    B. Japan

    C. Indonesia

    D. Bangladesh

36. What number marks India on the map?

    A. 2

    B. 4

    C. 6

    D. 8

37. How has Israel made up for its lack of natural resources?

    A. They have put everyone to work and have no unemployment.

    B. They have developed a strong technology sector of their economy.

    C. They have relied primarily on farming to keep their economy going.

    D. Israelis have refused to import oil, saving huge amounts of money each year.

38. What part of the Saudi economy is most fully under a command economic system?

    A. oil industry

    B. agriculture

    C. textile manufacturing

    D. technology production

Use the information in the box to answer question 40.

> • supports the modern State of Israel
> • dedicated to fighting anti-Semitism
> • belief that Jews have the right to live in Palestine as they did in the days of the Old Testament

39. What is anti-Semitism?

    A. denying women the right to vote

    B. hatred of Jews simply because they practice Judaism

    C. refusal to allow immigrants into your country

    D. refusal to allow the practice of religion of any kind

40. What do the phrases in the box BEST describe?

    A. Islam

    B. Zionism

    C. Orthodox Judaism

    D. the Palestine Liberation Organization

41. Why did the United Nations form a coalition to stop Iraq from taking over Kuwait in 1990?

    A. The United Nations wanted to completely destroy the country of Iraq.

    B. The only job of the United Nations is military action around the world.

    C. The economies of many countries depend on oil and Iraq's actions threatened that supply.

    D. The United Nations has to intervene whenever any member nation has a conflict with another country.

PLEASE GO ON TO THE NEXT PAGE.

42. How has the Indian practice of cremating their dead on the banks of the Ganges and the practice of factories dumping industrial waste and chemicals been a problem for other people who use the river?

   A. People are not allowed to go near the river when cremations are taking place.

   B. The banks along the river regularly catch fire and threaten Indian homes built there.

   C. Factory owners cannot use water once human ashes have been thrown into it upstream.

   D. The ashes of the dead, as well as partially burned bodies, and the waste from the factories are constantly floating down the river.

43. All of the following contribute to air pollution in China's largest cities EXCEPT

   A. growing population.

   B. burning coal for energy.

   C. huge numbers of automobiles and trucks.

   D. gradual drop in the number of new factories.

44. What is the name of the Hindu sacred text?

   A. The Vedas

   B. The Quran

   C. The Middle Way

   D. The Four Noble Truths

45. All of the following statements are true about the populations of the countries in Southern and Eastern Asia EXCEPT

   A. Most countries have very large populations in this part of the world.

   B. Few people here still farm since most now live in cities and work in factories.

   C. People in this region often have to deal with the problems of air and water pollution.

   D. Many people choose to live along rivers and close to the sea where it is easier to make a living.

46. The biggest concern people in Bangladesh have in terms of climate is

   A. extreme cold during long winter.

   B. annual drought brought on by hot desert winds.

   C. storm surges and flooding during heavy monsoons.

   D. hurricanes and tornadoes caused by global climate change.

SOCIAL STUDIES

CRCT PRACTICE TEST

47. What is the Hindu belief in reincarnation?

   A. there is only one god

   B. the cow as a sacred animal

   C. people should treat each other with kindness

   D. a soul returns to life in another body after death

48. What is the "caste system"?

   A. the Hindu priesthood

   B. the voting system used in Southeastern elections

   C. division of all the people in a society into categories that are hereditary

   D. the name for the way labor in India is divided between men and women

49. What is the Buddhist teaching that shows its followers the way to live their lives?

   A. the Bible

   B. the Quran

   C. the Five Pillars

   D. the Middle Way

50. How did Confucianism come to play an important role in Chinese society?

   A. Confucianism has replaced all other religions in China.

   B. Confucius led an army to take over the Chinese government during his lifetime.

   C. Confucian philosophy had little effect on Chinese society until the 20th century.

   D. A Chinese emperor hired Confucian scholars in 121 BC to help organize his government.

SOCIAL STUDIES

CRCT PRACTICE TEST

Use the chart to answer questions 51-52.

Country	Type of Government	Who Votes	Role of Religion	Design of Government
Japan	Constitutional Monarchy	All citizens 20 years old or older	No direct role; the government is considered secular	Elected parliament (the Diet) and a prime minister chosen by the Diet members
China	Communist Party	All citizens over the age of 18	Religion is not encouraged by the Chinese government	National People's Congress with leaders chosen by the congress
India	Democratic Republic	All citizens over the age of 18	India is a secular government	Elected parliament with a prime minister chosen from the majority party

51. Which best describes the Japanese government?

    A. monarchy

    B. theocracy

    C. federal democracy

    D. constitutional monarchy

52. In what way are these three governments alike?

    A. Only males over the age of 18 may vote.

    B. The Communist Party rules the parliaments of the countries.

    C. The governments of these countries have a monarch with little power.

    D. They have governments that are not linked to the practice of a particular religion.

53. The "Great Leap Forward" and the "Cultural Revolution" were examples of China's attempt to

    A. end communist rule.

    B. improve the economy.

    C. sell more goods overseas.

    D. control population growth.

54. The "Green Revolution" was India's attempt to improve

    A. education.

    B. air quality.

    C. agriculture.

    D. iron and steel manufacturing.

55. India leads many other countries in the area of

    A. health care.

    B. military weapons production.

    C. modern farming and agriculture.

    D. technology and service industries.

56. How did the "Four Modernizations" affect Chinese agriculture and industry?

    A. Many farmers were forced off the land and had to move to cities.

    B. Factories involved in heavy industry were moved to rural areas to provide jobs.

    C. Farmers were forced to sell all surplus agricultural products to the government.

    D. Farmers were given better seeds and equipment; factories began to increase the production of smaller consumer goods that were easier to sell.

Student Name: _____

Assignment: _____

Period: _____

Marking Instructions:

- Use a No. 2 pencil (no ink or ballpoint pens)
- Fill the circles in completely
- Erase completely to change your answer
- Make no stray marks

Student ID Number

0	0	0	0	0	0	0	0	0
1	1	1	1	1	1	1	1	1
2	2	2	2	2	2	2	2	2
3	3	3	3	3	3	3	3	3
4	4	4	4	4	4	4	4	4
5	5	5	5	5	5	5	5	5
6	6	6	6	6	6	6	6	6
7	7	7	7	7	7	7	7	7
8	8	8	8	8	8	8	8	8
9	9	9	9	9	9	9	9	9

Example:

   A   B   C   D

1 ○ ● ○ ○

Score:

[ ]

1 A B C D
2 A B C D
3 A B C D
4 A B C D
5 A B C D
6 A B C D
7 A B C D
8 A B C D
9 A B C D
10 A B C D
11 A B C D
12 A B C D
13 A B C D
14 A B C D
15 A B C D
16 A B C D
17 A B C D
18 A B C D

19 A B C D
20 A B C D
21 A B C D
22 A B C D
23 A B C D
24 A B C D
25 A B C D
26 A B C D
27 A B C D
28 A B C D
29 A B C D
30 A B C D
31 A B C D
32 A B C D
33 A B C D
34 A B C D
35 A B C D
36 A B C D

37 A B C D
38 A B C D
39 A B C D
40 A B C D
41 A B C D
42 A B C D
43 A B C D
44 A B C D
45 A B C D
46 A B C D
47 A B C D
48 A B C D
49 A B C D
50 A B C D
51 A B C D
52 A B C D
53 A B C D
54 A B C D

55 A B C D
56 A B C D
57 A B C D
58 A B C D
59 A B C D
60 A B C D
61 A B C D
62 A B C D
63 A B C D
64 A B C D
65 A B C D
66 A B C D
67 A B C D
68 A B C D
69 A B C D
70 A B C D

GLOSSARY

A

acid rain a name given to the moisture that has reacted with sulfur dioxide and nitrogen oxides which can come from the burning of fossil fuels

Afghanistan a landlocked, mountainous country located NW of India and E of Iran in Southwest Asia

air pollution the human introduction into the atmosphere of chemicals, particulate matter, or biological materials that cause harm or discomfort to humans or the environment

animist a person who believes that spirits are found in natural objects and surroundings

antiretroviral drugs (AVTs) drugs that are able to slow down the progress of HIV-AIDS infections

anti-Semitism hatred of the Jews simply because they practice the Jewish faith

apartheid the legal separation of the races

Arab a member of a Semitic people inhabiting Arabia and other countries of the Middle East

Arabian Gulf another name for Persian Gulf

Arabian Sea the NW arm of the Indian Ocean between India and Arabia

arable land soil that is suitable for farming

Ashanti a group of people found in the modern country of Ghana

Association of Southeast Asian Nations (ASEAN) an organization that was organized to help the member countries cooperate on economic matters, encourage cultural exchanges, and to help keep peace and stability in the region

Atlas Mountain Range a group of mountains that separate the coastal regions from the great Sahara Desert in northern Africa

autocratic government system a government in which the ruler has absolute power to do whatever he wishes and make and enforce whatever laws he chooses

automobile emissions the carbons and other chemicals that come from a car's engine

B

Bantu a member of any of a large number of linguistically related peoples of central and southern Africa

bartering a system in which goods and services are exchanged instead of using cash as a payment in a traditional economy

Bill of Rights a document stating the basic freedoms that all citizens may enjoy

Brahman the name Hindus have given to the gods they believe are part of a supreme spirit

Buddha the name given to the priest of the Buddhist religion; also known as "The Enlightened One"

Buddhism a belief that people could find peace if they could reject greed and desire

C

cabinet a group of advisors

capital goods the factories, machines, and technology that people use to make products to sell

capitalism an economic system in which the means of production and distribution are privately or corporately owned and developed

caste system a belief that a social class is inherited

ceremonial emperor a ruler with no power

Chinese Communist Party the name of the ruling party in China

Christianity the belief that Jesus Christ is the Son of God

civil disobedience the refusal to obey laws even if the result is punishment

civil war a war within the same country

climate the state of the atmosphere at a particular location over a long period of time; usually discussed in terms of temperature and rainfall

Cold War a state of political tension and military rivalry between nations that stops short of full-scale war, especially that which existed between the United States and Soviet Union following World War II

collective all ownership and decision making is in the hands of the government

collective farm   where people work together and share whatever they produce

command economy   an economy in which a government planning group makes most of the basic economic decisions for the workers

communist   an economic structure or government that promotes the establishment of a classless society based on common ownership of products and property

confederation government system   a system in which the local government holds all of the power and the central government depends on the local government for its existence

Confucianism   the philosophy or ethical system of Confucius which is based on good deeds and morality

Congo River   begins in central Africa near Lake Tanganyika, flows through central and west Africa through the largest rain forest in Africa for almost 3,000 miles before it reaches the Atlantic Ocean

constitutional monarchy   a government in which the powers of the ruler are restricted to those granted under the constitution or laws of the nation

cooperatives   farms that are owned by the government; workers are told what they may produce

credit   the ability to borrow money

Cultural Revolution   a name given to China's attempt in the 1960s to improve its economy by reorganizing its farms, businesses, and most of society

currency   something that is used as a medium of exchange; money

D

deforestation   the destruction of trees and other vegetation

democracy   originates from the Greek word "demos," which means people; another name for democratic government system

democratic government system   a political system in which the people play a much greater role in deciding who the rulers are and what decisions are made

Democratic Republic of the Congo (Zaire)   a large country in central Africa with a coastline on the Atlantic Ocean

desalination   the process of removing salt and other chemicals from sea water

desertification   the process of land becoming like a desert, due to deforestation and drought

Diet (the)   a two-house legislature that is elected by the Japanese people

district council   a group elected or appointed as a legislative body

dominion   having control or the exercise of control over another country

Domino Theory   a term meaning if one country fell to communism, all the others nearby would fall as well

drip irrigation   a system, using computers, that measures out how much water each plant receives

drought   an extended period of time without rainfall

E

Egypt   a large North African country located along the banks of the Red Sea and the Mediterranean coast

Eightfold Path   the eight rules for conduct that a person practicing the Buddhist religion is to follow during his or her lifetime

embargo   a trade barrier in which one country announces that it will no longer trade with another country in order to isolate and cause problems with that country's economy

emperor   the male ruler of an empire

entrepreneur   creative, original thinkers who are willing to take risks to create new businesses and products

ethnic group   a group of people who share cultural ideas and beliefs that have been a part of their community for generations

Euphrates River   one of the longest rivers of Southwest Asia which begins in Turkey and flows through Syria and Iraq

exchange rate   a system of changing from one type of currency (money) to another

extinction   a dying out of a species of plants or animals

F

famine   extreme and general scarcity of food

federal government system   a political system in which power is shared between the national and local governments, including executive, legislative, and judicial branches

federal republic   a government in which elected individuals make decisions for the people

Five Pillars of Islam   five things Muslims must do during their lifetime in their practice of Islam

fossil water   water that has been underground for centuries

four main castes   the division of the caste system in the Hindu religion

Four Modernizations   a name given to China's attempt in the 1970s to reorganize its economy

Four Noble Truths   the four phases of the Buddhist religion

free enterprise   a business governed by the laws of supply and demand, not restrained by government interference

G

Ganges Action Plan   a plan begun in 1985 to try and clean up the Ganges River

Gaza Strip   a coastal region at the southeastern corner of the Mediterranean Sea bordering Israel and Egypt

Golden Rule of Behavior   a belief from the religion of Confucianism religion that "What you do not like when done unto yourself, do not unto others"

Grand Canal   one of the world's oldest and longest canal systems (built more than 2,000 years ago) connecting the Yangtze and Huang He rivers

Great Leap Forward   a name given to China's attempt in the 1950s to reorganize its economy

Green Line   the place where the cultivated land ends and the desert begins

Green Revolution   a name given to the time period in India in the 1960s when they tried to modernize their agricultural system by introducing new types of seeds and grains, and fertilizer and pesticides were made available

gross domestic product (GDP)   the value of all the final goods and services produced within a nation in a given year

H

hereditary monarchy   the government is led by a king who comes from a family that has ruled the country for several generations

Hinduism   the worship of many gods that are a part of a supreme spirit named Brahman

Holocaust   a time when over six million Jews were killed in concentration camps set up by Germany

human capital   the knowledge and skills that make it possible for workers to earn a living producing goods or services

hydroelectic power   electricity produced from the energy of running water

I

income   the monetary payment received for goods or services, or from other sources, as rents or investments

Indian National Congress   a two-house legislature made up of representatives elected from all across the country of India

invest   to put money to use in something offering potential profitable returns, as interest, income, or appreciation in value

Iran   west of Afghanistan; one of the largest countries in Southwest Asia

Iraq   a country west of Iran which has the advantage of having two of the largest rivers in the region, the Tigris and Euphrates

irrigation   providing water for crops

Islam   the religious faith of Muslims, based on the words and religious system founded by the prophet Muhammad

Israel   a republic in SW Asia, on the Mediterranean Sea; created in 1948 by the United Nations as a home to the Jewish people of the world

J

Jordan River   a smaller but important river that begins in the southern end of the Sea of Galilee and flows into the Dead Sea

Judaism a religious group of Jews who believe in one God

K

Kalahari Desert a great desert located in the southern part of Africa

kami the divine spirit that followers of the Shinto's religion believe live in nature; means superior in Japanese language

Karma the belief that one's actions determine one's fate

Kenya a country located along the eastern coast of Africa bordering the Indian Ocean

Klerk, F. W. de the South African president who, in 1990, freed Nelson Mandela from prison after he had served 27 years

Kurds a distinct ethnic group that lives in the mountainous areas where Syria, Turkey, Iran, and Iraq come together

L

laissez-faire a French phrase that means to allow them to do as they please

Lake Tanganyika one of the largest freshwater lakes in the world and one of the deepest lakes in the world, located in the Great Rift Valley

Lake Victoria the largest lake in Africa

literacy the ability to read and write

loess another name for the silt or sediment that is deposited along a river's path, creating rich soil for farmers

Long March the name given to the 6000 mile journey that Mao Zedong and his followers took to avoid capture by the Chinese government

M

MacArthur Constitution a name given to the constitution that was written by General Douglas MacArthur (the American commander of the occupation forces) after World War II for Japan

MacArthur, General Douglas the American commander given the job of rebuilding Japan after World War II

Mahatma a name given to Mohandas K. Gandhi, a politician in India, who was instrumental in helping India gain its freedom from British colonial rule; means "Great Soul"

Mandela, Nelson South African statesman who fought against apartheid and was released from prison to become the nation's first democratically elected president in 1994

market economy an economy in which a society's economic decisions are made by individuals who decide what to produce and what to buy

micro-credit industry the extension of very small loans to the unemployed and to others living in poverty that are not considered a good financial risk

Middle Way (The) the goals that were to be accomplished by following what Buddha called the Eightfold Path (eight rules for conduct) in the religion of Buddhism

mila local beliefs the Swahili follow; for example, spirits can possess a person and there is a close link between their religious beliefs and the practice of medicine and healing

mineral deposits a mass of naturally occurring mineral material, usually of economic value; such as lead, zinc, gold, or silver

mineral resources a natural resource such as coal, iron ore, gold, or silver that are of economic value

Ministry of International Trade and Industry (MITI) a group that helps companies decide what products will sell best on the global market

mixed economy an economy that has characteristics of both market and command economic systems

monarchy a government where a king and his advisors make most of the decisions; it is a type of unitary government

monsoon a seasonal prevailing wind, lasting several months, bringing heavy rains often causing great hardships for those living in the area due to flooding

Muhammad an Arabic prophet who founded Islam

Muslim a name given to the followers of the Islam religion

Muslim League a group organized in 1855 in an effort to put more power into the hands of Indians

N

National People's Congress a group of people elected every five years by a vote of the Chinese people

nationalism the loyalty to a group with whom one shares a common history, culture, and/or religion

natural resource something that is in or supplied by our natural environment and can be consumed or used by people

Niger River originating in western Africa, it is the third largest river in Africa, flowing from Guinea over 2600 miles to the African coast

Nigeria a large nation on the coast of West Africa that has nearly every kind of habitat found in Africa

Nile River the longest river in the world which begins in the central mountains of Africa, runs through Ethiopia, Sudan, and Egypt, and flows northward over 4,000 miles until it reaches the Mediterranean Sea at Alexandria, Egypt

Nirvana name given to reaching a state of perfect peace in the religion of Buddhism

nomads people who move from place to place, usually traveling by camel, looking for water or food

non-violence a lack of violence

O

oasis a small place where trees are able to grow and where people can live with grazing animals and a few crops

oil one of the most important and valuable fossil fuels

oligarchy government system a system in which a political party or other small group takes over a government and makes all of the major decisions; government by the few

OPEC Organization of Petroleum Exporting Countries founded to set oil prices and policies

Operation Desert Storm another name for the Persian Gulf War

Operation Iraqi Freedom an invasion led by the United States in 2003 to stop the development of nuclear weapons by Iraq

Ottoman Empire an empire that controlled much of the Middle East or Southwest Asia from the 1300's until the end of World War I

P

Pan-African movement the desire for people of African descent, no matter where they lived in the world, to think of Africa as a homeland

parliament the name given to the group of people elected to run a parliamentary system of government

parliamentary democratic government a democratic form of government in which the people vote for those who represent the political party they feel best represents their views of how the government should operate

peninsula a body of land that is surrounded by water on three sides

per capita (GDP) the amount of goods and services produced compared to the number of people

Persian Gulf one of the main shipping routes for oil to be shipped out from the rich fields of Kuwait, Saudia Arabia, Iran and other countries that line its shores; also known as Arabian Gulf

Persian Gulf War a military force used to liberate Kuwait from the Iraqi invasion in 1991; also called Operation Desert Storm

Persians people who live in the modern country of Iran

Political Bureau of the Communist Party a small group of men who make all of the decisions on how the Chinese government and life in that country should be organized

premier a name given to a chief administrator of a government

president the chief executive of a government

presidential form of democratic government sometimes called a congressional form of government; in this type of government a president is chosen to be the leader

prime minister the name given to the head of government; chief executive of a parliamentary democracy

productive resources the use of natural, human, and capital to produce goods and services that you expect to sell for a price high enough to cover production costs

protective tariff a tax placed on goods coming from another country

Q

qanats underground tunnels in Southwest Asia that bring water from the hills to dry plains

quota a way of limiting the amount of foreign goods that can come into a country

Quran the holy book of the Islam religion

R

rainforest areas with hot, humid, tropical climates and dense, evergreen forests with trees hundreds of feet tall

rate of return the gain or loss of an investment over a specified period, expressed as a percentage increase over the initial investment cost

Red Army a name given to the communist army in the Republic of China

Red Guard the name of the new army of young people Mao Zedong used to enforce his policies in the 1960s

refugees people who have to leave their homes as the result of war

reincarnation a belief that the soul does not die with the body, but enters the body of another being, either a person or an animal

religious group a group with a belief system in a god or gods, with a specific set of rituals and literature

reparations the payment for damages done to property

republic a state in which the supreme power rests in the body of citizens entitled to vote

Republic of Sudan located just south of Egypt in southeastern Africa, Sudan is the largest country in Africa and also the largest among the countries that make up the Arab world

respiratory disease those diseases of the lungs, bronchial tubes, and trachea in the human body

robotics using mechanical techniques with robots to assemble goods or products

Rub Al-Khali a desert in southern Saudia Arabia that means "empty quarter"

S

Sahara Desert the largest desert on planet Earth covering over 3.5 million square miles

Sahel a dry, semi-arid region south of the Sahara Desert covering almost 1,800,000 square miles that is slowly turning into desert land. It serves as a transition region between the harsh desert to the north and the grasslands and rain forest to the south and stretches from the Atlantic Ocean to the Red Sea. The word Sahel means "border" or "margin."

Saudia Arabia the largest country of the Arabian Peninsula in Southwest Asia; controlled by a monarchy

savanna a vast area of both grassland and more tropical habitats in the middle of Africa close to the equator

savings the money that you have not spent after buying things you want

secular a word meaning it favors no special religion

sediment the topsoil, silt and minerals from the mountains that is gradually spread along the path of a river enriching the farmland and creating a large, fertile delta at the mouth of a river

Shia Muslims the second largest denomination of Islam

Shintoism the earliest religion in Japan which means "way of the gods"

silt rich topsoil, carried by floodwaters

South Africa a country located at the very southern tip of the African continent that is mostly a broad plateau with large stretches of grasslands in the interior

Special Economic Zones a name given to those areas that were set up along the coastal areas to try to encourage foreign companies to do business with China

specialization those products a country makes best and that are in demand on the world market

specialize to train or devote oneself to a particular area of study or occupation

O

oasis, 26

oil, 60, 84

oligarchy, 39, 99, 157

Operation Desert Storm, 125

Operation Iraqi Freedom, 125

Organization of Petroleum Exporting Countries (OPEC), 56, 84, 103, 113

Ottoman Empire, 120

P

Pakistan, 188

Palestine, 121, 124

Pan-African Movement, 72

Panchayat, 162

Parliament, 40, 159, 163

parliamentary form of democratic government, 40, 101, 103, 159

peninsula, 128

People's Republic of China, 156, 157, 162, 169, 197

per capita (GDP), 58, 97, 115, 153, 178

Persian, 88

Persian Gulf, 76

Persian Gulf War, 125

Political Bureau of the Communist Party, 162

pollution, water, 82

polytheistic, 146, 148

premier, 163

president, 40, 159

prime minister, 40, 103, 156, 159, 162,163

productive resources, 185

protective tariff, 56, 176

qanat, 86

quota, 56, 112, 177

Quran, 103, 148

R

rainforest, 11, 29

Red Army, 197

Red Guards, 197

Red Sea, 76

refugee, 124

reincarnation, 146

reparations, 195

republic, 162

Republic of China, 196, 197

Republic of South Africa, 17, 52, 59, 68

Republic of Sudan, 17, 44, 48

Republic of Vietnam, 189

respiratory disease, 137

River, Congo, 11

River, Ganges, 127, 134

River, Indus, 127

River, Mekong, 128

River, Niger, 11,22

River, Nile, 11,22

River, Yangtze, 127,135

River, Yellow, 127

robotics, 183

Rowlatt Act, 187

Rub al-Khali, 85

S

Sahara Desert, 11, 25, 26

sahel, 11, 24, 25, 27

Satyagraha, 193

Saudi Arabia, 78,103,109

savanna, 11,28-29

savings, 63

Sea, China, 128

Sea, of Japan, 128

Sea, South China, 128

Sea, Yellow, 127

secular, 162

sediment, 127

self-sufficient, 175

Shatt al-Arab, 75

Shia Muslim, 88,89,94,103

Shinto, 148

Shintoism, 148

silt, 22

South China Sea, 128

South Korea, 140,142

Southern Asia, 127-187

INDEX

Order Form
CRCT Test Prep

Clairmont Press

Phone: 1-800-874-8638   Fax: 1-800-874-9190   E-mail: gacrct@clairmontpress.com
1494 Bellflower Court   Lilburn, Georgia 30047

Ship to:

Name   Position

School/District

Street Address   (not PO Box)

City   State   Zip Code

Telephone

E-mail Address

Bill to:

Name   Position

School/District

Street Address or PO Box

City   State   Zip Code

Purchase Order Number

Item #	Quantity	Title/Description	Price	Total
978-1-56733-099-1		**6th Grade** CRCT Test Prep TEACHING THE GEORGIA PERFORMANCE STANDARDS		
978-1-56733-098-4		**7th Grade** CRCT Test Prep TEACHING THE GEORGIA PERFORMANCE STANDARDS		
978-1-56733-097-7		**8th Grade** CRCT Test Prep TEACHING THE GEORGIA PERFORMANCE STANDARDS		

* Shipping and handling charges:
• For orders of less than $500.00, add 10% for standard shipping and $5.95 for handling.
• For orders of $500.00 or more, add 10% for standard shipping and handling.

Subtotal	
Shipping and Handling*	
TOTAL	

You may charge this order to your VISA® or MasterCard®

Card type (please check one): ☐ MasterCard. ☐ VISA   Signature _____

Credit Card Number: ☐☐☐☐ ☐☐☐☐ ☐☐☐☐ ☐☐☐☐

Expiration Date: ☐☐ / ☐☐
M M   Y Y

CVV code on back of card ☐☐☐

Credit Card Billing Address: _____
Street   City   State   Zip

150+ Copies	$ 9.00 each*
100-149 Copies	$10.00 each*
30-99 Copies	$11.00 each*
11-29 Copies	$13.00 each*
5-10 Copies	$15.00 each*

Minimum Order is 5 books. Above pricing applies to total number of books ordered (a combination of all grade levels) with a minimum order of five (5) books.

TEACHERS: The answers to all questions and tests can be found at **www.clairmontpress.com**

Click on GA CRCT Test Prep and complete **registration** for the password. Passwords are e-mailed after approval.

* Prices are subject to change without notice. Please contact Clairmont Press to confirm pricing and availabilty.